NINE SAPIENS:

BIOLOGY AND EVOLUTION OF PERSONALITY TYPES

OR HOW A **HUNTER-GATHERER** IMPACTED WALL STREET

CLAUDIA NARIO AND **HUGO KRÜGER**

Our gratitude

To our parents, for having always been by our side.

Our recognition

To Robert Sapolsky, Lars Penke and Yuval Harari, for having inspired our thinking with their work.

A tribute

To Bertrand Russell, for having put his intelligence at the service of a better world.

NINE SAPIENS

© 2021 by Claudia Nario and Hugo Kruger
Illustrations by VALF

ISBN (Print): 978-1-09834-771-0
ISBN (eBook): 978-1-09834-772-7

INTRODUCTION

This book is the bastard child of an improbable romance between two worlds that rarely converse: recent advances in Science on the biological basis of behavior, and a personality model called the Enneagram. Science, a very composed and educated lady, and the Enneagram, a long-haired drifter, committed to personal development and other immaterial things.

The authors were friends of both, and we were convinced that, if not made for each other, they could at least get along very well. This is how these two, who perhaps would never have even met, were struck by the arrows of the winged son of Venus.

It all started as an arranged date, which both were very hesitant to attend. The Enneagram told us: "I don't think this relationship will work. She is too rigid, cerebral, everything has to be under control, and I need my freedom...why do you insist on introducing me to her?"

And Science: "What do I have to do with that *New Age* hippie and his messy life? A guy who's more interested in making up stories than finding the truth? What could he possibly contribute to me?"

We had a hard time convincing them to attend the meeting. Our main argument for Science was the following: "We know that you have already had many dates with other personality models, and that you like the factorials very much[1]. But deep down, you know that while they are very mathematical and orderly, they are also very superficial. Give the Enneagram a chance.

---

1   Reference to factorial models of personality, developed through the application of factor analysis (a statistical technique) to personality survey data.

In spite of its dark origin and fantasy mind, it has a lot to contribute. You will be surprised to hear it, for you will find many coincidences between what he has to say and what you have already discovered."

And we said to the Enneagram: "You don't know what you're missing. She has many ideas that will interest you and that could even change your perception of yourself. If you listen to her, we are sure that you will achieve an even more realistic vision of who you are, and a more solid base to fulfill your purpose of development. You have nothing to lose!"

This is how the first date happened. And at the risk of betraying our confidentiality agreement, we transcribe here what we remember from that first encounter.

Science: Hello, Enneagram. I've heard the craziest things about you. Tell me the truth about yourself.

Enneagram: Truth? My thing is not so much about truths, but about falsehoods. It is about discovering the false Ego and freeing the essence.

Science: I don't understand you, but your wordplay is interesting. You are enigmatic. What is your object of study?

Enneagram: The human being.

Science: Too broad. You have to be more specific.

Enneagram: What about "behavior"? Would that do?

Science: Still broad, but it works for now. If you like, I can tell you what I know about human behavior. And then you tell me what you know.

Enneagram: But…I don't really need you to tell me anything, for I don't have any questions, I have answers. Besides, the questions are always the same.

Science: Of course the questions may be the same, but not the answers! The answers are always changing. There are better ones today than yesterday, and today's may not be as good as tomorrow's!

Enneagram: I don't know if I would be interested in anything you have to say. My answers come from very far away.

Science: Hmm…where do your answers come from?

Enneagram: Well, I don't really know. My origin is lost in the beginning of times.

Science: Then you may be interested in knowing what I know about the origin of the behavior. And I can tell you exactly where I get my information from. Are you interested?

And then, oddly enough, the Enneagram remained silent for a moment and with a small flirtatious smile on his lips, he winked in agreement. Science and the Enneagram walked to a new bridge standing at the end of a wall. The waters of the river of knowledge below ran unstoppable, generating waves, foam, and an unmistakable sound of water and stones. From the bridge could be seen an intricate complex of buildings, large, small, old and new. Some buildings were still under construction, and all of them were connected to one another through countless roads and bridges.

They stopped at the highest part of the bridge.

Enneagram: You will not come to me with "if the river makes a noise…"[2]

Science: Of course not, that is already evident. What I want to show you are the three buildings where the research teams that have produced the ideas that I will discuss with you have been working for the past 20 years.

Enneagram: But…you can see many different buildings from here.

Science: Indeed, there are many. I want to draw your attention to three of them. See that new building in front of that complex, surrounded by woods, and roads interconnecting them?

Enneagram: Yes, it is a peculiar set. The buildings are quite different from one another.

Science: That's right. The new building is for Behavioral Genetics. You will see that there are some closer and others farther away. There is that of Neuroscience, that of Genetics, with its north wing called Epigenetics, that

---

2   From Spanish proverb: "If the river makes a noise, it's because water is running", equivalent to "Where there's smoke, there's fire."

of Ethology, and that of Psychology. A little farther on is the Mathematics and Statistics complex, which has bridges that connect it to almost all the others. The largest is the Biology complex, which gives its name to this whole section of the campus. In the neighboring section you can see the buildings of Anthropology, Sociology, Paleontology, Archaeology. And that very old one, surrounded by ivy, is the Philosophy building.

Enneagram: Wow, these are all very large buildings.

Science: Of course. And all have collaborated, for a long time, in the effort to understand human behavior. Today I want to tell you about all the findings in Neuroscience and Genetics.

Enneagram: I understand. And the third building?

Science: The third is that little one, connected to the Psychology building. It is called Evolutionary Psychology. The team working in that building seeks to understand psychological traits and personality as mechanisms of adaptation to the environment, governed by the laws of Natural Selection. They do not like to be confused with Developmental Psychology, which is another small building that cannot be seen from here. That one deals with the study of the psychological development of individual human beings, from childhood onwards.

Enneagram: I see that the Evolutionary Psychology building has several buildings connected to it as well. There are some small ones that even have bridges.

Science: Yes, everything connects with everything. The little ones over there are those of Game Theory and Artificial Intelligence. A little farther is that of Zoology. And that big one you already know.

Enneagram: I see.

Science: These are the sources of the ideas we will be talking about.

When they got tired of walking, they stopped at a bar. After a long chat, a fruit juice for Science and a couple of glasses of wine for Enneagram, he told her about the nine personality types. Science looked animated, and as she listened to Enneagram, she kept connecting the dots between new and old ideas inside her head. When he finished talking, she stated her comments in the form of questions.

Science: What you are proposing raises some doubts. I invite you to work together to answer four questions.

First, is it possible to relate what you call Personality Types to behavioral patterns already identified by other branches of Science?

Second, is it possible to identify "biological mechanisms" that could explain the basis of each type? Which ones?

Third, if these mechanisms exist, would this imply that your nine types would be partly hereditary?

And finally, if they are inherited, can we trace their evolution over time? Do they have an adaptive purpose? When would they have appeared?

Enneagram: I confess that I feel excited. These are questions that I consider important to supplement what I already know. What is more, I am beginning to have my own hypotheses.

Science: Good. To work then. And if something doesn't make sense to you, we continue to investigate. The beauty of this is that we never get to sit on our laurel wreath. We are always checking whether what we held as true yesterday, can still be considered as valid today. Every time something new is discovered, in any of the buildings we saw today or even some that are still under construction, all of our convictions could be changed. It is part of the game.

Science and the Enneagram left the bar and sat down under the trees, ready, for the first time, to have a real dialogue.

What's so sexy about this model?

The model known as the Enneagram was outlined by Oscar Ichazo (1931–2020).[3] This Bolivian philosopher made a synthesis between Neoplatonic writings and texts taken from different religious traditions, to substantiate his teachings on what he called the "nine passions" of humankind. He coupled his model with a graphical representation, a symbol he had borrowed from George Gurdjieff (1866–1949), a self-proclaimed spiritual teacher of Armenian origin.

This model, still incipient, was taken by the Chilean psychiatrist Claudio Naranjo (1932–2019), and transformed into a personality typology. Naranjo had been trained at Harvard and Berkeley with some of the most outstanding researchers of his time in the scientific study of personality: Gordon Allport and Raymond Cattell.

Naranjo reflected his ideas in the books *Ennea-type Structures* and *Character and Neurosis.*[4] Even then, he built his description of the types based on findings from different lines of research in psychology, psychiatry, and biology of human behavior.

As a theoretical model, the Enneagram combines a series of virtues that, in our opinion, no other existing personality model to date has been able to provide.

Like factor models of personality, the Enneagram allows us to describe (and potentially measure) personality traits and their interindividual differences. Like psychodynamic models, the Enneagram allows for the understanding of the subjective experience of the individual, and provides a valuable aid for the development of a higher level of well-being.

Secondly, the Enneagram incorporates a systemic view, seeking to explain the dynamics of the interactions between its different parts. Like

---

3   Founder of the school of personal development known as the Arica Institute.
4   Naranjo: Ennea-type Structures: Self-Analysis for the Seeker (1990), Character and Neurosis (1994)

any complex system, personality could be characterized as a set of traits in permanent interaction with each other and with the environment, giving rise to emergent "properties" that cannot be explained on the basis of their isolated elements. Its internal dynamics appear chaotic and unpredictable, but the system is ultimately governed by laws that can be deciphered. As in every complex system, according to this model, the "whole" of personality is more than the sum of its parts. Individuals of different types may share what seems to be the same behavior, yet both will respond to different causes and will elicit different effects.

Thirdly, the nine types described by this model present clear parallels with behavioral patterns that have recently been identified by branches of biology and neurology. In some cases, the descriptions of these scholarly articles in the field of behavioral biology seem to be taken out from an Enneagram text. For those who already know the model, you will see that this is the case for Type Seven. Other types present striking similarities, such as Types One, Two, Five, Six, and Eight. A few have proven more difficult to track down, as is the case with Types Three, Four, and Nine. However, for all of them, there is evidence taken from behavioral biology that would explain an important part of the traits that the model describes.

Finally, the structure of the types, around "central traits" and with "fuzzy edges" between one type and another, is better adjusted to the behavior of personality traits at the genetic and clinical level: the traits have a normal statistical distribution, it is not "bipolar" nor does it have "arbitrary" borders, as models like the MBTI seem to suggest.[5]

From the point of view of the scientific community, all these potential contributions of the Enneagram could only materialize if the model is "real"; that is, if it can be verified, through scientific methods, that it truly reflects the "reality" of the phenomenon we call personality, as opposed to being a beautiful and powerful construct that is only found in the collective

---

5   Sutton, 2007, pg 28

imagination of its "believers".[6] At the time of writing this book, there are already several studies that support the existence of the nine types. However, the volume of these studies is still small, and from a scientific point of view, totally insufficient. And to honor the truth, there are also some studies, fewer, that fail to verify their existence.

One of our motivations for writing this book is precisely to encourage more and more researchers to collaborate with this validation effort.

Will Science want to be seen hand in hand with the Enneagram?

Let us recognize that it could be threatening for the Enneagram to accept an invitation from Science. Perhaps she will criticize him and expose him as a phony. Or she may just accuse him of being negligent for not doing his homework.

The Enneagram has existed for sixty years now, accumulating generations of authors who have been adding, modifying, and introducing new variants and emphasis on the original models proposed first by Ichazo and then by Naranjo. From the simplicity of the nine-type model, concepts have been added by the dozen: wings, levels of development, points of stress and well-being, lines of integration or disintegration, instinctive biases. So many subtypes, variants, and manifestations have emerged, that it is difficult not to feel trapped in a maze.

Unfortunately, only a few authors have attempted to base their observations on something stronger than their own intuitions and opinions. This has led the scientific community to look at this model with deep mistrust, generating a sidereal distance between them and the community of "believers."

This proliferation of different theories about the Enneagram has not only created a growing schism with scientific psychology, but has also lent itself

_____

6   Sutton, 2012

to the creation of "factions" within the Enneagram community, generating a true competition between schools; something that is almost ironic for a model devised in the first instance as a tool for personal development.

Will the Enneagram want to go to the movies with Science?

Let us now look at the other side of the wall: the scientific study of personality has been gaining *momentum* over the past 20 years, but it is still surprisingly fragmented and riddled with internal struggles.

Personality psychology is torn between factorial models and their search to describe individual differences in a "scientific" way, and the psychodynamic models, derived from clinical practice, with a vocation to explain internal processes and to aid in the development and well-being of individuals.

Within each of these macro worldviews there are dozens of different concepts, constructs, and theories, and very few efforts to integrate.

Amidst this chaos, the battle for scientific validity in the last few years seems almost won by the Five Factor Model[7], as a very high percentage of academic research on personality has gravitated in its direction.

However, for those of us who work in developmental, educational, or clinical psychology, the *Big Five's* approach to personality may resemble a 19th-century anatomist's understanding of the mysteries of how the human body works. The Five Factor model is limited to describing "components" and measuring their magnitudes and differences, but it is totally incapable of explaining the dynamics of personality, of understanding the subjective experience of each person, and of telling the story of how each one of us came to be "who we are."

---

7   The Five factor personality model (FFM), also called the "Big Five", proposes five broad dimensions of personality that were initially discovered through a statistical technique called factor analysis (Goldberg, 1993).

In the last two decades, two elements have appeared on the scene that promise a new disruption in the "building" of personality psychology.

The first is the Theory of Chaos. From this theory's perspective, personality can be seen as a "complex system" in which the whole has emergent properties that cannot be fully explained by the sum of its parts. One of the fundamental implications is to relativize the idea of determinism regarding behavior. A certain set of temperamental traits does not necessarily determine a specific set of behaviors. Another implication is that human behavior could be defined by the complex interactions of these components with one another and with external stimuli, and that a purely factorial model would be insufficient to comprehend this phenomenon.[8]

The second disruptive element is the recent and enormous advance in the knowledge about the biological and genetic basis of behavior. The discoveries that encompass not only the physiological correlates of emotions and behavior, but also the interaction between hereditary and environmental components during the different phases of development, are surprising and revealing.

In the face of these discoveries, Evolutionary Psychology has finally managed to find evidence on the specific mechanisms that could explain and support many of the theories that they have been proposing for some decades, about personality as a mechanism of adaptation to the environment.[9]

Sitting on the wall

We, the authors, have long sat on the wall that divides the world of the Enneagram and that of scientific research, without deciding to jump to either side.

---

8   Capra, 2003
9   Panksepp, Jaak; Montag, 2017; Penke, Jokela, & Mu, 2016; Pinker, 2009.

We are licensed psychologists, with postgraduate degrees in mental health and organizational behavior, linked to the academic world for a long time and with more than 25 years of experience using different personality models.

We perceive the Enneagram as a powerful tool, we feel portrayed by the descriptions it offers, and as psychologists, we have used it both to predict behavior and to guide the development of our clients. It has a "taste of truth" for us.

That said, our position is highly critical of the *status quo,* both of scientific psychology and its prevailing models, and of many of the current approaches and debates that we witness in the Enneagram world.

With respect to the Enneagram, we view the growing proliferation of variants and hyper-detailed descriptions with great skepticism. They seem to us unlikely, overly deterministic, and poorly founded. Nor do we like the fanaticism that we observe in some of its defenders, who pose it as a "revealed truth", beyond any need for verification.

We believe that the only way the Enneagram will be able to consolidate its potential and contribution is by voluntarily submitting itself to the rigors of the scientific method. Only in this way will it be able to establish its credibility, testing the validity and veracity of its different elements, and "purifying," integrating, and clarifying the model. Needless to say, the Enneagram would gain a lot if it drank from the fountain of behavioral biology. It could prove to be a fortifying, and why not, transforming drink.

Perhaps even more important: those who study the Enneagram to understand their own personality and to advance in the path of their own development, will obtain a more solid body of knowledge and a more realistic understanding of themselves and of the levers that can be used to achieve greater psychological well-being, instead of remaining confused in a Byzantine network of concepts that, at the end of the day, will be of little help.

With the same strength, we reject the dogmatism that exists within the scientific community, which impedes any dialogue with other sources of knowledge or with traditions that come from outside its own, closed kingdom.

We do not agree with the positivist reductionism that encourages factorial theories, nor with the relativism of postmodern approaches, which state that each individual is unique, unfathomable, unpredictable, and inexplicable.

And above all, we believe that the "scientific" models of personality need to be more self-critical of the degree of subjectivity that each of them has. "Human trace" can be clearly detected in the many subtle individual decisions that shape, name, define, and describe each of their constructs.

If the scientific community manages to break through its prejudices, it could benefit from a model that it would come to recognize as the valuable product of centuries of observation of human nature, and the genius intuition that shaped it, incorporating vast knowledge of modern psychology into its design.

Because ultimately, neither the social sciences are as exact as they would like to be, nor did the Enneagram emerge so far removed from science, as is sometimes claimed.

We don't want to jump to either side of the wall. What we want is for the wall itself to become permeable.

What's in this book

Without wanting to make a *spoiler* of what you may be discovering, we anticipate some of what you will find here.

The first part of this book presents some concepts about the biological basis of behavior. We will give you only the fundamental pieces that are necessary to understand what comes next.

Then you will find a description of nine personality types, accompanied by some hypotheses about their possible biological basis and about their adaptive purpose, seen from an evolutionary perspective.

You can come and go as your adventurous spirit and curiosity dictate. If you want to go step by step, you will enjoy a structure that goes from the general to the particular. If you like specific detail and scientific precision, you will find an abundance of references about the studies that support the discussion.

We will also invite you to a totally intuitive approach based on short stories that will illustrate the adaptive advantages of each personality type in the age of the hunter-gatherers.

With all these elements we hope you enjoy the adventure of crossing this wall as much as we do.

For those of a more scientific mind, a word of clarification: The statements that appear in this book are not "proven." We do not claim to have the final "truth" about personality. Nor do we believe those who claim to have it today. Our contribution is limited to "connecting the dots" between actual scientific findings, and our interpretation of the nine-type model. We present our sources in a transparent manner, so that the reader can go deeper and form his or her own opinion.

For our readers who already know the Enneagram model, the following message: The traits hereby presented for the types represent our personal vision of what constitutes the true "core" for each of them. In our view, all other traits are secondary, culturally determined, and therefore may vary. We have come to this conclusion, after a thorough review of how genetics and biology work in interaction with experiences and environment, in the process of the making of our personality.

PART I: THREE THINGS YOU SHOULD KNOW BEFORE FINDING YOURSELF

You are sitting just like that, with precisely that expression on your face and a certain emotional atmosphere inside, because you ARE like that. It is usual for you to be like that. You have lived with yourself, from the moment you were born.

Since we already know that you do all this, we could predict that, in the future, you will repeat gestures, behaviors, and emotions that are similar to those you have right now. And if we knew more of your behaviors, those that are relatively stable over time, we could group them together and talk about your "personality," your particular way of being.

Your personality is formed by the set of cognitive, emotional and behavioral patterns, related to each other, that characterize your way of interacting with your environment. These patterns, which we usually call "traits," remain relatively stable throughout a person's life, and they show important differences between individuals.

To present this model of Nine Sapiens we want to start by explaining the foundations of our hypotheses. We will do so in this first part, which we have divided into three sections.

We will start with the place where our personality is "housed". The brain. We will describe in the simplest form, how its basic systems and functions operate. In the second section we will analyze personality from the perspective of Evolutionary Psychology, which understands it as a mechanism of adaptation to our environment. And finally, in the third section, we will review the implications of heredity and environment in the formation and development of personality.

The first thing: It all started in the brain

Scientist Björn Brembs says that the ability to choose between different behavioral options would be common to most brains.[10] Do you feel represented? Watch out! Brembs is referring to flies! And to agree with him, we will tell you that the neurons in our brain are not very different from the neurons in a fly. The main difference is that a fly's brain usually has one hundred thousand neurons and ours, eighty-six thousand million. And the way in which our neurons are organized, product of thousands of years of evolution, allows us to do many more things than to prowl around trash cans, said with respect for the commendable ecological work of flies.[11]

Millennium after millennium, our brain evolved into a sophisticated adaptive organ. Thanks to it we are here, with time to make comparisons with flies, while other animals live in an economy of survival or submitted to us in one way or another.

Let us pause to acknowledge *Homo sapiens'* brilliant race to position himself at the top of the food podium, in just a few evolutionary steps and with greater speed than any other species, subjecting and reducing many others to extinction. This race was sustained by the evolution of our brain, consisting of a gradual increase in its capacity, a growing specialization, and an increasingly integrated functioning.[12]

---

10 Brembs & Hempel De Ibarra, 2006
11 Roth & Dicke, 2005
12 Friedman & Miyake, 2017

The process of specialization of our brain was a very long road, which took it from being just another unit within a bundle of undifferentiated cells collaborating with one another, to becoming a sophisticated central nervous system with highly specialized structures and substructures. It could be compared to going from spinning around in a small wooden raft, to the complex subdivision of tasks and technology necessary to command a nuclear submarine. Throughout this process, our neurons were grouped into small units or areas, assuming increasingly differentiated functions, each working in its own role: interpreting environmental stimuli, decoding sensations in our own body, activating the movement of an arm to pick an apple from a tree, or triggering emotional responses that would motivate an "other" to become our sexual partner, just to mention a few.

The same can be said of the integration process. These specialized groups of neurons needed to function and respond in a coordinated manner. When our visual neurons detect a hungry lion with its eyes suspiciously resting on us, the neurons of our amygdala should be alerted as soon as possible, so that they can take care of activating our sympathetic system, which in turn will ensure that our blood is timely directed to our skeletal muscles, all this to prepare us to fight like Tarzan or run away like Mr. Bean.

Let us recognize that the neurons in our brain do a great job as a team, as they enable us to do many things, that can go from running away from those who want to have us for breakfast, to scaring away a fly that wants to land on our nose. A movement that, by the way, should contemplate that our eyes only register static images, sending them to the brain in the form of flashes. The bad news: human eyes average 60 flashes per second and flies' average around 250. Have you ever wondered why it is so hard to catch a fly?

Our neurons have much to communicate to each other, and through-out evolution their messages have become more and more complex and full of subtleties. And this communication had to be faster and faster. So neurons branched out and connected with each other in the most efficient way they could. In time, they developed a very ingenious code to transmit the messages to each other, similar to our alphabet, because they were able to say everything they needed using very few elements. Just a handful of different neurotransmitters, with their respective receptors and some mechanisms to regulate their quantity.

Remember the picture of a neuron? They all have a star-shaped body and a long tail called an "axon," which can extend from 4 micrometers in the neurons of our cerebellum, up to 1 meter in length in the case of the neurons responsible for moving your toes.

The body of the neuron is surrounded by "dendrites", small branches in charge of "capturing" the "messages" that come to it from its neighbors "upstream". Each time a message arrives, the neuron "decides" if it is strong and clear enough to be retransmitted. If it does, then the message is sent along its axon by means of an electrophysiological pulse, and when it reaches the end, the message is "fired" to all the neurons that are communicated with it, "downstream". And how is this message triggered? Small amounts of neurotransmitters are released from the end of the axon, into the space that separates the neuron from its neighbors "downstream".

The economic aspect in all this is that the same neurotransmitter means different things to different neurons, depending on their role, and the place where they are located. And some neurons may be more sensitive to the action of a certain neurotransmitter, since they have a greater number of "receptors" for it. Others have fewer receptors and therefore will be more "deaf." They will have to be yelled at louder and more often so they can "hear."

On the other hand, after the message has been sent, there is always some amount of those neurotransmitters that will remain as leftovers, floating in the synaptic space. It is important to get this waste out of there as quickly as possible, so that the neuron "downstream" does not interpret that it is being spoken to again. For these purposes, we have "cleaning systems," capable of recapturing the excess material for future reuse (very ecological); or simply breaking it down and discarding it by means of enzymes (less ecological, but equally effective).

We were saying that, as our brain evolved, the neurons of the different specialized units connected with each other as efficiently as they "could." Let us imagine these groups of axons as if they were the streets and avenues of a big city. There are a little over one hundred thousand kilometers of these "streets and avenues" within our brain. Some are main avenues, because they concentrate a lot of traffic, as is the case of the roads that connect our left and right hemispheres with each other. Others are full-blown streets that connect well-established neighborhoods, such as the roads linking "*downtown*" Amygdala with the affluent suburbs of the Pre-Frontal Cortex. Some of these streets are direct and fast, point-to-point, and others follow completely ridiculous routes, inherited from the past, as if they were the great detour to surround an old cathedral, or the road that used to circle the old city walls. Other streets are still very new, seldom trodden, and unpaved, and they could disappear at any minute if they fall into disuse. But as it happens with a big city, it is a living, dynamic phenomenon, the transit is always changing, and new streets emerge every day. We will come back to this when we touch on the subject of neuroplasticity, and the role it has in our capacity to change our way of feeling, thinking, or acting as individuals.

Now, we have mentioned some of the "neighborhoods" within our brain. These are specialized units. Some of them are very old in evolutionary terms, such as our autonomous nervous system, responsible for regulating the correct functioning of our internal organs. Others emerged somewhat later, such as our limbic system, associated with many of our emotions, whose primitive role was simply to mobilize us towards everything that was positive for our survival, and to avoid everything that was harmful.

The high point of the brain's evolution was the emergence of the Pre-Frontal Cortex. Something like the "presidential palace " within this city. A great "center of operations," capable of directing "thought" and orchestrating "will" and "decision making."

No more flies or cities for now. Some of you may think that we've taken a long detour, and that you've had enough with the biology classes you already had in elementary school.

We ask you to bear with us for a few more minutes, because we will be resorting to some of these basic concepts along the book: the different types of neurotransmitters, receptors, and waste-disposal systems, and the different degrees of integration or specialization within the brain, as we explain the mechanisms underlying personality types, how they operate, and how they are inherited.

We leave you with two key ideas that we will return to later:

KEY IDEA 1: The evolution of our brain has consisted of a gradual increase in capacity, a growing specialization, and an increasing integration or coordination.

KEY IDEA 2: Our neurons "talk" to each other using neurotransmitters, and they "listen" to each other through receptors to those neurotransmitters.

Second thing: Personality is a radar to navigate the social maze

We, the *Homo sapiens*, owners of an increasingly refined "intelligence," have become capable of understanding sophisticated cause-effect relationships and of better predicting our environment. And when a mutation made us capable of developing a more precise language, it revolutionized our ability to organize ourselves into ever larger social groups, multiplying our options of achieving collective goals. Hunting mammoths, building boats, or making it clear to our hostile neighbors that we are willing to fight as brothers, were all achievements unthinkable for the individual, but possible in the collective.

However, larger groups do not only bring advantages. They also bring headaches. Thus, we were forced to learn how to navigate a complex web of relationships, alliances, betrayals, and hierarchies. Not that they didn't exist before. All social animals experience these problems to some extent. For primatologists, the difference between a gang of chimpanzees and a band of adolescents is that the latter are dressed and listen to music. Having said that, let's admit that *Homo sapiens* has taken this complexity to a whole new level. We have won an Oscar and three Bafta's.

Managing the social tangle required a very different set of adaptive skills than avoiding being a cat's dinner or being bitten by a snake. Our brains were forced to evolve more sophisticated adaptive strategies, such as balancing the subtle challenges of being able to collaborate in some cases while competing in others, of being sincere, without being naive, or of being righteous, but not relentless.

Evolutionary Psychology has come to the same conclusion: all social animals had to develop certain behavioral patterns to adapt to living in society. In order to know when it was appropriate to display each behavior, we had to sharpen our cognitive "radar" in a way that allowed us to understand the subtleties of our social environment. And to mobilize us to action, we had to extend our basic "emotions" to a more social function. It must have been millions of years of evolution, generation after generation.

Intuitively, we have always known that there are different personalities. Philosophers and theologians, psychologists and psychiatrists, neurobiologists and playwrights, poets and people with common sense, since time began, have recognized that there are certain distinctive patterns in the behavior of different human beings. It has been much more difficult to agree on "what" these patterns are. It is not unusual then that so many different personality maps coexist, each with its own emphases, methodologies, and ways of interpreting the world. How can we know which map is closest to the "truth"?

Evolutionary Psychology has entered this discussion relatively recently, offering a less arbitrary way of making sense of individual differences. They argue that all social animals have personality, and that we have developed it as a mechanism to adapt to life in society. That it would have a hereditary biological basis, and therefore, would be subject to the mechanisms of natural selection. That personality is not "neutral," but that it profoundly affects our adaptive capacity. And that the individual differences that have survived throughout evolution represent the distinct genetic variants that have been successful in overcoming the typical adaptive challenges that each species must face.[13]

The ideas that we propose in this book are, to a great extent, a construction derived from the hypotheses of Evolutionary Psychology.

KEY IDEA 3: Personality is, fundamentally, an "adaptation" mechanism to live in society.

The minefield: Invisible challenges of living in society

Here is a list of some of the typical "adaptive challenges" that our species has had to face, repeatedly, millions of millions of times, over millennia.[14] Raise your hand if they sound familiar:

---

13   Buss & Penke, 2012; Penke et al., 2007; Arslan & Penke, 2014; Panksepp, 2011; K. L. Davis & Panksepp, 2011; Montag, Widenhorn-müller, Panksepp, & Kiefer, 2017; Buss & Hawley, 2011; Kasper, Schreier, & Taborsky, 2019.
14   Adapted from Penke et al., 2007

- *Friend or Foe*: Choosing the best among the available partners to establish collaborative relationships and detecting potential cheaters.
- *You scratch my back and I'll scratch yours*: Forming coalitions to achieve ambitious goals and solving conflicts that might weaken collaboration in the group.
- *The network*: Facing threats to our status or our inclusion within the group and surviving in case of isolation or exile.
- *In love and war*: Attracting an effective partner for reproduction and/or breeding, confronting "sexual competitors," and fending off "poachers" who might want to steal our partners.
- *Watching them grow*: Procuring help to take care of our children and to support them during the long time they are unable to fend for themselves.
- *Through thick and thin*: Providing resources to our families within a universe of limited resources.
- *Quo Vadis*: Detecting personality traits and monitoring the emotions of the people around us.
- *No means no*: Defending ourselves from unwanted sexual advances.
- *All animals are equal but...*: Obtaining a position of hierarchy starting from a position of subordination.
- *The Fight Club:* Defending ourselves from attacks by hostile humans.

Evolutionary psychology argues that different personality patterns represent alternative responses to these typical "adaptive challenges." If you look closely, you will see that the vast majority of these challenges are primarily social, although some relate to aspects of our biology, such as the fact that human "puppies" require so much care and for so long just to survive into adulthood.

Throughout our evolution, human beings have developed psychological mechanisms to quickly detect and process all relevant information regarding these challenges; and to make decisions about how to face them and solve them.[15]

Given their constancy over time, it is intuitive to think that natural selection has "fixed" some of our adaptive strategies: emotions, cognitive biases or preferences, so that they guide our reactions quickly and "economically." Thus, we would not need to "relearn" each of our most basic behaviors from scratch; every time a new individual was born. It begins to make sense that our personality has evolved to "record" some of its components into biology and heredity. Although Skinner might be turning over and throwing stones at us from his grave, it seems that our behavioral flexibility has certain "systematic" limits.[16]

KEY IDEA 4: Different personality "patterns" represent the different responses that have proved to be successful in the face of a finite number of typical "adaptive challenges" that have remained constant for millennia.

A subtle difference

Let us now return to evolution. The history of our personality is the history of our brain's evolution. And this evolution operated as it always does, through random mutations and natural selection.

Generation after generation, each one of the specialized areas of our brain presented small mutations, totally by chance.

Watch out: this is not something that happened in the past. Our genome is composed of about 25,000 genes, give or take; and we all carry mutations, which could occur in any of these genes.[17]

---

15   Buss & Penke, 2012, pg 11-12.
16   Barrett, 2006; Apicella & Barrett, 2016; Penke et al., 2007
17   Technically, these mutations can also occur in any section of the genome specialized in the regulation of the expression of those genes (Akey, 2009).

You and I, in all probability, carry about 70 new mutations on average. Most of these mutations will be neutral for our adaptation, and many will be passed on to our children and grandchildren, because they will not interrupt the functioning of our organism. But the odds are that at least two of the new mutations that you and I carry will be harmful. In many cases, the damage will be slight and therefore our children will also take their share. And so it happens that many mutations tend to accumulate from generation to generation. Our grandparents did the same thing with us, which means that we all live with about 500 slightly "disruptive" mutations in our brains.[18]

Carrying harmful mutations doesn't sound very sexy. So far, only bad news. The good news is that, very occasionally, mutations occur that are beneficial for adaptation. Natural selection gives a standing ovation when this happens, and the mutation tends to perpetuate itself in the generations to come, for the joy and benefit of all.[19]

A small mutation, in a gene within 25,000, may seem like a small thing. However, any of these seemingly tiny mutations, when they affect the subtle mechanisms within our brain, can generate enormous variations in the way we react and behave. This could mean the difference between life and death. Or, to be less dramatic, the difference between life and death of another. Or the difference between having many children and having them survive; or having none at all.

KEY IDEA 5: Our brain has evolved from random mutations that are passed on from generation to generation, following the laws of Natural Selection. These mutations affect the way we react and behave.

---

18   Buss & Penke, 2012; Keightley, 2012; Keller & Miller, 2006
19   Buss & Penke, 2012, pg 27.

Grow and multiply

In the past, natural selection was understood as the "survival of the fittest." Today we understand adaptive success as the ability to pass on our genetic material to the next generations. The more replications of our genetic material, the more adaptive success. Sounds like more fun, doesn't it?

From the point of view of natural selection, the most important quality of any living organism is its "fitness," which is nothing other than the statistical probability of transmitting its genes to the next generations.[20]

Obviously, in order to pass on our genes, we would have to meet a series of intermediate challenges, which can be summarized as four: surviving at least until we reach sexual maturity; being able to access sexual partners and reproduce successfully; having our children and relatives survive until sexual maturity; and establishing reciprocal collaborative links with unrelated individuals in order to increase our chances of survival.

The intense emotions associated with our own survival, with motherhood and fatherhood, with "falling in love" and finding a partner, with establishing a home, and with bonding with our closest relatives, would be a reflection of how the brain has evolved to "mobilize" us to ensure the transfer of our genetic material. The basis of these emotions is linked to the nucleus of our brain and operates quite automatically.[21] On top of that, we can always add a little bit of romanticism. One thing does not rule out the other.

With this new logic, not only the strongest would multiply, but also the most astute, the most cautious, the most daring, the most peaceful, the most creative, or anyone who would achieve a reasonable number of living children, whatever their method. And although we still have much to understand, many studies already confirm this suspicion: our personality influences our "reproductive success."

---

20   Penke et al., 2007, pg 574; Sapolski, 2017.
21   Sapolsky, 2017.

KEY IDEA 6: Adaptive success is about being able to pass on our genes to the next generations.

Rock, paper, scissors

The blue-throated "spotted" lizard is willing to do whatever it takes to protect its mate and its territory. Above all, he must defend himself from orange-throated males, which are large and aggressive bullies, and whose favorite sport is stealing away the partners from their blue-throated companions. These orange-throats, on the other hand, usually have so many sexual partners and such wide territories to take care of, that they are exposed to plundering by the yellow-throats, which, pretending to be female, sneak into their territories to steal their mates. Thus, the males of this species of lizard (*Uta stansburiana*), in their three chromatic versions, compete with different strategies for the same females.

This competition for reproductive access has been compared to the Rock, Paper, Scissors game. And biologists have observed that it leads to genetic oscillations, making the least common variant in one generation become the most common in the next, and so on. All three strategies are efficient under certain conditions, and none of the three is permanently the most successful. It all depends on the circumstances.[22]

This selective mechanism, called "Balancing Selection," means that different variants of a trait can be adaptive depending on the circumstances, so that genetic variation will be maintained throughout evolution.[23]

---

22   Sinervo & Lively, 1996; Arslan & Penke, 2014
23   An alternative hypothesis to Balancing Selection would have been that many of the personality variations that currently exist are due to recent mutations that have not yet been able to be "cleaned up" by the process of Natural Selection. However, Selection only takes about 10,000 years to "fix" a non-adaptive mutation. If this were the case, these personality variants could be specific to one or a few related populations and would not have a "universal" presence as has been proven through various studies. This presence across different populations and cultures implies that these mutations would have emerged before the different "branches" of our species were separated (Keller & Miller, 2006).

This mechanism explains why evolution has preserved different personality types. It is because all of them have proved to be adaptive in the face of several of the recurrent challenges that we human beings face, at least under certain circumstances that are also recurrent. If there were a single "optimum personality," selective pressure would have led to all of us sharing the same personality traits.[24]

Since we humans are faced with a varied range of adaptive niches, especially from the point of view of our social environment, different personality styles would be more or less successful in each of them. And let us remember that part of our heritage is also endowed by an enormous behavioral plasticity and learning capacity, the crown jewels of our brain's evolution.[25]

KEY IDEA 7: Evolution has preserved different personality types because they have all been adaptive to the recurring challenges and circumstances we face as a species.

Tell me how you invest your energy and I'll tell you who you are.

Our energy (and time) is limited. Our personality determines which aspects of our environment are presented to us as more visible or "priority" when it comes to defining where to invest our energy. For example, some of us may choose to prioritize our own well-being; others, the attraction and retention of sexual partners; and still others, the protection and care of our children.[26] The different personality traits will also determine which strategies we will use to solve these challenges, and which of them we will tend to solve more successfully.

---

24   Some evolutionary psychologists argue that, unlike personality, our intelligence would have evolved steadily in the direction of greater "robustness" (Penke, 2010).
25   Buss & Penke, 2012
26   Lenton, Fasolo, & Todd, 2009; Penke, 2010; Buss & Penke, 2012.

And on what basis do we select our strategies? It is generally an unconscious decision, forged from our early childhood, as we go along responding spontaneously according to our "innate tendencies." Little by little we learn the impact that these responses have on our environment. Over time, we will be able to actively select the environments where we feel that our "pool" of capabilities has the greatest likelihood of adaptive success.[27]

All personality traits carry adaptive advantages and disadvantages. A high sensitivity to stress, for example, will allow a greater capacity for alertness, and better detection of potential dangers, both physical and social, while involving an unpleasant subjective experience, and a potential damage to the health of its bearer.[28]

KEY IDEA 8: Our personality determines which adaptive challenges we will prioritize and the strategies we will use to address them.

KEY IDEA 9: We will choose environments where our innate tendencies and preferred strategies give us more guarantee of success.

Step by step and little by little

Let us consider that evolution measures its times in thousands or millions of years. Nothing happens overnight. It may surprise you to know that a significant part of our genes has not changed much since the Pleistocene.[29]

Some of the personality types we will describe later must have had an adaptive sense since the dawn of our species. Some may have emerged even earlier, from mutations that occurred millions of years ago, carried over from our shared evolutionary past with other mammals. Have you ever identified with the reactions of a deer or a lion?

---

27   Buss & Penke, 2012
28   Nettle, 2006 ; Penke et al., 2007.
29   Penke, 2010

Other personality traits only seem to acquire adaptive value after the "cognitive revolution" and the development of language, which according to theorists would have happened some 70,000 years ago, giving way to "modern" *Homo sapiens.*

And it is also very likely that many personality traits have continued to evolve since the advent of agriculture, when the process, far from stagnating as was once thought, may have accelerated due to the rapid increase in population that it brought along.[30]

In spite of this "recent" acceleration, in general terms, evolution occurs very slowly. Let's do an exercise to place ourselves in the orders of magnitude. Some estimate that the first hominids would have emerged more than 5 million years ago. The most accepted theory is that *Homo sapiens* emerged at least 200,000 years ago, but others calculate that our evolution was much longer and intertwined with that of our "first cousins."[31]

If anthropologists mark the beginning of "modern man" at 70,000 years ago, we would have spent at least 60,000 years living as hunter-gatherers. This is equivalent to 86% of our evolutionary time as modern humans, even without considering the hundreds of thousands of years that we were already *Homo sapiens*, or the millions of years of our evolution as hominids.

We do this reflection partly as an exercise in humility, and partly because it allows us to better understand why some of our personality traits do not

---

30   There is evidence that the speed of the evolution of Homo sapiens would have accelerated in the last 10,000 years, due to the advent of agriculture and the explosive population growth it brought with it. As there were more births, there were also more mutations to which selective pressure was applied. Moreover, the direction of this selective pressure may have changed with the transformations brought about by sedentary life: less varied diet, more exposure to disease transmission, less risk of dying in accidents and greater risk of dying in war or from simple starvation, just to mention a few. Above all, sedentary life introduced the possibility of accumulating wealth, social classes, great political conflicts and, in general, a greater risk of being abused by other homo sapiens. Our social life escalated to a new level of complexity, also exerting a new selective pressure on our personality.   Evolution as an adaptation mechanism is a living process. (Lee, 2018).

31   Lee, 2018.

seem completely adequate to adapt to our post-industrial and post-modern environment. Something within us seems to miss the savannah.

This is not only true for the evolution of our personality. It is also true for many other adaptations that we carry in our bodies. Our taste for sugar, for example, and our ability to gobble up large quantities of chocolate or cookies, even beyond what is necessary for the caloric needs of our day (however guilty we may feel...). Our ancestors were rarely fortunate enough to encounter a bunch of grapes or an apple tree. And if they did, they usually had to compete against birds, monkeys, or other fruit lovers. Nor did they have many options for storing or carrying them for long periods of time. The most adaptive thing to do was to stuff everything that fit between their chests and backs, with little danger of ever committing an excess.

Therefore, when we consider the adaptive value of different personality traits, we have to go through imagining what were the challenges that our hunter-gatherer ancestors had to face. This gives us a basis for understanding their adaptive value along the 10,000 years we have lived in sedentary and agricultural societies, and in the 200 years after the industrial revolution.

We are convinced that many of the genes that rest at the foundation of personality, yours and ours, were already carried by some of our ancestors of that time. If they had not survived and reproduced then, neither you would be reading this book, nor would we have written it.

KEY IDEA 10: Our brain and personality evolved slowly, over millennia, adapting to the challenges of our life as hunter-gatherers.

Evolution is a great recycler

Before finishing this section, we want to share with you one last quality that characterizes evolution, which is particularly informative regarding brain and personality development.

Evolution never "creates" from scratch, and always "works" with the elements it has at hand. It is not an "inventor," but a great "recycler." If our brain needs to develop a new functionality, it will "reach out" to the "closest" function within those that already exist, trying to "expand" its duties in order to accommodate the new purpose. The brain "hijacks" a primitive function to devote it to a more sophisticated one.[32] For instance, in the following pages we will see how the area of the brain responsible for perceiving physical pain, eventually expanded its job to also take care of the perception of emotional pain. We will also see how the same brain mechanism that lays at the base of repugnance for decomposed food, became responsible for feeling "moral repugnance."

KEY IDEA 11: The more sophisticated functions of our brain were "assumed" by primitive areas that were performing "similar" functions.

And the third thing: Born or made?

It's in my blood

And after the thousands of years of evolution of *Homo sapiens*, it was our turn to be born. Almost by chance, we come with a genetic "package," a legacy from all our ancestors. To what extent does this "package" determine our personality?

The evolutionary perspective rests on the assumption that personality is, at least in part, hereditary. But is this a confirmed fact? And...does this mean that I am predetermined to be like my parents and grandparents? To what extent? Here we go.

---

32   Sapolsky, 2017.

Did you say "heritability"?

What do genes have to do with humans having a pair of eyes and a pair of ears? Everything, because it is a totally inherited trait. What is the heritability of that trait? Zero, because there is almost no variation around that average pair of ears and pair of eyes. What's the catch? A "hereditary trait" is actually something quite different from the "heritability of a trait."

If the usual value of a trait is highly influenced by genes, then that trait is strongly inherited. On the other hand, if the genes influence the degree of variability of that trait, then that trait has a high *heritability*.

Let's understand the difference through an example. Let's imagine that, in a delivery room, a father waits anxiously to know how many ears their child will be born with. The last one came with three....If this were true, the number of ears would be a feature of high heritability. If, on the other hand, the idea doesn't even cross that father's head, it's because 99.99% of children only have two ears. As this is the case, then we are talking about a trait that is highly inherited but has very low heritability.

On the other hand, there are many behaviors that, without being hereditary, do correlate with our genes. For example, wearing a skirt in most of the Western world is highly correlated with having two X chromosomes. However, there are exceptions. If you have a Y chromosome, have been born in the Highlands of Scotland, and were brought up with strong patriotic values, you will tend to wear a tartan skirt, ideally with bagpipe music in the background.

In other words, when we talk about the hereditary component of personality, we are actually talking about its degree of *heritability*. That is, the percentage of the variation of each personality trait that is attributable to genetics.[33]

---

33   Sapolsky, 2017

The fruit does not fall far...

"He has his father's eyes," "she's so talkative, it runs in the family." Many individual differences, cognitive abilities, and personality traits are largely heritable. You suspected as much. What's more, we are going to share with you a piece of striking information: the greatest individual predictor of any personality trait is how our parents score for that trait.[34] It is understandable if you leave the reading at this point and think for a moment about your parents. Then you can continue.

Let's imagine we open today's newspaper and read: "Scientist succeeds in cloning human being from test tube obtaining an identical twin. One will be raised in New York, and the other will be sent to New Guinea. A 20-year longitudinal study will reveal important relationships between genetics and behavior. Scientific team celebrates with Dom Pérignon Vintage champagne." No. We are not going to read that headline. No one would dare to experiment by cloning human beings and separating them at birth. No one? Correction, it has happened, courtesy of Nature and Chance.

Science has taken advantage of this great natural experiment to collect findings that have traditionally been the greatest source of information about the genetic basis of personality. After thousands of studies, follow-ups, and meta-analyses, calculating the similarities and differences between identical twins, non-identical twins, and twins separated at birth, and after having collected data on millions of pairs of twins, experts have managed to agree on an approximate figure for the heritability of personality: between 40% and 60%.[35]

Much more recent is the technique of Genome Wide Association Study (GWAS), which has allowed scientists to analyze hundreds of thousands of differences in DNA, estimating the genetic match between individuals; to then examine their similarities and differences at the level of visible features.

---

34   Penke, Jokela, & Mu, 2016.
35   Plomin et al., 2016; Polderman et al., 2015; Hill et al., 2018

This is a difficult technique, as it requires distinguishing what is important and what is accessory within many thousands of differences at the DNA strand level, in many thousands of individuals. It is very easy to overlook or underestimate the impact of a small difference. Another technique is the study of "candidate genes," which are chosen for their repeated association with some particular personality traits. Unlike GWAS, this technique starts from an existing hypothesis, and uses genomic analysis of large populations to explore its validity.

Genomic analysis techniques are very promising, but have not yet been able to corroborate the heritability found in statistical studies with twins. Despite this, the consistency of the latter's findings is such, that their conclusions are still considered valid.[36]

Finally, some studies and meta-analyses have explored the extent to which personality evolves throughout life. These studies have shown that 80% of the traits that remain stable have a hereditary root.[37]

KEY IDEA 12: Between 40% and 60% of our personality is the product of hereditary variations.

And I leave half of my genes to each of my children...

Now, what exactly is inherited? If we consider inheritance from the point of view of its literal meaning, nothing. Because to "bequeath" something in the form of an inheritance requires that we have first "owned" that something. Perhaps if we are entirely purists, we should refer to it as "passing on." We are temporary holders of certain genetic information that

---

36 L. K. Davis et al., 2013; Gaugler et al., 2014; Klei et al., 2012; McGue et al., 2013; Plomin et al., 2016; Rietveld et al., 2013; Vinkhuyzen et al., 2012.

37 Briley & Tucker-Drob, 2014; Plomin, Defries, Knopik, & Neiderhiser, 2016; Turkheimer, Pettersson, & Horn, 2014.

has been transferred to us and that we then pass on, and neither a will nor a testament will be necessary!

But enough of the technicalities, and let's return to inheritance, which is the term that biology has chosen to identify that which does not have an environmental origin: What is it, in precise terms, that is inherited?

All heritable psychological differences begin with genes that carry the codes to produce certain components, all of them key to the operation of our brain.

The slight differences in these genes generally translate into a greater or lesser production of certain neurotransmitters; a greater or lesser number of receptors for them in our neurons; or a more or less efficient "waste disposal" mechanism for collecting leftovers from our synaptic space.

Remember?

Any subtle variation in any of these "primary" neurophysiological mechanisms will lead to differences in our activation thresholds, our levels of reactivity, or our degrees of sensitivity to very specific stimuli.[38] In short, all this will influence our cognitive style, our most recurrent emotions, and the behaviors that come to be more spontaneous, effortless, or successful for us.

It is night, both are sleeping, and the neighbor's cat has jumped on the roof. Slight knocking sounds and some quick cat footsteps. One of the two opens his eyes and sharpens his ears. The other sleeps peacefully.

Same stimulus, different response. And the strength of the response may also vary. There will be those who will not only prick up their ears when the neighbor's cat walks by, but who will be alarmed, wake up their companion, turn on the lights, and go up to the roof to make sure that it is not a thief or an alien attack.

---

38   Plomin et al., 2016

KEY IDEA 13: The "heritable" component of our personality translates into a set of reaction thresholds and degrees of sensitivity to the stimuli that surround us.

All for one and one for all

In the pages that follow, we will mention many studies that have found a correlation between the presence of some specific genes and the manifestation of certain personality traits. In other words, these studies go far beyond defining what percentage of our personality is hereditary, or what could be the basic mechanisms that explain this relationship.

These studies have found, for example, that carriers of the variant 7R+ in the gene that encodes for dopamine D4 receptors (DRD4) in the Nucleus Accumbens, tend to be extraordinarily restless, curious, and fond of novelty, that they have a greater tendency to migrate, and a greater likelihood of consuming nicotine and practicing extreme sports.[39] What???

Well, not so fast. Let no one imagine that this heritability issue is a simple one.

To begin with, there is no such thing as "the gene" for Perfectionism, Anxiety, or Kindness.

Studies have shown that, very often, a single personality trait can be caused by an accumulation of genes with very small effects.[40-41] The key factor in this case seems to be a "collaboration" between genes. It is not yet known if their effects accumulate, and the trait is only expressed when they

---

39   Iversen & Iversen, 2007.

40   Plomin et al., 2016; Gratten, Wray, Keller, & Visscher, 2014

41   No single nucleotide has been shown to have an effect greater than a 1% increase in the probability of presenting the trait. The exception is some rare mutations, which have a large impact on the individual who presents them, but they are so rare that their impact on the general population is also very small (Chabris, Lee, Cesarini, Benjamin, & Laibson, 2015) (Plomin & Simpson, 2013).

achieve a certain "critical mass"; or if they interact with each other, so that a gene is only expressed when another gene is present.[42]

But this is only part of the story. It is also suspected that the exact opposite could happen. That is to say, the same gene—or set of genes—could be at the base of many apparently dissimilar traits.

Situation 1: She entered the church and immediately felt it. She was startled, as the eyes of everybody present fell on her. Could I be dressed inappropriately?

Situation 2: She worked for several hours without raising her head. She was against time. All her attention was focused on the task at hand. Her co-workers were unable to keep up with her. She didn't get up until she was done.

Situation 3: It was late, and she was alone. But she just needed to walk through that dark alley. If only someone came to walk with her. But no. Could she do it quickly perhaps? But if she ran, her fear would show...

The above example illustrates how monitoring social acceptance, maintaining a prolonged state of alert, and detecting environmental threats, being distinct behaviors, may share a common inherited root in the form of a hypersensitivity to stress.[43]

And the story does not end here. Many interactions between genes and environment have also been observed; that is, genes that will only be expressed in a particular way, when in the presence of certain environmental conditions. To be continued...

---

42 The mechanism that describes the summation effect of several genes at the base of a single trait is called polygeny, and is also observed for the heritability of intelligence, physical traits, or the propensity to develop certain diseases. The "non-additive" relationships, which describe an interaction between genes, in which the presence of one is a condition for the expression of another, is called epistasis (Penke et al., 2016).

43 This mechanism, a single gene responsible for multiple traits, is called pleiotropy (Buss & Penke, 2012).

KEY IDEA 14: The relationship between genes and personality traits is not one-to-one. A single trait can be caused by the joint effect of many genes; and at the same time, a single gene could be at the base of many apparently unrelated traits.

It is more than the sum of its parts

Let's go one step further. Biologists, geneticists, psychiatrists, and psychologists have long discussed whether the natural unit for studying personality corresponds to individual traits or to sets of interrelated traits; that is, personality types. To make it simple, let's talk about two main factions, those who support the "trait" thesis, and those inclined towards "types". Do you want to know who is winning?

In the world of psychologists and during the last twenty years, the balance of this discussion has been decidedly tilted in favor of those who defend individual traits, thanks to the influence of the factorial models of personality. In the world of psychiatry, the historical balance has been almost invariably tipped towards types, as sets of interrelated traits, known as diagnostic categories.

Of course, there are nuances, and both sides continually influence one another.

Is this match still in a tie? Probably yes. However, there seems to be a way out. Biologists and geneticists have entered this discussion in a much more dispassionate way, making contributions that, in our opinion, are hard to ignore.

In a 2018 publication, the renowned geneticist and psychiatrist Robert Cloninger describes the use of *machine learning,* a method from the field of artificial intelligence, to identify complex patterns in the millions of data obtained from numerous brain imaging and genome wide association studies (GWAS). Drum roll, please. The machine learning approach identified patterns at the genetic and brain functioning level, that were associated not to isolated traits, but to *sets of traits*.[44] We could be witnessing how the balance starts to tip in favor of personality types, as a preponderant model to explain behavior.

KEY IDEA 15: Recent evidence from genomic analysis and brain imaging indicates that we do not inherit individual traits, but rather sets of inter-related traits or "types."

Normal and abnormal are at least first cousins.

Both biology and psychology have been discovering for some time now that the frontier between normal and abnormal is not as clear as we would like to think. The difference between perfectionism and obsessiveness, between nervousness and anxiety disorder, or between social awkwardness and autism, seems to be only a matter of degree. Something that popular wisdom had sensed long ago.

On the one hand, there are indications that the same genes that are at the base of certain disorders are also "responsible" for the normal personality traits that resemble them. Genomic analyses have discovered that the genes "suspected" of causing some disorders are normally distributed within the general population. And, oh, surprise! The greater the concentration of those genes, the greater the presence of the disorder.[45]

---

44   Cloninger gives an example that is extremely clarifying: A person who scores high on three specific traits: Search for Novelty (impulsive and open to change), Avoidance of Harm (anxious), and Reward Dependency (warm and caring); often describes himself as "sensitive" because of the many internal conflicts that often arise with this set of traits. Another person who also scores high on Reward Dependency, but has low levels on the other two traits, will describe herself as fundamentally "reliable." These findings suggest that the genetic make-up of these two people would be different; and that the trait they share at the "descriptive" level would actually respond to different biological mechanisms and genetic patterns (Cloninger & Zwir, 2018).

45   Plomin, Haworth, & Davis, 2009.

Traits have also been found to "run" in families: relatives of patients with diagnosed disorders such as autism or schizophrenia often have similar personality traits, but within normal ranges.[46]

This would imply the existence of "degrees" in the trait, which could be caused by a greater or lesser quantitative accumulation of the "responsible" genes. It would also imply that mental disorders are quantitative extremes of normal personality variations. In other words, there would not be "disorders," but rather "quantities" of a given trait.

Even psychiatry, used to well-defined diagnostic "categories," has begun to align itself with this view. The *National Institute of Mental Health* is changing its diagnostic strategy to a model of "dimensions" rather than the "categories" used in the past.[47]

Danger alert! This continuity between "normal" and "abnormal" refers to the causes of a disorder, not to its consequences. Those who are afflicted with mental illness can experience it with great pain, and those around them as a great misfortune.

And of course, the degree to which a trait will be considered "pathological" will also depend, to a large extent, on the environment. A low level of "agreeableness" can be adaptive when the social environment is harsh.[48] Entering a butcher shop and roughly beating freshly slaughtered animals hanging from a bloody hook is probably highly inappropriate, except if your name is Rocky Balboa, in your spare time you collect debts for a Philadelphia loan shark, and while doing so you listen to Bill Conti's music.

KEY IDEA 16: Normal traits and the personality disorders that resemble them are a matter of different "degrees" on the same continuum.

---

46   Warrier et al., 2019; Persico & Napolioni, 2013; Sapolsky, 2010.
47   Insel et al., 2010; Plomin et al., 2016.
48   Penke et al., 2007; Nettle, 2006.

Till death do us part

Nature and nurture are meant for each other. Eternal and indivisible. Their relationship begins from the very moment the egg is fertilized and the embryo begins the adventure that will lead to its birth.

And of course, if heritability is responsible for 50% of the cake, the other 50% will correspond to its better half.

Now, getting to know what part of us has been contributed by genes and what part by environment … that has a steeper price. It is a very tangled, scrambled, mess of spaghetti. Here are a few clues:

And it all started...

The root of our personality is already there when we are inside the uterus. The seed of our genetic package begins to unfold, intensely influenced by the hormonal and nutritional balances of the intrauterine environment. If our mother suffers from a high level of stress (due to her personality or circumstances), we will feel so. A subtle change in the balance between oxytocin and vasopressin in the amniotic fluid could initiate a small snowball that, in perpetual interaction with the influences of my environment, would eventually lead to me winning the Nobel Prize in physics, or becoming the first woman president of my country. Or not. For evidence has been found that intrauterine hormonal balances can leave traces on personality until adulthood.[49] Much of our genetic information never gets to be expressed, or the way in which it does is modulated by the environment, both inside the womb and outside.

And then we are born. Psychologists in the past attributed enormous importance to the "parenting style" of our father and mother figures, over our personality and our level of mental health. Some of these theories

---

49   Sapolsky, 2017

generated many—unfair—guilty feelings on the parents of young people who were mentally ill.

The most recent studies indicate that there is no "single" aspect of our environment capable of making such a difference in our personality.

It is neither a dominant mother, nor a permissive father, nor the day when we forgot our character's lines on stage, or when we got the trophy and climbed up to the winners' podium. None of them is the sole cause of a certain way of being. Neither regressive therapy nor hypnosis will allow us to find the unique root of a trait in a single life event.

It is rather the accumulation of thousands of millions of micro experiences, apparently irrelevant, of small and cumulative effect, that build up over time slowly modeling our personality, in permanent interaction with our genes. For there is no such thing as the *tabula rasa*, no matter how bad it hurts Skinner and Watson.[50]

As children of the same father...

Human beings influence our own environment from the moment we are born. Let's face it, now that we trust each other. If they are docile, smiling, and sleepy, or if they are explosive crybabies and a nightmare to feed...well... we will do the best we can and that we know when dealing with them. Let him who is without sin cast the first stone.

There is much evidence that a child's personality influences the way in which the parents behave towards him or her.[51] Take this into account when you go to your psychoanalysis session.

And not only that. Even children who grow up in the same family do not share the same environment. Even in the case of twins. Not only will parents adjust their behavior to each child's style. Birth order, gender,

---

50   The most famous and recognized "hard-core" behavioural psychologists.
51   Avinun & Knafo, 2014 ; Klahr & Burt, 2014 ; Plomin et al., 2016

physical appearance, skills, and pure chance will also have an influence. Again, billions of micro experiences.

However, let's not underestimate the impact of our parents' personality either. Within our multiple experiences, having a perfectionist, anxious, detached, or violent parent will certainly create a common thread between many of them.

And of course, our parents behave according to their own genes as well. It is possible that their behavior towards us will come to reinforce the effect of the genes that they had already passed on to us. Again, the skein is pretty tangled.

In short, genetic factors can influence the behavior of both parents and children. But at the same time, the behavior of each party becomes an "environmental factor" for the other. If it seemed confusing to you, it is because you have understood...

Damn karma

And then we grow. We start leaving the protected—or unprotected— environment of our childhood home a little more, to encounter a world out there. And we meet our peers. Again, the imprint of our species, of millions of years of evolution, makes us want to belong, and we tend to define our identity in relation to the group. Even if it is from a deep introversion.

Without realizing it, I can evoke different reactions in others. If I like to shove other people around, if I am sweet and docile, or if I am determined and competitive in games, I will bring on very different consequences to myself.[52] Others might be afraid of me, take advantage of me, invite me to play, or steal my snack and call me names. And I will react, and they will react, in a back-and-forth movement that could follow me around throughout my life.

---

52   Buss & Penke, 2012

If I am big-sized and muscular, I will probably find it easy to approach problems in an outgoing way and I might succeed in solving conflicts by banging people up. If I am small and clumsy in sports, I may have the incentives to cultivate more conciliatory strategies.[53]

If I am lucky, and I do get into it, I may learn a little more about myself, to be a little less reactive and acquire a little more wisdom and freedom as I go through life. If I am not so lucky, then I will walk through life in action and reaction mode. Totally predictable.

Each to one's own

You have captured the idea by now. People are not "passive recipients" of the environment around them. In fact, we do everything within our means to choose the environment that best suits our preferences, our personality, our talents, and, say, our genetic predisposition.[54] Or did you think you had freely chosen your occupation?

Many of the decisions we make throughout our lives—our choice of friends, our partners, how to earn a living, where to live—are mediated by our personality. And each of them will have a direct impact on the social environment we will experience. There is evidence that genetic factors influence our taste for living in the city or in a remote place, or our decision to emigrate or "stay" in our home environment, despite the vicissitudes we may have to face.[55]

Think about it for a moment. When we select our environment, with a greater or lesser degree of awareness, we are selecting the type of problems in which we get into. If you love narcissistic types with that all-can-do macho air, then you may have to get used to the idea that one of the adaptive

---

53   Lukaszewski, 2013; Sell, Tooby, & Cosmides, 2009; Buss & Penke, 2012
54   McAdams, Gregory, & Eley, 2013; Plomin et al., 2016
55   Garcia, Mackillop, Aller, Merriwether, & Sloan, 2010

challenges that you will have to face is possible marital infidelity.[56] Are we saying that the bad workman cannot blame his tools anymore? But of course, we can always blame our genes, can't we? (To read the outcome please refer to the final chapter.)

Let's take it to the language of evolutionary psychology. The hypothesis is that, to the extent of our possibilities, we will always look for the niches in which our personality traits yield the greatest benefit (are most "profitable"), in terms of our own satisfaction and adaptive success.

KEY IDEA 17: We are not passive recipients of our environment. With all our genetic baggage, we actively shape, influence, select, and construct the environment around us. In turn, our environment influences the formation of our personality from the moment of our conception until our death.

---

56   Buss & Penke, 2012

PART II: PERSONALITY TYPES

Personality types?

The night has just ended, and it is cold. The breath condenses as it leaves his thin body and finds the almost zero degrees outside. A ship's siren can be heard in the distance. Behind those huge buildings and *containers* is the port. The unmistakable sound of gravel under a shoe alerted him to the presence of someone just across the street. A coughing sound gave away a probably male voice. A chill washed over her body, and she could feel the hair on her arms rise.

As you read this paragraph you might think:

1. That person should not be there.
2. She got the goosebumps because she found her beloved.
3. They are preparing for the New York City Marathon.
4. That mist must hide deep mysteries.
5. Breath goes from a gaseous state to a liquid one.
6. She would have to stop and assess what the person in front is doing.
7. It must be another passenger arriving early to a cruise.
8. She should cross the street and check who's there.
9. Most likely, they both know each other and are going to the same place.

It will all depend on your neurotransmitters, the events of your childhood, the history of your interrelationships, and how you currently make sense of all that.

In the following pages you will find a hypothesis about the existence of nine different personality types, the main traits that characterize each one of them, their possible biological bases, and a vision about the evolutionary advantages that each one had—and has—to adapt to their environment. The names that we give to each type have been inspired by the social roles each of them could have had some 20,000 or 30,000 years ago, based on their personality traits:

- Type 1: The Regulator
- Type 2: The Social Weaver
- Type 3: The Hunter
- Type 4: The Wizard
- Type 5: The Sage
- Type 6: The Guardian
- Type 7: The Explorer
- Type 8: The Warrior
- Type 9: The Peacemaker

For each type, we will present a story about its possible ancestral origin, generated by a specific "mutation" that affected the delicate neural mechanisms at the base of our behavior. We describe how each of these mutations would have generated a tendency towards a certain way of perceiving and reacting to environmental stimuli, giving rise to what we know as personality "traits." Along with describing these traits, we formulate a hypothesis about how they might have been adaptive in antiquity, giving clues about how and in what contexts they are adaptive today.

You will have to judge for yourself whether talking about nine basal structures makes sense to you, and whether it's ultimately helpful to understand the phenomenon of behavior.

Biological Basis

For each type we will have a section called "Biological Basis". It will contain a series of hypotheses about the probable biological mechanisms underlying each personality type. Subtle variations, of a hereditary nature, impact the way our brain works, giving rise to cognitive, emotional, and behavioral predispositions. These, in permanent interaction with environmental factors, would model our personality from the womb onwards.

Recent research in the fields of neuroscience, genetics, and behavioral biology have made it possible to identify recurring behavioral patterns in connection to specific brain mechanisms and genetic substrates. The association between these patterns and the personality types mentioned above is a contribution from the authors.

As we anticipated in the introduction, human behavioral biology is a branch of science that is still in its infancy. The two techniques that have contributed most in recent years to the understanding of the biological basis of behavior—functional magnetic resonance imaging of the brain (fMRI) and the analysis of the Human Genome—are still very recent, and present complexities that are not yet fully resolved.

On the other hand, research in this area is advancing with unprecedented speed, and we hope that in the next five to ten years, more information will be available to enrich, complement, or modify the content of the following pages.[57] One of the objectives of this book is to encourage a greater effort to connect these lines of research with the study of personality.

Evolutionary advantages

We will also propose how the core traits of each Personality Type might have been adaptive in a hunter-gatherer world. Why? Because, as we have

---

57   Meyer-Lindenberg & Weinberger, 2006

said, a significant percentage of our evolution as "modern" human beings has been spent living that way. Evolution is always a slow cooker.

In Part I, we discussed how the subtle, inherited variations that underlie our Personality Type would have arisen from mutations that occurred thousands or millions of years ago. If they hadn't been adaptive, they simply wouldn't have remained.

We believe that there is archaeological evidence from at least 32,000 years ago, indicative of the presence of motivations and traits that we might associate with the type we call The Wizard, whose ability to represent things that do not exist probably required an advanced use of language in order to be adaptive.[58] Evidence has also been found of our ancestors taking care of their sick and elderly in ways that seem characteristic of the type we call the Social Weaver, among the remains of hominids that lived in the Ice Age 1.8 million years ago.[59]

We also believe that other Personality Types that we will present in the next few pages could have emerged even earlier in our evolution, perhaps millions of years ago, since they have a very primary adaptive significance, and their behavioral patterns are hinted at in many other social animals. Examples of this are the Guardian, the Warrior, or the Peacemaker.

Core traits

In the upcoming chapters, personality types will also be portrayed through a short list of their most characteristic traits, possibly all derived from their genetic inheritance and the biological mechanisms that followed them.

Let's pause here to get some perspective. So far we have always talked about personality "types." What exactly do we mean by this term? What

---

58   Hohlenstein-Stadel cave; Wynn, Coolidge, & Bright, 2009
59   Remains of hominids found in Dmanisi, Georgia; Lee, 2018

is finally a personality type? According to this model, a type is made up of a set of interrelated traits that share the same genetic or biological basis.

Before we go any further, an important clarification is necessary: Can a person have more than one personality type at a time?

Yes and no.

Yes, because our personality structure seems to be determined by the joint influence of several types at the same time. Based on what we know about heritability and how it works, each of us could inherit genes for many families of traits at once.

No, because we believe that only one of these types is the one that is located in the "center" of our personality. It will possibly be the type for which we have a greater genetic load. The fact is that this type assumes a role of "conductor" in the organization of our internal world. Many other types will also make themselves heard in our inner concert: some will be the first violin, another the tuba, and another just a humble triangle, which is only heard once at the end of the first movement. Despite having all those influences, it will be our central type who really defines what music our psychic life plays.

This is why, even if we have more than one type, it is very important to discover our Central Type, the one responsible for our most fundamental and recurring tendencies, our most unconscious and difficult traits to redirect or modify. Our Central Type will mark our "identity" at a deeper level, ultimately defining the core of who we are.

If we represent our personality as a series of concentric circles (Fig. 1), our "Central Type" would be at the core. From there it exerts its organizing influence over our entire psychic life. Our most "deeply rooted emotions," our "cognitive biases," and our most "spontaneous reactions" will be housed there. We have called it "Central Type" to differentiate it from the influence that the other types that we also carry, to a greater or lesser extent, exert on us.

Figure 1

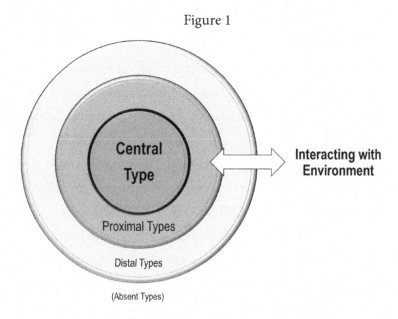

Our "Proximal Types" are those who also exert a major influence on our behavior, our motivations, and even our abilities, but without the overwhelming force of our Central Type. They will sound very familiar, close to us. That is why it is so common that, in the beginning, we get confused about which is our Central Type and which are proximal. To distinguish them, sometimes an honest introspection is enough, asking ourselves which set of emotions and reactions seize us more strongly and more frequently, even at times when they could cause us problems. On some occasions the boundaries between our Central Type and our other types can be more diffuse and the distinction can become more complex, making a guided process necessary.

Moving further away from the core we would find what we have called our "Distal Types." We will recognize them because we can still empathize with them, even though they are clearly more distant from our way of being. We will be able to understand the motivations of people who usually behave like this, and occasionally, we will exhibit some of these behavioral patterns ourselves.

Finally, there will be some Personality Types that will sound definitely alien to us. Empathizing with them will become much more difficult. Their motivations and behaviors may seem inexplicable and far-flung. We will be sure, crystal clear, that we do not belong to that type, and that we do not present any of their behaviors spontaneously, no matter how much we might want to sometimes. These will constitute our "Absent Types."

Let's illustrate this through an example. Imagine that your genetic makeup strongly predisposes you towards Type Six, but you have also inherited some predisposition towards Types One and Five, and to a lesser extent for Three, Four, and Seven. You may feel some affinity with the descriptors of all these types, but you will feel that those of Type Six are clearly stronger than any other. You also realize that you do not recognize any of the motivations of Types Two, Eight, or Nine in you. Your personality structure could be represented by the following diagram (Fig. 2):

Figure 2

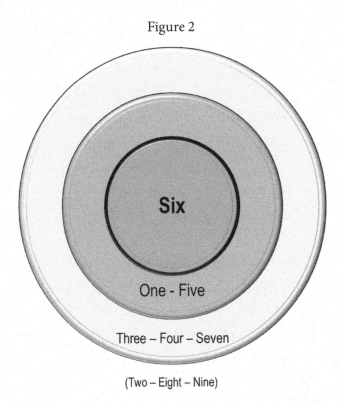

(Two – Eight – Nine)

We will return to this idea later, when we discuss how it is possible to use this information to get to know ourselves and, ultimately, to live better.

And if you are feeling that this model puts you inside a pigeonhole, allow us a clarification: although our traits would have a strong hereditary component, we conceive that our personality is much more than our type or set of types. We are ultimately unique and one-of-a-kind, because we are the result of millions of factors interacting with each other: thousands of genes determining reaction thresholds, sensitivities, and predominant tendencies, and an almost infinite amount of macro and micro experiences that have shaped us from even before we are born. And as much as all this may determine us, we are ultimately the only animals capable of "looking in the mirror" and reflecting on ourselves. Who we are will also be the result of who we want to be, and what we are willing to do in order to achieve it.

As Chaos Theory points out, a slight variation in any of these factors, occurring at any stage along the way, can lead to a totally different result. And as it often happens with the weather report, this model allows us to explain why we are who we are, but it does not allow us to predict who we will become.

A couple of clarifications before we start:

From now on, when we say that a person "is" of a certain Type, we will be referring to their Central Type, the one that provides "structure" to their personality.

For those readers who are already familiar with the Nine Types model, the descriptions may sound "minimalist." Once again, we would like to stress that what we describe here is what we believe to be the "core" of each type. In our view, the most relevant thing to understand is precisely this core, because everything else may vary.

We will present the types following the order from one to nine, respecting the numbers of the types according to the original model proposed by Ichazo and Naranjo, even though, in our opinion, their order of appearance throughout the evolution of our species was probably different.

Type One: The Regulator

Or how a child distributed with justice what was collected by all

A FIRST GLANCE

Please go back 30,000 years. Your little band is made up of twenty people. You have just returned to the cave, after spending the last four hours collecting fruits and grains. Next to the place where you usually sleep, you had left a spear you have been working on for some time. You now want to continue your work, but you realize suddenly that your spear is gone. The big guy, the one who sleeps just a little farther away, has taken it. You go and claim it, but the man gives you a strong push and a threatening look, fist in the air. You see no choice but to swallow your anger and walk away from the dispute. You approach the fire and share the situation with the rest of the bunch. Others have also been abused by this bully. It is known that he takes the females he wants and that when they go out hunting, he always grabs the tastier parts of the animal for himself. What can you do? Surprise him when he is distracted and give him a good whack with your club? Group up with others who have felt abused and lead a collective assault? Sue him and take him to court? Wait, no, you can't, courts don't exist yet. Would you like to confront him and tell him that he's not collaborating? No one has postulated the Harvard method so far. Would you force him to comply with the rules? Sorry, there are no rules in place.

Let us imagine that this is the state of events and a man or woman emerges, gifted with a great capacity to detect any sign of social disorder or transgression in relation to what should be and to what is fair and correct. A person also endowed with the ability to promote greater justice in your small society, so that human beings start behaving "correctly." Not only will you recover your spear and avoid disastrous outcomes for the big guy and for your gang, but this *fella's* contribution may have a lasting impact on our species' ability to organize ourselves into more equitable, orderly and stable societies. Finally, you might even be able to pass on your spear to your children.

These men and women must have been the first carriers of a mutation that we believe is at the base of Type One personality.

What was going on inside their heads, without them suspecting it? We think that they carried a mutation that caused them to experience a reaction of visceral rejection towards everything they considered wrong, dirty, improper, imperfect or immoral.

This visceral rejection would be caused by a mutation in a specific area of the brain, initially responsible for the detection and avoidance of toxins, that would have evolved to take charge of the detection and prevention of moral transgressions, potentially dangerous for coexistence in society. Introducing Type One.

BIOLOGICAL BASIS

Or how the insular cortex knows what is rotten in the state of Denmark

The insular cortex or insula is an area of our brain that is activated whenever we eat or sniff anything that we find disgusting; and even if we imagine that we do. More interestingly, this area is activated every time we perceive or think of something that is morally repugnant to us.[60] In other words, this area of our brain triggers a visceral response every time we perceive a violation of a norm. And the greater the activation of our insula, the greater the intensity of our feeling of rejection in the face of that violation. Or should we say repulsion? Every time we judge a person to be lazy, conceited, or disorderly, our insula lights up like a Christmas tree.

According to evolutionary theory, our brain was at some point forced to develop adaptations to a more complex social life. It became necessary to evolve a specialized unit capable of detecting and preventing moral transgressions that could be dangerous for coexistence in society. And thus, the brain hijacked a primitive area, hitherto responsible for our not having a rotten deer for lunch and being able to distinguish a putrid egg from a perfectly yummy one.

---

60   Wicker et al., 2003; Gogolla, 2017; Ying et al., 2018; Sapolsky, 2017.

And so it happened that this humble area of our brain was elevated to the noble function of becoming our moral radar. Although this rise in status did not happen overnight, nor was it a voluntary decision by our brain... let us remember that evolution operates very slowly, and that mutations happen by chance.

Anyway, once it happened, blessed mutation. It was about time someone came and introduced some order! You can imagine why it came to be so adaptive. It is not the same to have someone keeping the lion's share, than to have everyone enjoy their fair share of the work done.

That said, things are not so simple inside our brain. The now lofty insular cortex has never forgotten her humble past, since she continues to carry out her former functions. And on top of her desk, both tasks often get mixed up. This is why, in our brains, there is much cross-contamination between the physical sensation of repugnance, and the disgust we often feel in the face of moral transgressions.[61]

This two-way relationship is reflected in the results of various studies and everyday phenomena. In one laboratory study, subjects who were subjected to physically repugnant images, tended to make harsher moral judgments in an apparently unrelated situation. In another study, subjects who were exposed to a foul odor in the workroom then tended to be more conservative in their responses to a survey.[62]

On a more everyday level, when we feel an intense repulsion in the face of a moral fault, we may feel nauseous, want to vomit, or literally get a bad taste in our mouth, to the extent that it influences how we perceive food.[63] It is not by chance that in many movie scenes, the way to depict a strong reaction in the face of a moral misdeed is to show its characters throwing up.

---

61   The same is true for all the primitive functions of the brain that have evolved into more sophisticated ones (Sapolsky, Lecture 15, 2010).

62   Sapolsky, 2017.

63   Sapolsky, 2017.

The purpose of physical repugnance is to protect us from pathogens. In a metaphorical sense, the purpose of moral repugnance is also related to protection against contamination. The metaphors we use in our spoken language seem not to be metaphors after all. They seem to be a reflection of the slight confusion that happens inside our brain, due to the *multitasking* nature of its specialized units.[64] In all the languages of the world, there are words related to physical filth, which are used to refer to moral faults. We can say that an act is repulsive to us, that something is rotten in Denmark, or that a perversion is disgusting. And this mixture does not occur only in language. It seems that when we feel guilty, we also feel an unconscious urge to wash some part of our body. Yes, like Pontius Pilate or Lady Macbeth![65]

The subjects of a study were asked to report a morally reprehensible action they had committed in the past. Then, as a sign of appreciation, they were offered a choice of two gifts: a pencil or antiseptic wipes. Those who confessed a fault were much more likely to choose antiseptics, compared to the control group who was asked to report a morally neutral event. In another study, subjects were forced to lie during a game. Later, in an apparently unrelated situation, they had access to wash their hands. The time they spent washing their hands was directly proportional to the seriousness of their lies.[66]

Evidence has even been found that people with a greater propensity to feel physical disgust have a greater concern for purity or cleanliness, a greater tendency to have moralizing attitudes, and are more likely to have politically or socially conservative views.[67]

---

64 Krolak-Salmon et al., 2003; Sapolsky, 2017.

65 The association between guilt and the urge to wash one's hands has been documented in psychiatry as the "Macbeth effect," for Lady Macbeth's famous compulsion in Shakespeare's tragedy (Sapolsky, 2017).

66 This same experiment was carried out with subjects originally from East Asia. They, instead of washing their hands, chose to wash their faces. Interesting cultural variation, which could be a brain metaphor for "saving face". (Sapolsky, 2017).

67 Sapolsky, 2017.

Inside our insular cortex, we mix things up. We assimilate dirty and messy with bad, and clean and tidy with good, and our visceral reaction is more or less the same.

Now, one thing is the visceral reaction, and a very different thing is the wave of emotions and thoughts that follow. Who committed the fault? Was it me or somebody else? How serious was it? Our subsequent reactions are much more complicated, diverse, and will have more to do with what we have learned from our environment.

For example, if we have committed a serious fault and have been brought up in an environment of individualistic values, we will probably feel guilty. If we grew up in a collectivist environment, we would probably feel ashamed.[68] The initial reaction of disgust is biologically determined. Our interpretation, and everything that comes after it, is learned.

However, regardless of our culture, the way we interpret our own faults is a little more merciful than the way we interpret the faults of others. FMRI studies[69] reveal that when we contemplate our own mistakes, the emotional part of our prefrontal cortex tends to light up, as we consider our intentions and the possible mitigating factors that conditioned our actions. When we contemplate other people's mistakes, the rational part of our prefrontal cortex is activated to a greater extent, an indication that we are judging them based on their visible actions.[70]

The obvious consequence of this trick of our brain is that we condemn others much more easily that we condemn ourselves. It seems that the proverbial "straw in someone else's eye" has a neurological origin. By extension, the more distant we feel from the people we are judging, the less we tend to consider their motives and the greater our harshness and outrage.

---

68 Sapolsky, 2017.
69 Functional magnetic resonance imaging.
70 The ventro medial prefrontal cortex (vmPFC) is more concerned with the interpretation of emotional stimuli, and the dorsolateral prefrontal cortex (dlPFC) with the purely "rational" ones (Sapolsky, 2017).

And watch out: when we are under stress, we tend to be even harsher in our judgments. Even more rational and less empathetic.[71]

Up to now, we've been talking about a mechanism that operates in all of us, independent of our personality type. What does all this have to do with Type One? According to our hypothesis, the Regulator would be the bearer of a mutation that would have increased the intensity of this mechanism. And surely, there are degrees as to the intensity of this mutation, even within the population of One's.

We have said that all personality types are somehow related to a kind of mental pathology, when their characteristic features are manifested in an extreme way. In the case of Type One, it would be Obsessive-Compulsive Disorders. Several studies have found an association between a higher tendency to feel physical repugnance and the probability of presenting obsessive-type traits both within normal ranges and pathological ones.[72] Another set of studies have found an association between obsessive traits, and a genetic variant that encodes for a serotonin transporter (polymorphism in the 5-HTT gene) that is specifically associated with a dysfunction in serotonergic neurotransmission at the level of none other than, the insular cortex![73]

Let us stop to consider some of the obsessive-compulsive traits that can often be found in psychiatric literature:[74]

- Perfectionism and obsessive checking whether something was done correctly
- Obsession with symmetry, and compulsion to count, order, or organize
- Rejection of dirt, and obsession with cleanliness
- Fear of losing control

---

71 Sapolsky, 2017.
72 Sadri et al., 2017.
73 Nicholson & Barnes-Holmes, 2012; Shapira et al., 2003; Matsumoto et al., 2010; Stengler-Wenzke, Müller, Angermeyer, Sabri, & Hesse, 2004; Hu et al., 2006; Perlis et al., 2008.
74 Wu & Cortesi, 2008; Watson & Wu, 2005; Wu, Clark, & Watson, 2006; Foa et al., 2002; Rosario-Campos et al., 2006; Moller et al., 2015.

- Inclination to establish rituals
- Excessive focus on moral or religious ideas
- Guilt and doubt associated with the fear of not being perfect

It does seem that Type One is a moderate, successful, and adaptive version of what, at more extreme levels, becomes a painful and difficult disease to deal with.

Interestingly, there is evidence that normal people who have a tendency towards a repressed personality, show a higher level of activation and a greater energy expenditure in their Prefrontal Cortex, the brain equivalent of the Superego.[75] This hyperactive prefrontal cortex has in turn been associated with a high level of discipline, a tendency to inhibit impulsive reactions, to control emotional expression, and to have a more structured and planned life.[76] It is the prefrontal cortex, making sure that our behavior is appropriate.

EVOLUTIONARY ADVANTAGES

Or how a hunter-gatherer defended the rights of his band in front of the clan

At a time of high mortality rates, when 70% of deaths were due to disease, individuals who were born with a mutation that made them particularly sensitive to detecting foods that were best avoided, and an urge to keep their family's environment clean, would have kept a greater number of their children alive. This would have caught the attention of potential suitors, making them very attractive as partners. Yet, we believe that the influence of the Regulator must have reached far beyond the private sphere.

As the clan grew, many things were gained: they could better defend themselves against hostile "others," they were able to hunt larger animals,

---

75   Sapolsky, 2017
76   Sapolsky, 2004.

they had access to a wider range of knowledge and sexual partners, and the possibilities of bartering or exchange increased. But a bigger clan also brought bigger problems. It became increasingly difficult to maintain the social ties that held the group together.

Collaborative hunting raids, in search of larger and more dangerous animals, must have involved several bands, and must have lasted for several days. The hunters must have returned to their camp exhausted, and often, empty-handed. And a successful expedition still posed a great problem: how to divide the meat among them? Who had shot the deadliest arrow or struck the best blow? Who then deserved the most precious piece or the biggest chunk? Many of these discussions between hunters, who no longer had such close kinship or trust ties, must have ended up with a wooden club to the head.[77] More than a few must have felt they received less than they deserved, and blood must have flowed, cave versions of the Hatfield's and the McCoy's.

There were more fights, more conflicts between neighboring bands, murders from behind just for disputing access to a female, or for the possession of a special object. Faced with this order of things, the Regulators had an innate talent to recognize the imperative need to establish agreements that regulated interaction. Only in this way would peaceful coexistence and collaboration between non-relatives be possible. Only in this way would the fragile balance of the social fabric be stabilized.

Why not divide the result of the hunt in totally equal parts? Thus, it would not matter which of the arrows had killed the tiger, the important thing would be that all the hunters and their families would be fed. They may also have thought of the sick or injured hunters who had not gone on that raid. Everyone could receive a share and reciprocate later.

---

77   It is easy to visualize this need if we consider that the most probable result of any hunting expedition, even in small groups, was failure. And, in case of success, probably more meat would be obtained than the whole family was capable of consuming. In the words of Robert Sapolski (2017): "for a hunter-gatherer, the best investment against future hunger is to put meat in other people's stomachs at the present time"; pg 324.

There is archaeological evidence of these early Regulators. Analysis of the bones of animals consumed by man 200,000 years ago shows that they have uniformly spaced and parallel cut marks. The evidence suggests that it was the same hand that cut and distributed the meat, in equal parts, and it is likely that this function did not fall on the most successful hunter, but on an individual chosen by all the members of the tribe because they trusted their justice more.[78]

The Type Ones of the time had to display their special talent—and their strong motivation—to articulate these norms, to generate agreement around them, to comply with them themselves, and to ensure compliance by all others. These agreements must have covered many areas of everyday life, not just how to divide the meat of a joint hunt. How to prevent the strong from abusing the weak, how to punish a cheat who did not want to keep his part of a bargain or return a favor as promised, are other examples of likely concerns of the early Regulator.[79]

They must have worked to convince the different parties involved in a conflict about the advisability of abiding by the agreements, and they must have solved many problems related to the social order of their day to day life. With the strength of their visceral reaction to what is wrong, they proposed limits to what can and cannot be done, named the faults, explained why they were wrong, detected the offenders, and motivated collective disapproval and punishment.[80]

Imposing rules and having them respected by all has never been an easy exercise. Not today, not then. Even in the fairest distributions, some

---

78 Sapolsky, 2017, pg 323.
79 According to Sapolsky (2017), the main norms that regulated the social coexistence of primitive hunter-gatherer tribes were indirect reciprocity, justice, and the avoidance of despotism.
80 In the case of hunter-gatherers, the most common forms of "cheating" were theft, refusal to share, attempts to seize power, use of witchcraft with malicious intent, betrayal of the group, murder, and breaking sexual taboos. In all cases, the punishments were apparently only applied after less radical sanctions had failed (Sapolsky, 2017).

of the hunters must have muttered that their portion of meat had been the smallest.[81]

Anthropologists believe that the weapons of social regulation used at that time must have been the subjection to public criticism or shame, the exclusion from certain benefits, the marginalization or expulsion from the group, the application of non-lethal physical punishment, and, as a last resort, execution.[82] And of course, for the mildest or politically complex cases, you could always get your hands on some good old gossip.

If we look at it in retrospect, the visceral reaction of disgust in the face of moral transgressions was surely one of the forces that drove the process of civilization of human societies. Over the millennia it allowed human beings to develop the rules and practices necessary to self-contain their most primitive instincts.[83]

Tens of thousands of years later, this same force pushed societies to organize themselves on the basis of more complex institutions to guarantee order and peaceful coexistence: the code of Hammurabi, the tables of the law, or the Roman senate.

And although we cannot know if the hunter-gatherers already had their own version of the ten commandments, it is likely that the One's of the time already recited some rules by heart, and passed them on from father (or mother) to son.

This brings us to the probable kinship between the Regulator's psychological world and the birth of organized religions, at least in their rational

---

81 Studies of current tribes still living as primitive hunter-gatherers report that tribal members consistently complain that their meat rations are smaller and that the distribution has not been entirely "fair" (Boehm, 2012).

82 Various studies document the existence of such "judicial killings" in almost half of today's hunter-gatherer cultures (Boehm, 2014) (Boehm, 2012).

83 Rozin & Haidt, 2013.

component[84]: their rules of conduct, their organization, and their rites. The first religious norms and rites must have arisen as a result of the verbal transfer, from generation to generation and from tribe to tribe, of the social agreements promoted by the first Regulators and their intuitions about what was correct and pure.

What could be more in tune with their souls, than a vocation to fulfill and enforce divine rules, aimed at making us perfect beings? What greater pleasure than organizing social life through rites of passage and rituals to mark agreements and commitments?[85]

It is certainly an occupation in which thoroughness and perfection pay off. It is not surprising that all organized religions have disciplinary and ritual aspects related to cleanliness, food preparation, and the importance of numbers.[86]

THE FOOTPRINTS OF SAPIENS REGULATOR

Scenes from a lost past

Scene 1:

A medium-sized deer for ten rabbits. The agreement was totally clear. But the hunter had stopped delivering the rabbits when they could be counted with the fingers of only one hand. There were still as many rabbits missing as there were fingers on the other hand. He had climbed the small hill three

---

84 Religions have other components: the "story" they share to explain origin, meaning, phenomena, and which represent their worldview; loaded with symbols, which appeals to emotions, and which probably proved a comfortable terrain for other personality types who completed the task.

85 Often religious leaders have been the best at designing and carrying out these rituals. The most disciplined. An area where thoroughness and perfection are rewarded. Many Ones probably earned their living through these jobs, so well-aligned with their inclination. (Sapolsky, 2011).

86 Sapolsky (2017) points to the relationship between these rituals and obsessive-compulsive traits.

times to demand that the deal be honored. Then he had no choice but to resort to the Regulator. He told the story of his deal and his demand: five rabbits. The Regulator listened. These breaches of agreements put him in a bad mood. This kind of behavior could not be tolerated. The entire system they had worked so hard to build was at risk. He accompanied the plaintiff up the hill. Upon arrival it was he who took the floor, demanding to know the truth. The debtor claimed to have made the commitment voluntarily, but that rabbit hunting had been rare. As for the rest of the deer, there was nothing left. The regulator set a deadline of five nights to finish fulfilling the commitment. If not, he would have to give up other possessions until the plaintiff was satisfied. And so it was done. On the fifth day, and not having satisfied the debt, the strong men of the clan came together and took from the debtor enough weapons and seeds to satisfy the commitment.

Scene 2:

Under the tree of the big shade, the young woman had accepted the courtship of both hunters. Both wanted her and both felt entitled to take her. Both had performed the courting rite under the tree. She should have warned the second young man that she could not be courted because the first had already sought her out. But now it was too late. It was a conflict that usually ended when one of the two young men gave in and withdrew from the courtship. But these young men had returned from their first hunt for the larger animal. Both were strong, they had driven the spear, both had their bed in the cave. None would yield. The three then went to the Regulator. She would know how to deal with this situation. She looked at the young woman with disapproval. First, she made it clear that the fault was hers. She should never have allowed two courtships in a row. Regarding the problem already created, the tradition of the tribe had to be respected. The first born would have the first option. The mothers were called, and they reported on the order of birth. The young woman was then paired up with the one who was born first. Before the dispute was concluded, the Regulator ordered the young woman to meet as many girls as there were nights between full moons, and to tell her mistake, so that *no young woman would ever again accept two courtships in a row under the tree of the big shade.*

Scene 3:

The Regulator saw the group of hunters arrive with a huge wild boar. He knew it was time to work. He went to the cave, where he zealously kept his tools. The largest flint knife was reserved for mammoths. He had already cut three. His father had cut five in his entire life. A large boar could be cut perfectly with his smaller tools. He opened a large leather pouch and took out his precious flints, each of them wrapped in thin animal skins. He took two of his best knives and closed the pouch again, leaving it in the same place from which he had taken it. He unfolded the skins and checked the condition of the tools. They were perfectly sharp, just as he had left them when he last put them away. He carefully folded the skins and went to meet the hunters. On seeing him, the group of hunters left the animal on the ground and began to gather green leaves. Everyone knew that the Regulator would not make any cuts if the animal was not on a bed of green leaves.

Scene 4:

The Regulator felt that his face was red, and the body fluids were swelling his head. He could not believe his ears. The hunting party had been attacked two nights away and now they were returning and telling about their expedition. When they were questioned about the bodies of the fallen, they confessed to having left them there to return safely to the cavern. The Regulator rarely used bombastic gestures when speaking. But now he gestured as no one had ever seen him before. What they had done was against all their customs. The fallen are given burial, in holes dug or covered with rocks. They are never abandoned. It is not done this way. The Regulator mounted a repair expedition. Six men joined him along the two nights' distance. When he got there, he again gestured and shouted. The scavengers had bitten the bodies. They dug the three graves and arranged the bodies according to custom. Head towards the sun, and arms next to the body. When they returned to the cave, they gathered the elders and proposed that anyone leaving an abandoned body should leave the tribe. And so they agreed.

CORE TRAITS

Let's now get to the heart of the matter. What do the Regulators who walk among us in our 21st century look like? Remember the caveats on the previous pages: Type One people come in many models, sizes, and colors. However, they have several elements in common, all of them explainable from their biological basis. In this section we make a proposal regarding what these distinctive and defining traits are, of what we call Type One personality.

Super-superego: Integrity

Regulators feel a strong desire to be right and to act in the right way. Much more than other people, they strive to be virtuous, to live according to their principles, to achieve perfection in everything they do, and to do it right the first time.

They tend to assign special importance to ethics, honesty, integrity, and justice as guiding principles in their lives. Oftentimes, they truly strive to be better persons. Type Ones are well-intentioned.

The dark side of this trait is that they tend to be perfectionists, sometimes going to extremes in their levels of demand with themselves and with others. They have something like a super-superego, an internal voice that is constantly reminding them of the right way to act, congratulating them when they behave well, and criticizing them when they don't live up to their own standards.

I feel disgusted: Repulsion towards what is wrong and impulse to correct

The perception of Type One spontaneously tends to fixate on anything that does not fit with their idea of what it should be. A lens is imposed on them to look at reality, in terms of what is right or wrong, what is good or bad, and metaphorically speaking, what is clean or dirty. This perception is supplemented by a strong urge to correct, to right the wrongs, to reform and amend, unconsciously wanting to restore order and balance.

At the root of these reactions is a feeling of revulsion. It is related to disgust, literally speaking. That is why it is so powerful. Only after this visceral reaction has already occurred does the prefrontal cortex of the One's appear, trying to explain and put into words what they already feel on an instinctive level.

On the one hand, this faculty gives them an innate ability to improve things, to detect what is not working and what is susceptible to being perfected. It also gives them the energy and motivation required to get the job done.

On the other hand, they feel anger or frustration when things don't work out. This emotion is especially strong in the face of what they interpret as ethical misconduct, whether it's their own or that of others.

Early to bed and early to rise: Discipline and self-control

In their effort to act the right way, Regulators tend to exercise strong control over their own impulsive behavior and emotional life.

This translates, on the one hand, into an enviable willpower and a fierce self-discipline. Within a Western culture environment, we could see them getting out of bed early, having a balanced breakfast, exercising or doing yoga before going to work, and in general, leading a sober, healthy, and orderly lifestyle.

When they set their mind to something, be it in personal or professional life, they are able to align their effort and resist the temptations of laziness or dispersion in order to move their purpose forward.

But so much discipline also comes with some costs. Without realizing it, they are likely to try to channel their impulses and emotional expressions into what is appropriate and what is "right." In mild cases, this can simply make them appear less spontaneous. In other cases, this may lead them to repress their real emotions, becoming unaware of their own anger, or any other "wrong" emotions. By suppressing the perception of their own emotions, they may stop perceiving or empathizing with the emotions of others.

On the other hand, repression is never bulletproof. From time to time, an intense emotion will manage to break their inner dam and come to light in an explosive or disorderly way. When this happens, Type One can be the most disconcerted, uncomfortable, or upset with himself.

The moral high ground: Tendency to judge

Another cost of Regulators' self-discipline is that they will expect the same from others. If they can, why can't others? This expectation, far from being neutral, may come hand in hand with sour recriminations whenever they feel let down.

Regulators have a tendency to judge severely and even harshly. The faults of others become very visible to them, being able to temporarily erase from their perception any emotional connection with the other person, or any consideration of these faults within a broader context. They can fall into a "tunnel vision," remaining fixated on the need for the perpetrator to acknowledge their faults or make an act of contrition in order to be able to "turn the page."

On the other hand, the severity of the Regulators begins with themselves, for no one will be as critical as their own superego. And if someone points out their faults to them from the outside, they will generally be willing to acknowledge them honestly and neutrally, with justice and without passion. This, as long as that someone has managed to convince them that they have made a mistake.

For Regulators often feel unconsciously in possession of the truth. When they look at themselves, the first thing that strikes them is their good intentions and their effort to act correctly. They are less lucid in perceiving their own negative emotions such as anger, or they see them but rationalize them as "justified."

Alone with my conscience: Autonomy and independence

Regulators feel alone in front of their own conscience. Their moral compass is fundamentally based on their own sense of what is right and what is wrong. This feeling has been forged throughout their lives, based on the sensation that no one tries as hard as they do to act correctly or to do things well. This often leads them to feel a degree of distrust in the opinions, decisions or actions of others, especially when it comes to people who they perceive as very different from themselves. Thus, Ones tend to become highly autonomous decision makers and judges of their own actions.

Although it is not in their nature to be disruptive or revolutionary, they will preserve tradition only to the extent that they feel that it is "correct." Otherwise, they will be able to stand alone before the world, denouncing all those who live in the wrong. Many religious reformers recorded in history are good examples of this.

OCD & Me: Taste for order and symmetry

Their instinctive rejection of filth and untidiness is at the base of their attraction, also visceral and instinctive, for orderliness, cleanliness, and symmetry. It is possibly the only type to whom sorting out and tidying up literally brings pleasure. Any teenager who has a Regulator mother or father will know what we're talking about: *Mom, I'm telling you there's no need to sort shirts by color!*

Rituals, as a way of ordering life, can be another way of satisfying this impulse. An innate taste for routines could manifest itself in different ways: from an extraordinary regularity in their daily habits, to a rigorous adherence to rituals.

If A then B: Love for Reason

Their attraction to order and symmetry is also manifested on a mental level. Their nature inclines them towards a taste for logical arguments and objective data, a love for concepts, numbers, and sequences, and an appreciation for mental order and organization.

These characteristics, together with their desire for consistency, their self-discipline, and their tendency to control, often make them extremely rational and reasonable people. They have an innate attraction to activities that involve structuring, planning, organizing, and evaluating.

And, thanks to their unique combination of rational mind and visceral conviction of being right, people of this type often become masters of debate and great at convincing others of their opinions and points of view.

Type Two: The Social Weaver

Or how a child stopped looking at himself and looked at others

A FIRST GLANCE

It was a real catastrophe. Many adult males had gone out in small boats to explore new hunting grounds. Many round moons had passed, and they had not returned. The rivers had grown, taking away much of the food sources. Now they were sharing a single large cave. There were the children without parents, the elderly, and the injured. There was hunger and disorganization. Some still had food reserves, but they jealously guarded them. The young woman approached one of the fatherless children and took him to one of the bands that still had some food. She explained how they could keep the child and integrate him into their group. He was an orphaned boy; he would probably die. But they could be his new parents. The boy could join the band. In a few years he would hunt for them. He would bring water. He would give his seeds to have new members. The idea was considered, and the little orphan was taken in. The young woman continued with her task by placing two other orphans in different bands. And it became customary. Children without parents would never be abandoned. She also promoted the sharing of food among the families. In the future, when there was an abundance, those who shared today would be compensated. This young woman came to be known as "She-wolf who helps" and she had many children. And her children begot many more. Her band was said to be the seed of "helping men and women."

Sitting comfortably in our soft 21st century armchair, our nuclear family offers safety and reference. Our extended family, in many cases, an important support network. Further away will be the different groups to which we belong—our soccer team, a political party, a foundation to save something we love, and a broader social organization whose leaders, in the best of scenarios, we elect by vote. And although nuclear families today can take shapes that were unthinkable before, ever since our beginnings, human groups have repeated a constant in the way of organizing our relationships, based on "concentric circles" according to the degree of closeness.

No one knows exactly how our hunter-gatherer ancestors were organized, but the analysis of their settlements makes us suspect a fairly similar structure, according to degrees of proximity.[87]

Consider the enormous value of being able to act collaboratively in ever larger groups. How decisive was the number when it came to competing for resources against other species that were much stronger, but less able to coordinate in large groups.

Reciprocal collaboration with the rest of the clan was critical for survival; despite the fact that these larger groups, with fewer and weaker blood ties, and less frequent interactions, were always more unstable and vulnerable to infighting, individualism, and lack of cooperation. Remind you of anything? We haven't changed much since then...

This clear evolutionary advantage must have been reinforced by the birth of individuals endowed with a greater inclination to form collaborative relationships, and a greater natural talent to do so. People with a mutation that brought about a tendency to feel an increasing number of individuals as part of their "family," establishing closer ties of collaboration with all those who could be considered worthy of being classified as "us."

BIOLOGICAL BASIS

Or how hormones take care of children and make friends

Today we can presume that the brain of these individuals carried a mutation that made it more sensitive to the action of oxytocin and vasopressin, two key substances in the regulation of animal and human behavior.

These substances play a key role as hormones, preparing different organs of our body for sexuality and nurturing. They also act as neurotransmitters,

---

87   Dyble et al., 2016; Hamilton, Buchanan, & Walker, 2018.

driving responses that support these functions at the behavioral level.[88] Both substances share an almost identical chemical structure, as they evolved from a common "ancestor," and orchestrate "similar" processes, oxytocin primarily in women, and vasopressin in men.[89]

We can see the same in other mammals. Let's talk about rats. During labor, mother rats experience a discharge of oxytocin in their brains, which activates their maternal instincts and triggers behaviors such as bringing their cubs closer, warming them, licking them and generally caring for them. But if the action of oxytocin is blocked, the young are abandoned to their fate. And vice versa. If we administer this substance to a virgin rat, it will look for others' offspring to adopt and care for. In the meantime, the male, as soon as he smells the birth of his children, will act paternally under the influence of a vasopressin discharge.[90] We are talking about rats. Between rats and human beings there is an enormous evolutionary distance. In fact, recent studies reveal that *only* 90% of rat's genes have a more or less obvious correspondence with human genes.[91] Blessed 10%...Where is my cheese?

Furthermore, monkeys and rodents who, as individuals, are more sensitive to the action of these hormones, are not only better parents. They also establish "more stable couples" with their sexual partners, and are more

---

88 We have long known the role of oxytocin as a hormone associated with milk secretion, motherhood and lactation in both humans and other mammals. Vasopressin, on the other hand, was known for its "antidiuretic" role acting at the level of the kidneys. Many years later, neurobiologists have rediscovered these hormones in another role, acting as neurotransmitters on various brain centers. The presence of receptors for these peptides in specialized areas such as the ventral tegmental area (VTA), the nucleus accumbens, the hippocampus, the amygdala, and the prefrontal cortex, was key to this discovery. Since then, many of its behavioral effects have been discovered (Sapolsky, 2017).

89 Oxytocin has similar, but "attenuated" effects on the brains of men; just as vasopressin has a secondary role in women (pg. 108) (Sapolsky, 2017).

90 When female rats give birth, they develop more receptors for oxytocin in their brain; and if the action of these receptors is blocked, they stop displaying maternal behaviors. The male's brain, in turn, develops more receptors for vasopressin when it smells a female giving birth to her offspring. A virgin rat that receives a dose of oxytocin behaves "maternally" with the offspring of others (Sapolsky, 2017).

91 Center for Human Genome Sequencing (Baylor College of Medicine)

"sociable" and prosocial in general.[92] A female tamarin carrying the oxyto-cin-sensitive gene spends more time in non-sexual physical contact with other monkeys, both male and female. She will enjoy hours of "pleasant chat", pulling out the fleas from one another, petting or grooming her friends.

The same has been observed in the differences between some related species. Males of mountain voles are polygamous, while those of prai-rie voles are almost always monogamous. Studying their brains, it was found that prairie voles had a greater number of receptors for vasopressin in their Nucleus Accumbens. And when these "monogamous receptors" were implanted in the brains of polygamous voles, many of them chose to "love" a particular female "forever." Bonobos and chimpanzees are similar in many ways, but they clearly differ in their social behavior. Bonobos are much more sociable and less aggressive, and while they are far from monog-amous, they use sexual exchange as a way to restore social harmony. You guessed it: bonobos carry a genetic variant more sensitive to oxytocin.[93]

And what about human beings? Let's take it one step at a time. First of all, it has been found that the simple application of an endonasal oxytocin spray can do wonders for our behavior. Within experimental settings this application is capable of:

- Improving our capacity to remember faces and to "read" emotions.[94]
- Increasing our tendency to trust other people and to display generous behaviors.[95]
- Increasing our sensitivity to social reinforcement.[96]
- When applied to couples discussing their problems, it increases their tendency to communicate positively and decreases their stress levels.

---

92 Walum et al., 2008; Curtis et al., 2005; Smeltzer, Curtis, Aragona, & Wang, 2006; Aragona, 2009.
93 Sapolsky, 2017
94 Savaskan, Ehrhardt, Schulz, Walter, & Schächinger, 2008; Domes, Heinrichs, Michel, Berger, & Herpertz, 2007.
95 Kosfeld, Heinrichs, Zak, Fischbacher, & Fehr, 2005; Zak, Stanton, & Ahmadi, 2007; Zak, 2017.
96 Hurlemann et al., 2010.

- In women, it generates greater attraction to babies.

- In men who are in a monogamous relationship, their interest in looking at pictures of attractive women, or in approaching other women, decreases.[97]

- In economic games like the *prisoner's dilemma*, players tend to "turn the other cheek" even after they have been "betrayed."[98]

Perhaps we are on the verge of the end of couples' therapies…a good inoculation of oxytocin and vasopressin, as the case may be, and problem solved.

As you might guess, there is an indication that autistic people have less oxytocin and vasopressin activity in their brain[99]; therapy with these substances tends to relieve their symptoms, improving their ability to establish and maintain eye contact with other people.[100]

And what about the more stable individual differences? It has been found that genetic variants associated with increased action of oxytocin or vasopressin in the brain are associated with more sociable and prosocial behavioral styles.[101] People who carry these variants are usually:

- More avid and precise collectors of social information.

- More likely to make frequent and prolonged eye contact and to better remember faces.[102]

- More accurate in perceiving other people's emotions, although with a certain bias towards capturing and remembering positive emotions better than negative ones.[103]

---

97 Sapolsky, 2017.
98 Campbell, 2010.
99 McDonald, Baker, & Messinger, 2016; Wu et al., 2005; Jacob et al., 2007; Liu et al., 2010.
100 Sapolsky, 2017.
101 The most studied is the OXTR rs53576 variant, but there are indications that the variant associated with these same patterns could vary according to population or ethnicity (Liu et al., 2010).
102 Sapolsky, 2017.
103 Rodrigues, Saslow, Garcia, John, & Keltner, 2009.

- More sociable and likely to establish close and stable relationships.[104]
- More socially skilled, being able to better understand the complicated web of interpersonal relationships.[105]
- More sensitive and responsive to signs of social approval or rejection.[106]
- More empathetic, altruistic, generous, and collaborative.[107]
- More inclined to a "sensitive" and warm parenting style with their children, and in the case of women, to greater physical and visual contact with their babies.[108]
- More likely to establish long-lasting relationships and rate them as stable and happy.[109]
- More likely to rate other people as "trustworthy."[110]
- Less vulnerable to anxiety or fear.[111]
- More optimistic and with a greater tendency to high self-esteem.[112]

However, not everything is lights. There is a dark side that needs to be mentioned. The same cocktail of oxytocin that makes us feel love towards our fellow humans, makes us reinforce the dividing line that separates us from the "others." The very same mechanism that makes us feel cohesion, protection, reciprocity, and belonging more intensely; can increase our hostility towards those who we perceive as strangers.

Everything stems from its primitive origins. From its root in the instinct of parental care. Remember that in the animal world, a mother or father can be extraordinarily hostile—and violent—when an intruder threatens

---

104 Hercules et al., 2016; Walum et al., 2008; Aspé-Sánchez et al., 2016.
105 Their "reading" of relationships has a certain gender bias: women seem to be more adept at reading relationships of kinship; and men, those of power or dominance (Sapolsky, 2017).
106 Tost et al., 2010.
107 Israel et al., 2009.
108 Sapolsky, 2017.
109 Sapolsky, 2010.
110 In laboratory experiences, they have a greater tendency to evaluate the faces of strangers as "reliable" (Sapolsky, 2017).
111 These hormones act on the amygdala, decreasing the reaction to frightening stimuli and allowing the activation of the parasympathetic system and the "calm" response (Sapolsky, 2017).
112 Saphire-Bernstein, Way, Kim, Sherman, & Taylor, 2011.

their family.[113] These hormones can decrease our tendency to collaborate with strangers, exaggerate our prejudices towards those who are not like us, and exacerbate the behavior of "us" versus "them." It is oxytocin in action: an elixir of love, all affection and generosity when it comes to "one of ours"; and a poisonous potion when it comes to the "enemy."[114]

Welcome to the intensely interpersonal world of Type Two.

EVOLUTIONARY ADVANTAGES

Or how a hunter-gatherer organized the care of the elderly and sick

At an evolutionary level, the emergence of collaborative behaviors with individuals beyond my blood ties is only explicable to the extent that these are also useful for the individual. The concern for the well-being of the weak, the elderly, the sick, can only be explained through the deep roots of our need to collaborate.

Hunter-gatherers were surrounded by great incentives to "save their own skins." In Maslow's pyramid we would have been in the first stage, trying to eat, to survive to the threats of animals, of nature, of some tribe eager for our females, when not cannibals, and even to the threats from rivals within our own group. In this state of affairs, the Social Weavers, surprisingly, showed a spontaneous interest in the welfare of others.

---

113 The association between high levels of oxytocin and vasopressin, the propensity to collaborate with those close to us, and to rival or attack "outsiders" has been confirmed by studies in animals and humans (Sapolsky, 2017).

114 The application of oxytocin generally increases the willingness to collaborate in economic games. The exception is when players believe they are playing against an anonymous stranger. There, the application of oxytocin produces the opposite effect: it decreases collaboration, increases envy when the other is winning, and bragging when the other is losing (Shamay-Tsoory et al., 2009; pg 116). Also, the administration of oxytocin in the laboratory situations exaggerated prejudices towards members of minorities and out-groups (De Dreu, Greer, Van Kleef, Shalvi, & Handgraaf, 2011).

Let's imagine for a moment how they lived. Their day-to-day life took place in small bands, made up of 20 to 25 members of an extended family, half adults, half children, plus one or two friends or relatives who "tagged along." These gangs almost always mobilized through already known terrain, settling in temporary camps, depending on the time of year, following the cycle of plants and the migration of animals. Their camps had about 4 or 5 "independent homes" (shelters with a place for fire), which some interpret as a sign of the existence, even then, of something similar to nuclear "families."[115] We do not know how flexible or stable these families were, and it is likely that they varied greatly between cultures. Some would have been matrilineal—women of the same blood family staying together, and men migrating to other bands to procreate. In others, the other way around, the paternal line must have been preserved.

Several bands formed a wider and more or less flexible "community," sharing common ancestors and migratory customs. These groups of bands, which today we call "clans," differed in size and complexity, ranging from close to one hundred to several hundred people.

This way of organizing is not really very original. Many of our close cousins, the primates, are grouped in a fairly similar way. More remarkably, this way of organizing ourselves has remained relatively constant throughout our evolution. As we know that there will be some skeptics who will mutter that we organize ourselves that way just out of habit, here are three possible reasons associated with collaborative challenges that are rooted deep in the biology of our species:[116]

Male-female collaboration: The very human combination of a large head to house our powerful brain and narrow hips to facilitate bipedalism brought about great complications to procreate. Natural selection pushed for our cubs to be born ever more premature. Have you seen a newborn

---

115   Dyble et al., 2016.
116   Dyble et al., 2016.

baby up close? Compare it to a foal. Ours are much uglier, helpless, and dependent. Excluding, of course, your own baby, who is undoubtedly the cutest in the world.

To make matters worse, our brains consume, from the very moment of birth, a great deal of energy. Human babies have a long childhood, and often have short intervals between births. A single mother is unable to satisfy the energy needs of her offspring on her own. Evolution pushed towards collaboration of the male and towards a certain sexual division of labor, to ensure the survival of the young.

No other species has a childhood as long as ours, and yet many have developed adaptations to share the heavy burden of parenting. In many cases, the male collaborates. In others, the females have developed creative solutions, such as the bat mothers who work together as a "team" to share parenting and take turns foraging for food. In one species of fish, individuals take turns in their sexual role, alternating from male to female and vice versa, to ensure fairness in the distribution of roles.[117] We can go comparing to see if we get some ideas ...

Collaboration between "relatives": Human beings spread out and occupied increasingly difficult environments. The probability of going out hunting and returning with food became increasingly unpredictable. On lucky days, we would bring back more meat than our family was capable of consuming. And on unlucky days, we would go hungry. Evolution favored an instinctive impulse to collaborate with our close relatives. *It doesn't matter if today went bad for me, because you will give me from your share. I will return the favor tomorrow.* This strategy stabilized the food supply and made it easier for everyone to survive.[118]

---

117 Sapolsky, 2010.

118 The size typically adopted by these "bands," of about five male hunters and a similar size of females of reproductive age, is thought to be a function of the optimal balance between "stabilizing" the supply, versus the need to distribute it among too many "heads" (Hamilton et al., 2018).

We are also the only species unable to give birth on our own. In most species, when the mother is about to give birth, she seeks solitude. In our case, since the head does not really fit through the birth canal, the child usually comes out in a position that makes it almost impossible for the mother to receive them. Usually it was other women in the family who assisted. So strong is this need for collaboration that women, if they do not feel supported at the time of delivery, produce a cortisol rush that can eventually slow the process.[119] Likewise, evolution must have pushed for greater collaboration from other adult relatives in the upbringing: grandmothers, grandfathers, aunts, or older siblings.

Collaboration between "non-relatives": The band was enough to ensure our livelihood, but not to defend ourselves in case of violent invaders or the need to hunt larger animals.[120] Nor did it offer a sufficiently wide "genetic supply" to prevent children from being born with some defects, since individuals in the band were usually all closely related. The clan was able to respond to these needs; and the bands integrated it as a dynamic entity, increasing or decreasing in size, merging with each other, or dividing, depending on the need. The young, male or female, used to migrate and join a new band in search of a sexual partner to reproduce.[121] And fortunately they did, because otherwise we wouldn't be having this interesting discussion.

Sometimes the clans constituted even larger and more complex groups, called "tribes." Tribes were a much looser unit of "our people", sharing the same language, beliefs, and customs; exchanging knowledge and "luxury goods" such as shells, pigments, or feathers; and occasionally gathering together to celebrate rites and religious festivals. Bands and clans must

---

119 Lee, 2018.

120 Hamilton et al., 2018.

121 According to experts, some cultures were "matrilineal," the females of the band were related to each other and it was the males who migrated. In others it was the other way around, the males of the band remained, and the females were integrated into the "family" of the male (Apicella & Barrett, 2016).

have competed and even fought over the same resources; yet the members of the same tribe must have recognized each other as "alike." This allowed them, at any given moment, to put aside their differences and unite to fight potential invaders.

As coexistence became more complex, and as our social life extended to members of nearby clans as part of a larger "we," these early "Social Weavers" were possibly the first to actually experience a "feeling" of "brotherhood" beyond their own families.

They were possibly the first to go to parley, to approach "others" that were no longer seen as such, and to shape broad collaborative alliances that proved to be a decisive factor in our prevalence over other species. They must have built bridges between initially rival clans. They must have pushed their peers towards a more "humanitarian" society, promoting the care of their weaker, wounded, and sick members. They helped forge bonds of reciprocity, gratitude and mutual trust, which became the foundation for the great social agreements of the future.

We can imagine them not only taking care of their own children with diligence, but also collaborating with the upbringing of their grandchildren or nephews, with more care, more attention, and more affection than their peers. At a time when half the children were dying before the age of 15, this certainly helped to perpetuate their own genetic heritage, and made them valuable and respected members within their communities. It also turned them into attractive sexual partners, as they "promised" careful and selfless parenting, and with it, more and stronger children. They had this natural ability to make other people feel close, welcome, accepted, safe, understood, and supported.

THE FOOTPRINTS OF SAPIENS SOCIAL WEAVER

Scenes from a lost past

Scene 1:

The young woman had already filled the pouch with water. But her work did not end there. Among the hides she wore to cover herself from the intense cold, she had yet another empty pouch. She filled that one too. She began the arduous task of climbing up to the cave with the two heavy pouches of water. She took breaks from time to time and rested. This also allowed her to chat with some members of her clan who were coming up from the river or were just coming down. Many were surprised to see that she was carrying two pouches with water. They looked around for the owner of the second one, without seeing anyone. When she told them that it was the pouch of the sick old man who slept under the elk's horns, they thought it was a strange idea. That old man was no longer procreating and had never procreated with that woman or her mother, or with the other daughters of her father. When she reached the cavern, the old man smiled at her and thanked her for the water and took the opportunity to tell her what had happened in the cavern during her absence. While this was happening, down on the river, there was talk about the "caregiver for the elderly."

Scene 2:

A small orphan had started to follow the band and was taken in by one of the women. He was introduced to the group of children, who were about to go on an excursion to the forest of the berries. It was one of their favorite excursions. If they were lucky, they could even return with some pieces of meat, some birds or a rodent. As the walk began, the little orphan began to fall behind. He didn't feel part of the group, he felt strange, he didn't quite understand what they were talking about, and he didn't know anyone. At that moment, another little boy stopped his march and approached him. He smiled at him, took his hand, and offered to walk together. He felt an urge to protect this little boy. He saw his weakness, and he wanted him to feel good. It didn't matter if he wasted valuable time to catch up with those that walked at the front. He explained the route they were taking and what they could find. He told him about rabbits and mice. He told him how at night by the fire, they would tell the stories about the excursion. They would no longer be separated. The little orphan trusted, and that contact sealed their friendship.

Scene 3:

She loved to talk. It gave her immense pleasure when they went down to the river to fetch water and they could tell each other stories and exchange gossip about the other members of the band and the neighboring bands: who had impregnated whom, who was a cheater, who had been the bravest hunter, and who was a bully. She collected in her mind, faces, anecdotes, ways of naming emotions and behaviors. She liked to look at the people she talked to. If they walked together, she liked to get close to her partner. She liked to smile and have them smile back at her. It made her feel warm inside. That's why she did not like it when a new way of carrying water up from the river was established. Someone would fill a bowl and walk a few steps to hand it over to the next, who immediately did the same and so on. It is true that it was faster, and that more water could be accumulated, but the charm of walking together and talking was lost. Fetching water from the river was no longer one of her favorite tasks.

Scene 4:

Taking a woman without the band's consent was considered a serious fault. When it also involved another clan, it was undoubtedly the moment of rupture for the always fragile relations between those who shared the same hunting territory, but not the ancestral spirit. And so the Wolf Hunters would have most likely taken up the spears against the Eagle Hunters. And so it would have been, if it weren't for the young man who came forward to parley. The young Wolf was known among the Eagles. Many times he had come to them before, carrying large quantities of fiber seed bowls. He had exchanged them for grains or other utensils. But if anyone was interested, the young man would teach them the secret of how to make the bowls. So, he would spend entire afternoons with them, talking and sharing stories. Several of his "apprentices" were now among those willing to take up the spears against the Wolves. The young man offered them to repair the damage caused with several gifts. And the possibility that if the woman wanted to return to the Eagles' cave, she could do it. The conversation brought them closer together and finally the conflict was avoided. The young Wolf came to be known as "the young man who talks to the Others."

CORE TRAITS

And what you may already be wondering: How to distinguish these beings, animated by oxytocin, when they approach you smiling, in the middle of a social gathering? Here goes a summary of the fundamental features that, to a greater or lesser extent, would be shared by the vast majority of Social Weavers.

"You've Got a Friend": Focus on relationships

From birth, Social Weavers are predisposed to take an interest in relationships and not be afraid of others. Oxytocin has the effect of a soft balm that bathes their amygdala, soothing their anxiety. Thanks to this increased sensitivity to this hormone, Types Two tend to trust themselves and others more, and to be more optimistic and cheerful than most people around them.

This disposition is at the root of the main motivation of this type: relationship, human contact, establishing connections with others. This drive has multiple expressions in their behavior.

They like to make eye contact with other people. Unlike others who are uncomfortable sustaining other people's gaze, Social Weavers actively seek it out, are able to hold it for longer, and enjoy it intensely.[122]

People of this type usually send off all kinds of friendly signals: they smile often, make pleasant comments, come closer, even in terms of physical proximity: a hug, a kiss, a handshake, a pat on the back. Sometimes, they simply place themselves a couple of centimeters closer to others when having a chat.

And behind all this promise of a relationship, there is usually a real intention to back it up. Connecting with others genuinely energizes them.

---

122 Sapolsky, 2017.

Like fish in the water: Emotional perception and social skills

Perhaps because they observe others with greater interest, they remember their faces better. Perhaps because they are interested in others, they perceive their emotions quite accurately. They can see when others are happy, sad, motivated, jealous, or exasperated.[123] Let's remember that there may be a slight bias in this ability. Evidence suggests that oxytocin makes it easier to perceive those emotions that are positive and happy, over those that are sad or upsetting.

That said, it seems that people of this type are usually more adept at emotional reading in general. They are also more adept at detecting the invisible ties that connect people: who is friends with whom, who is interested in whom, who is allied or in conflict, who is dominant and who is subdued.[124]

Social Weavers are equipped with an excellent "radar" that allows them to navigate, almost always successfully, the convoluted landscape of interpersonal relationships. In this territory they contribute their warmth, their positivity, their joy, spontaneity, communication skills, and charm. They are often sparkling and histrionic. They find it easy to engage in conversation with strangers and start new relationships, as they have this natural ability to make others feel at ease. Skilled readers of the political landscape, builders of alliances and coalitions, and agile in adapting to a wide range of people. The more friends, the better.

---

123   Skuse et al., 2014; Rodrigues et al., 2009; Hercules et al., 2016.
124   Sapolsky, 2017.

I will plant trees for your grandchildren: Prosocial behavior

Social Weavers tend to be spontaneous collaborators, even postponing their own interests or personal comfort to support, take care, or serve someone who requests it. They will not wait to be summoned or required, since they have a pair of "antennas" specially calibrated to detect the needs of others. People around them will often see them like this: as friends who are willing to support at the right time.

They often have a strong sense of family "ties." They will strive to forge a stable relationship with their partners and will tend to be loving and affectionate. They will often look for a partner who is, like them, relationship oriented.

Social Weavers tend to be involved, loving, close, and protective parents. In the extreme, they can become overly intrusive or "overprotective," causing their children to feel smothered and want to run away from them.[125]

Their friends and closest colleagues will become like an extension of their "family." The Social Weaver will often feel an impulse to act paternally or maternally towards the people they hold dear, extending to them their desire to protect, care, support or help. In many cases all this pro-sociality will be appreciated. But sometimes, when taken to the extreme, some friends and acquaintances might feel "invaded", consider it inappropriate, or simply reject to be treated "paternally" or "maternally" by someone who is neither their father nor their mother.

---

125 Sapolsky, 2017)

He loves me, loves me not...: Sensitivity to approval or rejection

So much concern for others comes with its costs. Social Weavers tend to be highly sensitive to manifestations of "rejection" or "indifference" by other people, especially if they are part of their immediate environment. They experience a powerful desire to please others, sometimes not quite consciously, and this desire is often at the root of many of their actions. They feel a deep satisfaction when they feel approved, wanted, needed, or loved. They especially like people who make them feel good. People who, like them, are responsive, considerate, empathetic, or generous.[126]

The flip side is that they resent any manifestation of detachment or coldness. This sensitivity can lead them to provoke just what they fear most: being rejected by others.

Their fear of rejection often leads them to be indirect and convoluted when expressing what they want, a communication style that others could perceive as "manipulative". Social Weavers may react strongly when they feel "excluded", and they may break down in the face of what they interpret as indifference. In the extreme, they may become acutely possessive or jealous, unconsciously seeking to be the only meaningful relationship for their partner, children or friends.

When experiencing these kinds of emotional demands, it is likely that others will run away and get lost. This causes a true "self-fulfilling prophecy," which becomes the great paradox of the Social Weaver. Their desire to connect is so strong that they can ultimately drive away people they care about.

---

126 Sapolsky, 2017

Friend or foe: Tendency to "tribal" behavior

More than other personality types, the Social Weaver tends to fall into an "us" versus "them" mentality. Of course, defining who makes up that "us" can be somewhat complex. Top of the list will be their family and often extensive network of friends. However, given their sensitivity to approval and rejection, the same person who yesterday was their close friend, today could have become their enemy by committing some voluntary or involuntary "betrayal." With the same intensity that they had previously felt positive emotions towards that person, today they may experience anger or spite. A very quick way to become a "them." This is an emotionally charged perception, which can vary according to the "heat" of the moment.

The same goes for their feeling of belonging to the group. Anyone who has chanted the anthem together with his national team and thousands of fellow countrymen, knows what it is like to feel like a "brother" with individuals you have never seen or will see again in your life. For a brief moment you savor the experience of being a Social Weaver, when he feels in communion with the group. By contrast, the members of the rival team can be felt, even momentarily, as enemies.

Defining "them" is equally complicated. It may be someone who hurt their feelings, who thinks differently from them, or who does not share their value scale. Or it may simply be people who belong to a "rival" area of their company, another political party, another ethnicity, religion, or nationality.

The emotionality of the Social Weaver within relationships will continue to be intense. Intense if it is a friend; intense if it is an enemy. Often, the way to punish the offender and vent their aggression will be reproaches, gossip, and complaints. In more extreme cases, they can become conflictive and feisty, even attacking only out of spite. This can be disconcerting for those around them, who are used to seeing them as generous and charming people.

Type Three: The Hunter

Or how a child did not want to be "a hunter," but "the hunter"

A FIRST GLANCE

He was already an old man and had not gone hunting in years. But by the fire, the children never got tired of listening to his stories and learning from them. The skills to camouflage themselves among the trees, to stay under water, to smell like a male bison, to make the best spear for each hunter, to manage to stay after the same prey for days and days. How to learn enough about your prey to be able to defeat it. Even at his old age, after those lessons, there were still females who wanted the seed of that old man who had once been called "the little hunter."

To own more than five bowls of animal fat for the winter. To show the highest number of successful hunts. To have water deposits in the same cavern, a greater number of coat hides, the more effective arrowheads. These were probably some of the signs that distinguished the most efficient hunter-gatherers. Today, in our contemporary Western society, it would probably be walking down Wall Street, or its equivalent in other countries, dressed as you should dress, talking as you should talk, and doing what you should do in order to be "successful." And within a community of Tibetan monks, we can imagine it as meditating the longest hours, owning the fewest robes, or enduring the severest fasts. The common factor is achievement. Being effective in attaining, whatever the objective, the geographic location, or the period in history.

The exploration of the biology of Type Three led us to investigate the biology underlying "goal-oriented behavior." We quickly realized that this is an overly broad concept, encompassing the entire spectrum of reward-based behavior. This is an inherent capacity not only in all human beings, but also in all animals, with a greater or lesser degree of sophistication. It is basic: it is a matter of procuring the means to survive. However, there seems to be something particular about Type Three.

What is it that characterizes this type? What is it about their goal-oriented behavior, and their relationship to success and achievement, that sets them apart from the rest of *Homo sapiens*? What is their "core" trait? The answer to these questions is less obvious than for other types. We will try to answer them via the hypotheses that follow.

BIOLOGICAL BASIS

Or how some hypothalamic neurons go big-game hunting

Hypothesis 1: Hyper-energization of goal-oriented behavior

A large percentage of the available research on goal-oriented behavior focuses on its "directionality": our ability to "persevere" and to "focus" attention on a particular goal, as opposed to the ability to "flex" our attention over several goals at the same time.[127] We do not think that Type Three behaviors are associated with any particular point on this continuum. On the contrary, we believe that Type Three is characterized by being very ductile to adjust their behavior, moving between these two extremes according to what is most useful in each situation.

However, a second component of goal-oriented behavior has been identified at a biological level. One that is less known and possibly more primitive in origin. It refers to the "energization" and activation of these behaviors, originally associated with the instinct to satisfy hunger.[128]

Technically, this "energization" is triggered by neurons in the Lateral Hypothalamus. They release a neurotransmitter called orexin, sending a message "downstream" to the Ventral Tegmental area and to the rest of the neuronal circuit that regulates the response associated with hunger. It

---

127 It refers to the "dopaminergic" axis of goal-oriented behavior (Friedman & Miyake, 2017).
128 Nieh et al., 2016.

is the mechanism that activates foraging for food and predation behaviors in animals.[129]

As we will see with respect to other primitive areas of our brain, throughout evolution, the function of this mechanism would have been "expanded" (or "hijacked") to energize "hunger" in a much broader sense: when we speak of "hunger for fame and fortune" we are not only talking about metaphors, since our brain uses the same neuronal circuits of hunger, to leverage this other "*mix.*"[130] We are talking about the evolutionary origin of the energization of all goal-oriented behavior, simple or sophisticated, necessary to adapt to an increasingly complex world.[131]

According to researchers in the area, these orexinergic neurons would influence a series of physical and cognitive processes, promoting not only the procurement of food, but also the energization and activation of the body in general, affecting bodily functions such as temperature regulation, digestion, and blood pressure, and temporarily reducing the perception of pain.[132]

Experimental psychology has also provided evidence of a connection between "hunger for money" and "hunger in general": A research team asked a group of subjects to answer a questionnaire regarding their degree of motivation to "make money". The experimental situation allowed these subjects to then eat as many chocolates as they wanted. The most "money-hungry"

---

129 Hills, 2005.
130 Sapolsky, 2017.
131 The entire system would have been expanded to give rise not only to behavior, but also to goal-oriented thinking (Hills, 2005) (Friedman & Miyake, 2017); (Sapolsky, 2012). Considering what is currently known about the lateral hypothalamus and the ventral tegmental area and their different roles in goal-oriented behavior, it is likely that the LH neurons are responsible for "energizing" or "driving" this behavior, while the VTA neurons are responsible for "directing" or "driving" it towards the goals or rewards that are relevant at that moment, modulating the value of the rewards through the dopaminergic system (Tyree & de Lecea, 2017).
132 Li, Hu, & De Lecea, 2014; Aston-Jones et al., 2010.

subjects ate significantly more chocolates, with the exception of those who were watching their weight.[133]

We are saying then that these neurons would be responsible for the degree of energy that we are willing to invest to carry out demanding tasks, sustained over time, in order to achieve a reward that we desire. And what is the reward that we desire? It does not really matter, since nature molded our brain so that we could adapt to the most varied challenges in the most diverse environments. In other words, whatever is needed. Furthermore, nature molded us to sustain effort based on our "anticipation" of reward. To such an extent that, at a brain level, the anticipation of a reward produces more "pleasure" than the reward itself.[134]

In short, the mouse runs to make the wheel spin. If it is convinced that spinning the wheel will bring about benefits in the long run, it can spend its whole life spinning the wheel. And with what energy! And although the life of an average Type Three is usually longer than that of a mouse, there will be no shortage of those who spend their lives "spinning a wheel."

Research on individual differences in how this mechanism works is still in its infancy,[135] but there are already some interesting findings. It has been discovered, for example, that people with a tendency to narcolepsy and excessive daytime sleepiness, that is, to generalized states of lack of energy, usually carry a genetic variant that determines a decreased activity of orexin within their organisms.[136] It has also been found that excess orexinergic activation is often associated with eating disorders, that is, literally, "hunger."

---

133 Briers, Pandelaere, Dewitte, & Warlop, 2006.

134 The Ventral Tegmental Area, the Accumbens Nucleus, and the whole dopaminergic system, are related to the "direction" of the motivation towards objectives. The focus of this behavior may vary as the rewards of your environment change (Tyree & de Lecea, 2017).

135 Pantazis, James, Bentzley, & Aston-Jones, 2019; Thompson, Xhaard, Sakurai, Rainero, & Kukkonen, 2014.

136 These are two variants in the genes that code for orexin receptors: OX1/HCRTR1 and OX2/HCRTR2 in human populations (Thompson et al., 2014)

Would it be possible that a similar mechanism lies at the base of excessive "hunger" in a broader sense? We believe that it is, and that if this mechanism has not been studied so far, it is possibly because it is not considered as a disorder. Unlike what happens with excess anxiety, aggressiveness, or obsessiveness, being excessively active or "workaholic" is perceived as barely a venial "sin," which any of us would be more than willing to confess in a job interview.

We believe that, if there are already clues about the relationship between this mechanism and a general decline in the energization of behavior, it will only be a matter of time before its association with a general increase of energization is discovered.

From an evolutionary perspective, our hypothesis is that Type Three would be biologically determined towards a "hyper-energization" of goal-oriented behavior, whatever goal they have defined as their own, from the influence of their culture, their mother, their grandfather, the Dalai Lama, or Lee Iacocca.

These unknown orexinergic neurons within the Hunter's Lateral Hypothalamus could be the main cause responsible for him being able to get up at 5 in the morning to go for a run before going to work, endure the pressure of being 14 hours in a row bidding for shares that go up or down; or spend four hours putting together an IKEA piece of furniture that "is not going to beat him."

Hypothesis 2: Testosterone and the "winner effect"

Type Threes, who from a young age were more energetic, skilled, determined, and competitive than most of their friends, must often have felt "the best." It is very likely that this feeling regularly triggered a discharge of testosterone that in behavioral biology is known as the "winner effect."[137]

---

137 Sapolsky, 2017.

What do we know about this effect?

- Every time we feel like a "winner" in a competition, we experience a rush of testosterone.

- This discharge occurs even whenever we "anticipate" a competitive situation, supporting the energization of behaviors aimed at "winning" it. This happens in the context of any competition, whether it deals with beating each other up until one is knocked out in a ring, or with something as intellectual as a game of chess.

- From an evolutionary standpoint, this discharge of testosterone would serve the function of increasing the aggressiveness of a defensive response, whenever individuals feel their status or social situation has been challenged.[138]

- Testosterone does not "generate" aggression, but acts by reinforcing, enhancing, and maintaining an already existing aggressive response.

This testosterone discharge has been associated with various cognitive, emotional, and behavioral consequences.[139] Some of them are:

- Sense of self-confidence, well-being, and exaggerated optimism.
- Decreased levels of fear and anxiety.
- Decreased level of empathy.
- Increased reactivity, impulsiveness, and willingness to take risks.
- Tendency to assume one's own opinion is correct, and to ignore the opinions of others.

Females or males endowed with a mutation that energized their goal-oriented behavior must have often experienced the "high" of testosterone as they felt they achieved, succeeded, or "won" in the multiple "competitions" that they had to face.

And testosterone allowed them to compete fiercely, too, whenever they felt their "status" was being challenged.

---

138 "Challenge Hypothesis" (J. C. Wingfield, Hegner, Dufty, & Ball, 1990); (John C. Wingfield, 2017)

139 Sapolsky, 2017.

EVOLUTIONARY ADVANTAGES

Or how a hunter-gatherer built a channel to bring water to the cave

200,000 years ago, we were an insignificant species. A few hundred bald, feeble apes, wandering around in handfuls, looking for fruit and roots, and taking the occasional opportunity to eat some carrion, after lions, hyenas, and vultures had already taken their share. The fact that, in such a short period of time, we have managed to build tools that allow us to communicate at a distance and travel through space, is almost a miracle of evolution.[140]

What is it that ultimately explains our prevalence as a species? If the reader is thinking about our great intelligence, stop for a moment and consider that the answer is not so obvious....To what extent was our intelligence an advantage to bring us fruit or to avoid being eaten by a lion?

Let us remember as well that our intelligence required the development of a huge head, which brought with it some enormous disadvantages. To begin with, it made both childbirth and parenting difficult, and forced us to procure much more food on a daily basis, just to meet our brains' tremendous demand for energy. What did we gain from all this?

The answer lies in our enormous adaptive flexibility. A capacity to adjust our adaptive strategies to almost any type of environment, and to overcome almost any type of difficulty.

In this context of natural selection, we could say that the personality type we call the Hunter, made "Adaptation" the central axis of life.

Everything characterizing this type—their pragmatism, their endless energy at the service of solving problems, their flexibility to adapt to changing environments or challenges, and their ability to overcome failure and to get back on their feet—are all qualities that could be attributed to our species in general. The Hunters, however, seem to experience this adaptive

---

140   Harari, 2014

drive more strongly than their peers. And as such, they must have acted as propellants for the advancement of *Homo sapiens* over the millennia. For these are the fundamental reasons why it is we, *Homo sapiens*, and not the Neanderthals, the elephants, or the chimpanzees, who have dominated this planet for at least the last, short period, of 70,000 years.

In what life situations were female and male carriers of this mutation especially effective? How did their relentless motivation and efficiency in solving practical problems show up? In what way did their high capacity to tolerate frustration help them? When and why were they chosen as sexual partners over other Types?

Natural selection tells us that the Hunters were able to solve problems that made the difference between life and death. Their own and that of their children. This mutation surely prompted them to make tools of wood and stone, to build portable "caverns" out of sticks and leather; to strive again and again to perfect the art of metals, or to try hundreds of designs for an arrow or spear until they found the most effective one. They may have been behind thousands of small improvements that made our daily lives more efficient, more bearable, or more comfortable, from the "handles" on a pot and the sewing needle, to the wheel.

The great legacy of the Hunter, their great contribution, seems to be precisely this "hunger" to achieve, survive, advance, and ultimately to rise above themselves. This "hunger" was behind the energy that, most probably, drove our ancestors to "get on their feet" to build a "better future."

THE FOOTPRINTS OF SAPIENS HUNTER

Scenes from a lost past

Scene 1:

She had never been known for being the best shooter. She was not a great runner either. Nor did they take her on their hunting expeditions. However, her band was never lacking for fresh meat. They were never short of warm furs. She had devised a system for catching her prey. She dug holes on the ground, which could catch any small game that happened to put their feet in the hidden opening. She also designed sophisticated traps at ground level, where a bait would attract her prey, which was then trapped by a scrambled web of branches, remaining defenseless against a spear stuck at close range.

Scene 2:

He wanted his spear to hit right where the first branches of the great trunk were born. But he failed. The spears were too heavy for his still young body. And although his ability to hit the target was superior to that of many men in the clan, he could not make his spears "fly" as far as he wanted them to. So he started testing different materials. The weight of the spear was important. It had to be capable of inflicting a fatal wound. The spears he could throw could barely hurt rabbits and other rodents. He wanted a good boar. So an experiment allowed him to discover a solution. He added weight to his best spear, the one that could fly easily, but only in the area near the tip. He tied up pieces of other old or broken spears. He shot with all his strength, and his surprise and joy were enormous, for he had managed to reach even higher. He calibrated the weight and practiced again and again until his shots were totally accurate. His first wild boar, of many that followed, earned him the name of Eagle Eye.

Scene 3:

She had a problem. She couldn't leave her young in the cave alone. She knew that there must be some way to solve it. That is when she came up with a way to carry her baby on her trips to the river. She knew that she needed her hands to remain free, so that she could carry the bowls back to the cave. She wrapped her cub in a thin hide and secured the package to her back with strips of wolf leather. Under the expectant gaze of women and men, she went to the river and returned with her baby on her back. The system became very popular and was soon copied in many other bands within the clan, and in time, within the whole tribe. In the end, the system was also adopted to carry their belongings whenever they migrated to a different camp.

Scene 4:

This is the fifth time he has stumbled and fallen. He complains, but not of pain. His complaint is against himself. With the impossibility that he is facing. He finally manages to stay upright on two feet, like everyone else around him. At his short eleven months of age, he feels the explosion of energy throughout his body. He wants to get up and explore the world. He wants to satisfy his compelling desire to move around and grab things, to smell them, to touch them. But he falls once again. And once again he gets up. And so, many times. Until he manages to take several steps at a time and hold onto a tree without falling. He laughs. He laughs and feels happy, smiling as he hears the approval of the adults who are watching. Years later he tried again and again to climb the smooth-trunk tree. He wanted to look at the valley from above and help with the surveillance. It was 15 or 20 failed attempts until he figured out how to do it. He improvised a makeshift ramp by resting a piece of wood against the trunk, helping him climb the smoothest part. From the top of the tree, before looking at the valley, he looked at those who were watching him and laughing at the feat. He raised an arm and shouted his victory.

CORE TRAITS

Let's agree that modern life no longer requires the skill to hunt elephants. At least not in most cases. However, we still have Hunters among us. What are their hunting grounds today? How to recognize them? We will review a series of traits that, according to our hypothesis, are rooted on the same mechanisms that turned the ancestors of Type Three into real Paleolithic superstars.

"Higher, better, faster, stronger"[141]: Hunger for "achievement"

The first characteristic of this type, the most structural, is their enormous amount of achievement-oriented energy. Achievement of what? Well, anything that the Hunters integrate as their "goal."

There will be big goals, those that were understood from a very young age as the most "desirable": to become the grand vizier, the painter who portrays the king, the richest merchant, the first woman president, the CEO of a Fortune 100, or the sexiest man of the year according to *People* magazine.

There will be smaller ones: giving a lecture, meeting a sales goal, finishing the report before the end of the day, winning a sports race, learning to play golf, conquering a partner, or fixing a leaky faucet.

Big or small, Threes tend to face challenges with the same attitude. Their body, their mind, and their emotions are perfectly aligned, in total activation, with the sole focus of getting their "prey." Their goal becomes the most important thing.

The Type Three hunter-gatherers must have felt something similar. Endowed with this instinct, sharper than their peers, they must have felt the "hunt" intensely. We can imagine their excitement as they prepared to go out on a raid. Their energy and focus, while chasing the boar for four days straight. We can also imagine their feeling of triumph when they finally made the catch. It is likely that the climax of their experience was the brief instant of actually catching the prey. Everything that came later, including the experience of being hailed for success, or the satisfaction of eating the meat with family around the fire, was less relevant to the Three.

---

141 Song by French duo Daft Punk, released in October 2001 as the fourth single from their second studio album *Discovery*.

Imagine today's Type Three with that same primal intensity. Their energy, their persistence in pursuing what they want to achieve, whatever it may be.

Success, a somewhat abstract and very popular term in our time, does not mean anything other than "having achieved it."

Only one will remain standing: Competitive and individualistic

Let's go back to the image of the hunt. When a lioness stalks her prey, there is a deep competition for survival. Let's imagine that for an instant they meet each other's eyes, and the lioness feels, "I'm going to kill you." If the lioness does not catch her prey, eventually she and her cubs will starve. There is no room for mercy or doubt. It is a competition that only has two possible outcomes: the lioness wins or her prey wins. With the hunting instinct, everything is about competition.

Type Threes face their challenges as if, in some way, they are "competing" against them. This tap "won't beat me," they will say as they try for the fourth time to find a way to fix a leak. This innate tendency to compete against the "goal" springs right out from their hunting instinct.

And what happens when this instinct is directed towards others? Well, it depends on their position in relation to the Three.

Those who compete "against" them for the same prey become their enemies. Whether they are of the same species, or a different one.

And of course, their hunting companions will be their allies. Type Threes' instinct tells them that they need each other to succeed. Now, there too, things can go wrong. As soon as one of their hunting companions no longer contributes to the achievement of the goal, he will automatically cease to be considered an ally. He may even be treated as an "obstacle."

And again, if it is not so much about the prey, but about being the "best hunter," things could get even more complicated. Their companions could become, at the same time, their rivals. The Hunter could inadvertently transfer this impulse to "compete" against the "prey," to compete against the others. To collaborate or to compete. It is the dilemma that the Hunter faces.

A recent study provides clues that corroborate this "primitive" connection between the sensation of "hunger" and the urge to "compete." In the first experiment, a group of subjects who had not eaten for hours were less likely to make donations to charity, compared with the control group who had eaten recently. In the second experiment, subjects exposed to a room smelling of food were less willing to collaborate during a business game than the subjects who played in a room without the smell.[142]

On the other hand, this is not just a consequence of their "hunger." Let's remember the role that testosterone plays in all this. Types Three will tend to experience a testosterone "high" every time they prepare to compete against an opponent, be it on a sports field, a negotiation, a meeting, or the annual performance review. We are talking about both men and women here. Under the influence of testosterone, the Hunters' competitive energy will be increased, boosting their faith in themselves, and reducing any consideration or ability to empathize with potential enemies. This is the "winner" effect in action.

"Just do it": Active, pragmatic, impatient, and hardworking

Programmed to feel "hungry" for "achievements," Hunters tend to view the world in terms of tasks and goals, and everything they have to do, or not

---

142   Briers et al., 2006.

do, to accomplish them. We will almost always see them doing something. Something useful, practical, something that produces results.

Vigorous and energetic, they tend to live in "high-speed" mode. They often see life as a constant race: there is so much to do, so many goals to meet, so many "miles to go before they sleep."[143] There is absolutely no time to waste on irrelevant things.

In extreme cases, many things can fall into this bag of "irrelevance": valuable aspects of life such as relationships with others, having fun, or taking some time to relax. Or even taking the time to pause and consider options before jumping into action.

"Doing" can become much more important than "feeling" or "thinking" in the inner life of Type Three. This makes them deeply pragmatic. Their cerebral cortex is busy, most of the time, devising the best strategies to achieve their goals.

Almost everything in the life of the Three tends to revolve around this axis: their concept of themselves is based on what they have been able to "do" or "achieve." Their perception of what is useful, or valuable, from the use of time, to any object or person, might come to be measured with the same yardstick.

There is a reason why they are often labeled as "impatient" or "workaholic." The Threes themselves, once they become more aware of themselves, often complain about this difficulty in slowing down and making contact with what they really feel and think.

---

143 Borrowed from Robert Frost, 1923, "Stopping by Woods on a Snowy Evening"

"No retreat, no surrender"[144]: Persistent and tolerant to frustration

A Hunter never leaves the job halfway and does not give up in the face of difficulty. When she has set herself a goal, she tries it over and over until she achieves it. "I just need to find the right strategy." She removes obstacles "at any cost."

They are biologically wired to behave this way. They have no incentive to stop before obtaining the prize. Lingering or getting frustrated are not useful strategies. The only behavior with a true practical sense, the only one that will bring them closer to their goal, will be "persisting."

Sometimes this very drive can lead them to "bend the rules a bit" to achieve their objective. It is not about bending the rules arbitrarily or willfully. This would only happen when the rules stand between them and their goal. When they become an "obstacle." Obstacles will be removed.

Can do, will do: Optimistic and high self-esteem

Type Three tends to display a "can-do," winning attitude. Their high self-esteem and self-confidence seem to have a biological basis, while it is likely that their experiences and environment will also play a role.

On the one hand, in the animal world, the active search for rewards is almost always accompanied by "positive" emotional states: motivation, curiosity, enthusiasm. The function of these emotions is, precisely, to mobilize the animal towards approaching behaviors.[145] A person that is biologically predisposed to "approach" rewards should naturally tend

---

144 American–Hong Kong action film from 1986 directed by Corey Yuen and starring Kurt McKinney and Jean-Claude Van Damm.

145 Unlike plants, animals have the power to approach that which sustains their life (rewards) and withdraw from that which endangers them. Withdrawal behaviors, such as freezing or flight, tend to be accompanied by negative emotional states (Ikemoto, Yang, & Tan, 2015).

towards "energized" physiological states and optimistic and extroverted emotional states.

On the other hand, the Hunters will possibly consolidate their self-image of "efficiency" from the experience of achieving what they set out to do, from a young age and throughout their life. This experience will probably reinforce their already existing visceral inclination towards a positive assessment of themselves and their abilities.

And that's precisely how others see them—confident. Even if they only superficially know what they are talking about, Threes could express themselves as if they were the ones who had invented the concept. Even if it's their first time playing that sport, they might seem experienced. Even if it is their first experience, we will see a veteran. We will see neither their doubt nor their insecurity.

The end justifies the means: Utilitarian

Types Three develop a particular skill to detect any element that "serves" their purpose. A way of dressing, a certain way of speaking, a diploma, belonging to a certain elite club, the right car, a Swiss Army knife, a hammer, or a studied "careless" look to their hair. Any element, if well used, can be a great tool.

The combination of their high self-esteem, their feeling of self-efficacy and their ability to detect which elements are "key" to success, often makes them skillful managers of their own image. Keep in mind that image is also a tool, at least when it comes to adapting to our social environment.

This combination is also the perfect cocktail to turn the Hunter into an able navigator of stages and auditoriums. They enjoy the spotlight, delivering the precise smile, the perfect word, the right silence, or the look that lingers just a couple of seconds longer on a particular member of the audience.

In their well-stocked toolbox we will often find great verbal fluency, vivid and engaging non-verbal language, and an almost infinite set of appropriate responses for the precise moments. It is naturally easy for them to sell their ideas.

All this can be transformed into a useful tool to close a deal, to influence a decision, to win an ally, or to ingratiate yourself with your boss. And if the right attitude for the moment is to demonstrate humility, they will usually know how to project that as well, even if it is not true. Because, let's face it, another tool in their toolbox is likely to be the ability to show themselves as more valuable or capable than they really are.

On the other hand, consciously or not, Hunters may come to see other people as means to their ends. Those who were initially attracted by their seductive charm may end up feeling used, disappointed, and disregarded.

I could tell you, but then I'd have to kill you[146]: Difficulty accepting mistakes

When our entire motivation and our emotional world revolves around "achieving," it is natural that "not achieving" becomes painful. To make a "mistake" is to "fail" in our fundamental purpose, the "focus" of our whole being.

It becomes so painful that the Hunter's automatic reaction will be to try to "get out of there" as quickly as possible. Their first impulse will be to act to correct it, but if this is not possible, they might react by denying its existence or by blaming others.

And if someone insists on forcing them to face their mistake, their first reaction might be to "compete" with a good "counterattack," in a reaction that may be disconcerting to people who were only pointing to a problem that needed to be solved.

---

146 Famous line in *Top Gun*, 1986.

Type Four: The Wizard

Or how a child who felt pain painted the cavern

A FIRST GLANCE

32,000 years ago, one of our ancestors worked for almost three months straight, carving an ivory statuette. The figure, over 12 inches tall, represented a man with a lion's head.[147]

---

147   Hohlenstein-stadel lion-man (Wynn, Coolidge, & Bright, 2009); (Harari, 2014)

A few years ago, we found the result of her work in a cave in southern Germany, although we will never be able to talk to the artist who sculpted it. What did this figure represent for its carver? Did she feel that she was carrying out an important task for her tribe, perhaps transcendental? And what did her peers feel? Did they bring food to the artist, so that she could continue with her sacred work?

No remains of tools or other signs of a domestic occupation were found in the cave. Just some flutes made of bone. And only a few miles away, in a different cave, another figurine of a lion-man was found. Smaller, but almost identical. Was it the same artist? There, too, bone flutes were found.

Would members of a same tribe enter that cave to contemplate those statuettes with emotion? What was the music of those flutes like? Would it be a ceremony lost in time? Today it is impossible for us to know.

What we can know is that it was one of the first representations of an "imaginary" being, portraying a reality that lay beyond what "is seen with the eyes." We can also speculate that the Sapiens who were behind those representations were able to intuit a whole landscape of emotions within an "inner world." Thus, they were able to make the "hearts" of their entire tribe resonate. And beyond.

This personality, delicately sensitive to the world of emotions and of great expressive power, seems to have emerged from a particular mutation.

It is likely that the first *Homo sapiens* who managed to touch their companions with a piece of music, a cave painting, or a story in the evening by the fire, were carrying a genetic variant that induced an increased sensitivity in a very specific area of their brain: the Anterior Cingulate Cortex (ACC).

BIOLOGICAL BASIS

Or how the Anterior Cingulate Cortex makes things beautiful

The Anterior Cingulate Cortex (ACC) is a brain region that is critical for processing the experience of pain. We are not talking about a purely sensory perception. That is the job of more primitive, basic areas of our brain, mostly linked to mere survival. The Anterior Cingulate Cortex is involved with the emotional experience associated with pain.

Suppose that you panic about injections. If your Anterior Cingulate Cortex were to be "deactivated," due to an accident or a tumor, and you were immediately given an injection, you would still be able to detect and locate the puncture. But you would no longer feel panic, not even a slight fear. What's more, the sensation of "pain" would be noticeable, but you wouldn't care in the least. The role of the ACC in humans goes far beyond the experience of physical pain.[148] Important notice: if any reader is thinking that it would be a good idea to have his or her own ACC deactivated, we advise that they finish reading this chapter before making the decision.

Originally, the role of the ACC seems to have been to mobilize the body to avoid elements of the environment that were causing it harm. Over the millennia, as our brain evolved to adapt to our intense social lives, the role of ACC expanded to include the processing of "social" or emotional pain. Studies using fMRI[149] in the brain show that our ACC is activated when we feel envious or when we are being excluded from the group.[150] Teenagers' ACCs must switch on and off like crazy while they are checking the "*likes*" on their social networks ...

---

148 Fuchs, Peng, Boyette-Davis, & Uhelski, 2014; Shackman et al., 2011; Shackman et al., 2016; Iannetti, Salomons, Moayedi, Mouraux, & Davis, 2013; Wager et al., 2013.
149 Functional magnetic resonance imaging.
150 Sapolsky, 2017.

Now the brain, in all its economy and efficiency, used ACC for an even more sophisticated function. Not content with putting her in charge of "feeling" our own physical and emotional pain, it also put her in charge of "feeling" other people's physical and emotional pain.

Thus, over time, the ACC was promoted to the honorable position of "chief manager of empathy" within our brain. Empathy, or the ability to "feel with the other."

Let's go back to the puncture example. Think for a moment of a menacing syringe. Now you see an unfriendly-looking nurse who takes that syringe and pokes someone else's hand. You guessed it. Your own Anterior Cingulate Cortex is activated just by looking at someone else's hand being pricked. But it doesn't stop there. Your own sensory cortex is also activated, exactly in the area corresponding to that part of your hand, making you "imagine" the pain vividly. Perhaps even your motor cortex is activated, and you slightly withdraw or contract your own hand.

And to complicate matters further, if the pricked hand belongs to your own child or your own mother, your ACC will be activated even more. If it is "just" a stranger you see for the first time, it will be less activated. And if the pricked hand belongs to an "enemy," and politicians on duty have done a good job painting the "enemies" as "subhuman," then your ACC may not activate at all.[151] Not a blink. We won't dwell on this point, since its implications are enough to write an entire book, but this reflection serves to understand the extent to which the mechanisms that regulate our social navigation are delicate.

So how does this mechanism work? A hint: we know that the Anterior Cingulate Cortex has many receptors for endorphins. We also know that

---

151 The activation of ACC in the face of the pain of others is a complex process, mediated by many cognitive processes. The level of activation of the ACC will be greater or lesser depending on the degree to which "the other" is perceived as "close." If it is seen as "one of us," the activation will be much greater. This belonging to an "us" is not only determined by cultural factors (in-group vs. out-group), but can also be manipulated or provoked by more or less explicit messages communicated by a "reliable" source (Sapolsky, 2017).

endorphins are endogenous opioids that, among other things, help reduce our experience of pain.

Endorphins ring a bell? If you exercise, if you eat chocolate...Well, you should know what studies reveal: that the mere action of endorphins on our ACC is enough to calm our subjective experience of pain; that the very real analgesic effects of many placebos can be associated with an activation of the endorphin systems acting on the ACC; and that the reduction of the experience of pain through hypnosis could also be mediated by this same mechanism. We can say the same about positive emotional states. We feel less pain when we are happy, and again, endorphins and ACC seem to be responsible.[152]

Another fact to consider: morphine, as well as other external opiates, acts on the same receptors, located in the ACC, when they reduce our perception of pain.[153]

Now, we are talking about a generic mechanism that is shared by all human beings. Almost all of us, in fact. The exception would be psychopaths, who arrived too late to the distribution of empathy.[154]

There is evidence that some people are born with a more reactive Anterior Cingulate Cortex than average. And indeed, these people are more "sensitive" to emotional pain, both their own and others'.[155]

The cause of these individual differences is not yet completely clear, but one of the main suspects is a genetic variant, the A118G polymorphism in the OPRM1 gene; a gene that codes for endorphin receptors. One study proved the "sensitive" variant of this gene to be associated with a greater

---

152 Navratilova et al., 2015; Wager et al., 2013; Rainville, 2002; Villemure & Bushnell, 2009.

153 The action of morphine on pain-free individuals, which is observed in addicts, does not act on the ACC but directly on the "pleasure circuit" and requires higher doses to have an effect (Navratilova et al., 2015).

154 Young people with psychopathic features present reduced activity in their ACC (as well as in the Amygdala and other associated areas) when contemplating the pain of others. The greater the severity of the psychopathic traits, the lesser the response of their ACC to empathic pain (Marsh et al., 2013).

155 Coghill, McHaffie, & Yen, 2003; Sapolsky, 2017.

reactivity to pain, both the one we experience when our hand is pricked and the one we feel when our group rejects us.[156]

Our hypothesis is that Type Four personality would be the product of an hereditary predisposition towards greater sensitivity to pain, both physical and psychological, and both one's own and that of others, caused by the presence of this genetic variant. In fact, neurobiology has already found many associations between specific patterns of behavior and the presence of this genetic variant or other individual differences in Anterior Cingulate Cortex function. Some of these patterns are:

- Increased ability to recognize one's own emotions and those of others: Several studies have found a direct relationship between the level of activation of ACC in humans, the ability to distinguish one's own emotions, and the ability to empathically recognize and predict emotions of others.[157]

- Self-absorption: You may think that an excess of sensitivity to the pain of others, inevitably leads us to enroll in Doctors Without Borders, or Greenpeace. This is not the case. In fact, the opposite is often true. Intensely feeling the pain of others is a painful experience in itself. And this psychic pain can become so strong, so distressing, that it becomes our main focus of concern. Hypersensitive people often turn over on themselves, in an effort to ease this pain. As a result, they are often less likely to act prosocially.[158] No Greenpeace. Better a poem.

- Tendency to think "liberally" or "unconventionally": Some studies have found an association between the amount of gray matter in our ACC, and our tendency to express "liberal" ideas in opinion polls. It may

---

156 Bonenberger, Plener, Groschwitz, Grön, & Abler, 2015.
157 Bernhardt & Singer, 2012; Sapolsky, 2017.
158 Laboratory experiences have shown that people who feel others' pain more intensely, measured as activation of ACC with an fMRI or as increased heart rate, are less likely to act prosocially in simulation activities (Sapolsky, 2017).

sound like an odd idea that our way of thinking might be related to our biology, but many studies tend to support this finding.[159]

EVOLUTIONARY ADVANTAGES

Or how a hunter-gatherer created a symbol that united the clan

Hunter-gatherers were like us. In our modern "egocentrism," we want to think of them as animalistic or "primitive," but if an accidental trip in a time machine were to deposit us 30,000 years ago, we would surely be surprised by the familiarity.

We would meet human beings with projects, with intellectual interests, with aspirations to be "valued" within their clan. We would find people who chat, laugh, and work together every day. United to their loved ones by bonds of affection, and although more accustomed to the certain possibility of an early death, often moved by the grief of losing their partner, their father, or a dear friend. We would see them burying their companions with loving care. We would see rivalries, envies, and competition. We would see the "cool" group, made up of those who feel most powerful, weaving their alliances and coalitions. We would see others striving to belong. Or preferring their independence. In short, we would see human beings like us.

In a world like this, we can imagine the impact that a man or woman gifted with a special sensitivity must have had.

It is true that, had it appeared too early in evolutionary time, this mutation might not have been particularly adaptive. What is the use of being extraordinarily sensitive if I cannot express it? When coupled with an increased cognitive capacity and a more sophisticated language, the impact of this personality trait on our development as a species must have

---

159   Sapolsky, 2017.

been enormous. The Fours of the time must have been able to interpret the deepest feelings of their peers, and through their art, their symbolism, or simply their ability to represent, they knew how to touch and bring hearts together.

Let's imagine we are there, coming back to our camp in the evening, tired, after a day of collecting or hunting. We sit by the fire, once again, surrounded by other faces that are so familiar to us. And the Wizard begins to tell a story. It is a story full of magic, which tells how our nimble and brave ancestors, descendants of the lion, managed to pull through when the earth shook and the mountains spat fire. It tells of the birth of our clan, of "our people," and why we are different from the "others." It tells the story of the river, the tree, and the mountain, which gave us wood and stone so that we could make tools. We forget our fatigue, and for a moment, close to the heat of the bonfire, we feel transported to that magical world.

It wasn't just the feeling of those hunters at the end of the day, around the fire. The next morning, those hunters still felt stronger and more invincible, because they were the children of the lion. And the scattered bands of the same clan could finally unite as "brothers," as "sons and daughters of the same spirit" to fight against the "invader." And who knows, it maybe that 32,000 years ago, many members of that tribe heard the melody of the flutes and paid their respects to an ivory statuette of a lion-man, inside a cavern.

Even then, Type Fours must have been very valuable in creating this "parallel reality" and in talking about "things that don't exist." Things that eventually become more real than reality itself, in the minds of us human beings.

The Wizards must have been incredible interpreters of their peers' emotions, powerful storytellers, creators of shared symbols and "meanings," mitigators of the uncertainty created by the forces of nature, generators of a sense of belonging beyond close family ties, all around a common legend. And in some cases they must have been, simply, the creators of something beautiful that provided a moment of solace, of being transported to a kinder reality, when contemplating a painting, listening to a melody, or following a story.

Because, at the end of the day, if we had to choose the greatest adaptation of *Homo sapiens*, the one that most explains our success as a species, we would have to lean towards our ability to establish large networks of collective collaboration. The Four's ability to create common symbols and meanings was essential for these large groups to be possible, without internal conflicts disintegrating them. If you don't believe us, think of the strength that a piece of cloth that we call a flag, or the image of a young man hanging from a cross, can have to this day.

THE FOOTPRINTS OF SAPIENS WIZARD

Scenes from a lost past

Scene 1:

The children could not understand the wizard's excitement. He kept looking at their feet. He demanded to know where they had been. The children, curious, escorted him to the small cavern where they had been playing. That was where he first saw it. The ochre tone of the earth was similar to that of the children's feet. Depending on the tone of the skin, the ochre was softer or more intense. Images of different shades of ochre crowded his mind. He closed his eyes and saw a hunting scene. It was just a mixture of colors associated with sizes and shapes on a certain coloration of the rock. And there it was. A mammoth, a hunter, a fox, a wolf pack. They did not move like the real ones, but it was clearly their spirits that allowed them to be seen. Painting them was like giving them life, it was like creating them all over.

Scene 2:

The wind season left an unexpected balance. The wizard had followed a sweet whistle sound coming from the mountain. He had discovered that the wind was blowing inside a small cavern that had openings to the sea. When the wind slipped through some of the holes, the pitch would change. But after the wind season was over, when the branches of the trees no longer moved and the perfumes of the forest remained, the wizard was determined to meet again with the whistle of the wind. He had an idea. He worked hard on a hollow bone, so that it would also have outlets for the air. But drilling the bone without breaking it was a very difficult task. His attempts failed many times until he found a suitable stone. He discovered that drilling by abrasion was much more efficient than hitting. He managed to make three holes in an old bone, which did not need cleaning, as the insects had accounted for the fatty pulp in its center. He blew and was disappointed with the result. It barely sounded like a whistle. Then he took it firmly to blow harder. The little flute was pushed forward so that only a small section received the blow. The sound came out perfect. Then he tried covering and uncovering the holes. The sweet and penetrating whistle attracted the attention of the clan to the first of many concerts of the wizard.

Scene 3:

Many times she walked alone in the forest. She would spend long periods in silence, contemplating or simply feeling the wind on her face. She liked the smell of the sea. The perfume of the forest mixed with flowers, fruits, animal remains, wet wood. She claimed that it was sometimes possible to see the perfume moving through the air. You could even see it coming closer, before you could perceive it with your nose. She liked to listen to the language of animals and insects. She spoke just enough, never without being asked. She preferred to listen. To listen and to listen. The stories, the fights, the arguments, the tales that the wizard told. One night in the cavern, wizard did not show up. They waited for him by the fire to hear the story of the great hunt. When it was clear that the wizard would not come, the girl stood up, and began to relate the magnificent adventures of that story. She used the shadows and the blinking light of the fire and it seemed that her characters had come to life. She knew the story by heart. And told by her it seemed even more real. The painted figures on the walls seemed to move. She imitated the war cries with her voice, the comments of the hunters, the laughter, the sounds of pain and fatigue. In the culminating moment she imitated the animal's last breath. They could see the animal dying. The wizard, who had watched in silence from behind, knew. He had already told his last story.

Scene 4:

Uru had been the best hunter of the clan. He knew when to surprise the animal. He knew the exact day to go hunting, how many men would be needed. The largest game had been obtained by following, listening, and hunting alongside Uru. But he was no longer with them. They had wrapped him in his favorite hides and they had left him in the cavern of the dead under the death stones. So now, when they wanted to know when to pursue the great bison, it was necessary to consult the shaman. He could talk to Uru. He could only ask him specific questions. The thicket of the forest in front of the cave of the dead, the smoke from the fire, and the invocations did the rest. He could talk to any spirit. But the spirits should be disturbed only if there were clear questions for them. Uru's spirit now walked through other forests and hunted in other mountains. But they would always be brothers, having hunted together under the spirit of the white wolf. A brother wolf will always help another. That was the oath. That's why when the shaman asked, Uru answered. He kept his promise and helped the clan.

CORE TRAITS

You are already wanting to meet this guy (or gal). Sounds fascinating, or at the very least, intense, right? Well, not so fast, because Type Four has a lot of charm, but like all the other types, they also have their ebb and flow. We are now going to dive into the intense world of the Four, in order to understand the shared traits of all those who identify with The Wizard as their Central Type today.

Your pain hurts me: Sensitivity to emotions, especially painful ones

The Wizards experience their emotions and moods intensely. By being "painfully" aware of their own emotions and those of others, they will tend to be especially empathetic, compassionate, and sensitive to other people's suffering.

Their tendency to experience painful emotions more strongly, might sometimes make them vulnerable to fall into states of sadness or melancholy, without an evident or immediate cause.

At a cognitive level, they are biased towards perceiving what is "missing" or what "hurts" in situations, in themselves, or in others. At times, this could lead them to overlook what is positive in the present moment, focusing attention on things that cannot be, or things that are already past.

This inner murmur could lead them to spend much of their time in a rather serious "emotional tone." They make their "home" and find it "comfortable" to inhabit emotions in the realm of melancholy; and, in some cases, they may even experience a feeling of being "alien" to themselves in moments of great joy or fun.

Sapiens, know thyself: Inward focus

Given the intensity with which they experience their emotions, it is likely that Type Fours are naturally inclined to focus their attention on their own inner world. This has many consequences for their psychic life.

Firstly, it brings on the possibility of developing a high level of self-awareness or what Daniel Goleman would call "intrapsychic intelligence."[160] This means an above-average ability to distinguish a wide range of hues and shades within their own emotional world. Like the myth of the Eskimos

---

160   Goleman, 2017.

and their fifty words for snow, the Wizard will tend to perceive the subtleties, nuances, and slight variations of emotional life, both their own and that of others.

This same intensity makes inner life become very important for Types Four. Perhaps the single most important thing in their lives. This may be the reason why we often see them making a great effort to be true to themselves, to their own internal world. The Wizards strive to be authentic, value genuine self-expression, and are highly sensitive to perceiving truthfulness or the lack of it in others.

Another direct consequence of this inward focus is that Fours tend to be reserved, as if absorbed in their emotions or thoughts.

And as we have already mentioned, feeling the pain of others intensely does not necessarily lead to generous actions. In the case of Type Four, this pain could become so intense that it leads them to turn on themselves and their own suffering, rather than helping or connecting with others, no matter how much they feel for the other's pain. Thus, Wizards could come to be perceived as "individualistic."

I am not made for this world: Vulnerability to "longing" and "deprivation"

Type Four seems to be equipped with a lower threshold to suffer from the emotions in the family of "nostalgia": feeling one is lacking, deprived, or longing for something that is, for some reason, impossible. Once under their spell, they seem to experience these emotions more intensely than the average person.

They tend to be more sensitive to feeling excluded or rejected in social situations, and they are more vulnerable to the effects of frustration.

In their relationships they tend to establish strong, meaningful, and authentic connections. However, their hypersensitivity could lead them to feel disappointed or disillusioned with relative ease. They may go from zero to a hundred, and from a hundred to zero, in an emotional swing that would be disconcerting or exhausting for those who love him.

They also tend to be more sensitive to the effects of envy, that is, to perceiving others through the lens of what "they have, and I have not."

Beauty is truth, truth beauty[161]: Expression through artistic creation

While our rationality seeks to express itself through numbers, syllogisms, and words, our emotions prefer the alternative language of artistic creation.

For, how can emotions be expressed? What can the sweet sound of a cello communicate, or a piano sonata heard at sunset? What do we feel when we contemplate eyes portrayed on canvas, playing with shapes and colors? What can a poem tell us about the fear of death, or a novel about the heroism and sacrifice of a man?

Many Fours are driven by an urge to express their emotional authenticity through these diverse languages. If we think about it, at the end of the day, "art" is nothing but a language that allows us to communicate emotions directly to the emotionality of another human being.

This does not mean that all Fours are artists or that all artists are Fours; but it seems that people with this type of personality tend to seek and enjoy artistic expression, be it as professionals, amateurs, or mere spectators.

And possibly, the artists who possess this type of personality will stand out from the bunch, because their art will flow from their most authentic emotional expression. And although they may be hurt if no one recognizes their accomplishments, and they may suffer if nobody is interested in buying

---

161   From "Ode on a Grecian Urn", written by the English Romantic poet John Keats in May 1819.

their work, they will prefer that to betraying what is most precious to them and "selling" themselves to what the masses want.

They will often be drawn to the special, the intense, the beautiful, the profound, the authentic, and the extraordinary. They will seek to be original, unique, to follow their own path and inspiration, their intuition, and their way of looking at reality. They will want to find themselves and to express themselves from their innermost beings.

ꝯ ꝗ꠱ ꒰꒱꒲꒳꒴꒵꒶꒷꒸ [162]: Sensation of being "different"

Possibly due to the permanent experience of perceiving themselves as more "sensitive" than their peers, they gradually come to the conviction of being "different." While their classmates were playing ball or jumping rope, they possibly preferred to talk with their friends, go for a walk in the garden, or listen to music at their special corner. Depending on the moment and according to their mood, but also more deeply influenced by the environment in which they lived during their early development, Fours may feel that this difference makes them "unique and special," or simply "inadequate," "misfits," and "misunderstood."

Rebel without a Cause[163]: Against establishment

The world of emotions is difficult to order and regulate. It cannot be "boxed in," however much the mind wants to. Perhaps for this reason, Fours show a tendency to rebel against establishment, structure, uniformity, and everything that means limits to their freedom.

---

162 "I'm Different"; in Tengwar, one of the languages created by J.R.R. Tolkien (1892–1973); from https://funtranslations.com/elvish

163 American drama film about emotionally confused suburban, middle-class teenagers, directed by Nicholas Ray, and starring James Dean (1955).

They seek to create spaces for difference, for the new, the spontaneous, that which springs from the flow of the most authentic emotions. Many times we will see them pushing to break schemes, to get out of patterns and not sticking to precedents.

Type Five: The Sage

Or how a curious little boy wanted to explain the world

A FIRST GLANCE

For many days he had observed how it had grown, under a weak leak. It was one of the plants that they used to collect on the plain. When they left that cavern, four full moons had passed. And the plant had grown up to deliver a hard, dry grain. An idea crossed his mind, what if it had to do with the grains they had collected? The following year, when the rains ended and the grounds began to dry out, they returned to that cave. He secretly reserved some grains and put them under the drip. Once again, the plant grew. Excitement kept him from sleeping. The next season, when the band returned to the same cave, he had already decided that he would put many more grains in the ground. Soon his discovery passed, by word of mouth, to the other members of his clan.

A random mutation, in the brain of a very ancient human, changed the course of the planet's history. This humble mutation, in a tiny gene, allowed our language to make a quantum leap.

We do not know exactly when that mutation occurred. Most scientists claim that it happened around 70,000 years ago, only in the brain of *Homo sapiens*, and that, in a few thousand years, it would have transformed the fate of our planet. Quite a cognitive revolution.

Others take it more easily. They don't swallow the story of *Homo sapiens* being so fast and exclusive. They observe the rate at which the primitive languages that still exist today develop, and they do the math. Based on their calculations, they set the date of the beginning of this process at least 200,000 years ago or even before we became a separate species.[164] Raise your hand if you are able to distinguish the differences between 70,000 and 200,000 years. These are the figures that evolution uses to count time. Regardless of when it happened, this mutation marked a turning point in our destiny as a species.

Our language became infinitely ductile and allowed us to talk about things that "cannot be seen." And we began to "see" with our mind's eye. We saw things that had never been seen before, and we even saw things that did not really exist. We ate from the forbidden apple...

---

164 Perreault & Mathew, 2012.

Before posing our hypotheses, we invite you to remember one of the findings of behavioral genetics: "there is a continuum between normal and abnormal traits." In other words, the border between healthy and pathological is rather a difference of "degrees."

Thus, our hypothesis is that these men and women had a greater-than-average predominance of short-axon neurons, favoring a more local—as opposed to global—connectivity in their brains, and a more "specialized" way of operating. What did you just say??

We are describing one of the biological bases that have been associated with "autism spectrum disorders," which, as we will see, share many characteristics with Type Five, although the latter presents them in a normal and decidedly adaptive version.

BIOLOGICAL BASIS

Or how short axons send rockets to the moon

Cognitive functioning is very demanding and requires a very efficient use of brain resources. The optimal organization of the human brain requires two principles: the specialization of the different parts of the brain in differentiated functions, and the integration or coordination of these areas for their orchestrated functioning.[165]

Important individual differences have been discovered in the degree to which our brains function in a specialized or integrated manner.[166]

It has also been found that these differences in the way our brain functions are reflected in anatomical features. People with more "specialized" brains have a greater proportion of neurons with short axons, with "local" connectivity, that is, much communication between neurons in the same region of the brain, to the detriment of their proportion of neurons with

165 Maximo, Cadena, & Kana, 2014.
166 Sapolski, 2010b.

long axons, that connect with neurons in other regions, lobes, or hemi-spheres. People with a more "integrated" brain have just the opposite: a higher proportion of neurons with long axons and greater connectivity between different and more distant regions of the brain.[167]

Like everything in life, both styles of connectivity bring along benefits and losses. By having their "long-distance service" a bit interrupted, the neurons of Type Five would have fewer "cross conversations" between areas that, although distant, would have to agree to perform some complex func-tions. For example...*here comes Mike, with a big smile. It is strange because yesterday we had a strong argument. Could it be an ironic smile? Could it be that he wants to apologize? Could it be that he hasn't seen me? Or has he received a blow in his frontal lobe?* To decode and to react accurately to social stimuli, we need to integrate different areas of our brain at "synaptic" speed. This can be very difficult for Type Five.

On the other hand, it is thought that local over-connectivity could translate into a brain that is hyper-specialized in the execution of certain tasks. Something like an organization that works "in silos," with functional units whose team members have very strong bonds and coordination with one another, but that work in relative isolation from the rest of the organi-zation. This is exactly what happens in the brain of autistic people, although to a much higher extent.[168]

Autistic spectrum disorders have two main sets of features: one is social in nature, and the other is cognitive.[169] Cognitive traits are related to specific patterns of interests and ways of perceiving and reasoning. Let

---

167 (Noonan, Haist, & Müller, 2009) generally converging on the finding of reduced interregional coordination, or underconnectivity. Underconnectivity has been reported between many brain regions and across a range of cognitive tasks, and has been proposed to underlie behavioral and cognitive impairments associated with ASD. The current study employed functional connectivity MRI (fcMRI.

168 The degree of severity of autistic symptoms has been shown to be directly and quantitatively related to the degree of "sub-connectivity" at the cortical level (Maximo et al., 2014); (Courchesne & Pierce, 2005).

169 Warrier et al., 2019.

us quote the authors who first described these disorders. They identified the following characteristics:

- A "strong interest in identifying patterns"
- A need for "order and predictability"
- An "excellent memory for data"
- A "strong focus on inanimate objects" and on "understanding how things work"
- A fascination with systems, which generally obey a set of precise laws or variables, and which, for the same reason, tend to be inherently predictable and repetitive
- An unusual focus (or specialization) of interests[170]
  Today's authors also include the following features:
- A drive to "identify" cause-effect relationships, and to understand the laws that govern specific systems
- Motivation to analyze and/or build systems
- Greater attention to detail[171]

There are indications that autistic individuals would not only have a greater drive, but often have a greater ability than the rest of the population to perform these tasks.

The following features have been identified within the "social" realm:

- Diminished capacity for empathy, that is, to perceive and react emotionally to the emotions of others[172]
- Difficulty in obtaining satisfaction from their relationships
- Difficulty communicating and interacting with others[173]

It is important to bear in mind that many experts suspect that what is now diagnosed as "autism" is not a single disorder, but many different

---

170 Asperger 1944 and Kanner 1943; in Warrier et al., 2019; Cederlund, Hagberg, Billstedt, Gillberg, & Gillberg, 2008.
171 Study conducted on 650,000 subjects, including 36,000 autistic individuals (Greenberg, Warrier, Allison, & Baron-Cohen, 2018).
172 Baron-Cohen, Richler, Bisarya, Gurunathan, & Wheelwright, 2003.
173 Baron-Cohen & Wheelwright, 2004; Warrier et al., 2019.

disorders, which only resemble each other in some of their manifestations. Here we will refer only to the type of autism characterized by preserved or even superior intellectual abilities, paired up with a deficiency in social skills.[174]

It has been proven that autism spectrum disorders are largely hereditary, and that personality traits of the "autistic" type tend to run in the families of these patients, without reaching pathological levels.

And although attempts to explore its genetic basis have not yet yielded clear answers and much remains to be investigated, science offers some important findings about the patterns of brain functioning that typically characterize this style of behavior.[175]

The following fact could be delicious for a winter discussion with your partner: On average, men's brains, compared to women's, have a higher proportion of short axons, greater local connectivity, and less volume in the *Corpus Callosum* (the "highway" connecting the right and left hemispheres).[176] So when a man says that he's watching the game and can't do anything at the same time, it's usually true. The causes of this contrast are not entirely clear, but the simplest explanation could be the effect that hormonal differences between men and women have on early brain development. Men are from Mars; Women are from Venus.[177] Or at least, it seems that female brains tend to a more "integrated" way of functioning. These gender differences could help explain the higher incidence of autism spectrum disorders in men than in women, in a ratio of four to one.[178]

We have no evidence to imply that Type Five is more common in men than in women. It could also be interpreted that women carrying the

---

174 Maximo et al., 2014; Abrahams & Geschwind, 2008; Warren et al., 2011; McPheeters et al., 2011; Brix et al., 2015.

175 Hoekstra, Bartels, Verweij, & Boomsma, 2007; Constantino & Todd, 2005; Warrier et al., 2019; Sucksmith, Roth, & Hoekstra, 2011; Persico & Napolioni, 2013; Abrahams & Geschwind, 2008.

176 Sapolsky, 2010a.

177 Book written in 1992, by American author and relationship counsellor John Gray.

178 Rubenstein, 2010; Greenberg et al., 2018.

mutation would be less likely to develop the most extreme version. It will remain to be explored in the future.

Some alternative hypotheses

The hypothesis of a more "specialized" functioning of the brain is not the only one that attempts to explain the biological basis of the autism spectrum. There has also been evidence of an association between autism and other differences in brain function, although it is possible that all of them are related.[179] Some of these differences are:

1) Brain processing of "important signals" vs "noise"

This mechanism has to do with the main inhibitory neurotransmitter in our brain, "GABA," which holds a fundamental role in the differentiation between "figure and background." Evidence has been found that the hippocampus of autistic patients has fewer receptors for this neurotransmitter, and that the severity of autistic symptoms is directly proportional to the level of deficiency of GABA action in the brain.[180]

An interesting fact is that a deficiency in the "inhibitory" pathways would lead to an overstimulation in the brain and an inability to filter out excess sensory stimuli. This would affect our ability to distinguish important sensory signals over and above general sensory "noise," something which could potentially influence our neural systems, and our cognitive, behavioral, or social patterns.[181]

We could draw a parallel with an association between the traits of "Introversion" and "sensory overload," often found by personality

---

179   Rubenstein, 2010.
180   Collins et al., 2006; Blatt et al., 2001; Hussman, 2001; Brix et al., 2015.
181   Hussman, 2001; Mahdavi et al., 2018; Rubenstein, 2010; Jing-Quiong & Barnes, 2012.

psychologists.[182] According to this hypothesis, introverted people could quickly feel saturated in situations with a large number of stimuli.

2) Increased growth in the prefrontal cortex during gestation and early life

Children with autism spectrum disorders have been found to have a larger prefrontal cortex and cerebellum compared to other children. This larger size could be interpreted as the result of evolutionary pressure towards increased capacity in areas of the human brain such as the prefrontal cortex, the center of complex thinking, planning, and decision making. While this increased size tends to be observed only during childhood, it could be due to a greater "genetic load" in this direction in the case of autistic children.[183]

3) Less action of oxytocin and vasopressin in the brain

As mentioned in earlier chapters, some studies have found a connection between a reduced processing of oxytocin and vasopressin, and the presence of autistic disorders. The same genetic variant that is associated with this decreased processing of oxytocin and vasopressin, has been found in the relatives of autistic children and in people with a tendency to "social withdrawal."[184]

EVOLUTIONARY ADVANTAGES

Or how a hunter-gatherer sorted out medicinal leaves

Our hunter-gatherer ancestors needed an enormous amount of information just to stay alive. Unlike today, they did not carry a mobile phone on which they could perform a quick internet search for the likely location of migrating animals, how many moons were left until the next high tide,

---

182 Smolewska, McCabe, & Woody, 2006; Aron & Aron, 1997.
183 Rubenstein, 2010.
184 Sapolsky, 2010a.

what types of rods did not rot in humidity, or what variety of mushrooms is not poisonous.

Hunter-gatherers needed to stay up-to-date on where to find nutritious food, what signs predicted a drought, how it was possible to detect whether a cave was safe, or whether a terrain would be exposed to wolf attack. They needed to know if that flint vein was good for making arrowheads, or what was the treatment for a fractured skull. Whether the buffalo in this region would migrate to the plains or to the mountains.

Today, human society as a whole has a vastly more extensive knowledge than our ancestors did, but on an individual level, each of us manages far less information than the average hunter-gatherer.[185] In our 21st century, we are used to coming home tired in the afternoon, after a long day at work, in blissful and total ignorance of how the machine that transported us home actually works, or of the internal mechanics that operate our TV. And we don't have a clue about the toils of the legion of people who participated in the long chain that finally brought food to our table.

40,000 years ago, men and women who had a great capacity to observe even the smallest detail, capture any new piece of information, and add it to their "mind map," became extremely useful for the survival of the collective. Just to start, their excellent memory for data would have turned them into true living "encyclopedias." But their contribution went far beyond memorization. They were men and women capable of "seeing" with the eyes of their minds, much more than their brothers or sisters. They were especially gifted at observing, understanding, and predicting.

It was a time when mankind's knowledge was at a very primitive stage. Even so, the Sage must have ventured precarious explanations for the causes and effects of many of the phenomena that surrounded them, offering them to his astonished companions. Why, if you put those seeds in the ground, does a new plant grow? And why do they grow here and not there? Why

---

185   Harari, 2014.

did the earth tremble? Why do owls come out at dusk? Where does the tide come from? Why does the sun hide on the horizon?

Thanks to their powers of observation, their natural curiosity, and their understanding of cause-effect relationships, men and women with this personality type must have accumulated a great deal of valuable knowledge. Those who survived to old age must have been recognized far beyond the confines of their own band. People must have come to consult them from neighboring bands and nearby clans. It must have been an honor to have one of them in the family.

They must have been more introverted than their peers, and this may at times have resulted in a less active search for sexual partners and fewer offspring. However, we believe that the Sage more than compensated for it thanks to their enormous social contribution, which brought them prestige and attractiveness as reproductive partners. Both for themselves and for the direct members of their family, who were likely to carry the same genes.

THE FOOTPRINTS OF SAPIENS SAGE

Scenes from a lost past

Scene 1:

They returned to their burrow in an orderly line, carrying some small red fruits on their backs. The boy had never seen those fruits, but he had seen ants. Many times. He had interrupted their rows with water, explored their burrows, eaten those stinging insects, and become an ant expert. And he had a theory: whenever they found sweet fruits, there were ants. He followed the trail to the origin, because wherever the ants were collecting the sweet fruits, they could too. And indeed, there was the prize. It was a huge bush loaded with red berries, sweet as honey. When he returned to the camp carrying a heap of fruits, he handed them to someone else and indicated where to find more. Then he hurried to the watchmen's rock, for it was already dark and he wanted to watch the night's sun rise, which, according to his calculations, would be larger than the night before.

Scene 2:

She wasn't sure she wanted that. She had seen it many times. If a woman lies with a man, then her belly swells. They get heavy and find it hard to walk. And then a kid comes out. They scream a lot, it hurts, and many die. If her belly swelled up, she wouldn't be able to discover new things. Others also think that it is better if she does not die, because despite being young, she already knows many things. She knows what plants to grind to close the wounds. She knows what plants to chew to remove pain from the body. She knows which part of the river is best for catching fish. She would like to be like her grandmother, a wound healer. They visit her from other clans to ask for her help. Her clan's totem is famous. And although she does not want her belly to swell, men want to breed with the daughters and granddaughters of her wise grandmother, to have offspring who know as much as she does.

Scene 3:

He had never been very fast or very skilled with the spear, but he knew exactly how many days away the prey was, just by looking at its droppings. He had never had much strength to carry water, but he knew where all the wells lay. His meager musculature did not allow him to cut the bones of the mammoth, but he had discovered how to obtain the pulp by making two small holes and blowing. He liked to go for walks alone, and the others often did not understand him. But the truth is that he had earned everyone's respect.

Scene 4:

Everyone loved honey. Every time they discovered a beehive, it was cause for celebration. One afternoon, on one of his walks, he noticed a fire that his companions had tried to light near the forest. They had used wet branches.

What fools! But something caught his eye. Abundant smoke billowed up to a nest of bees hanging from a nearby tree. He could see the very instant when the entire colony left the nest. Did they escape the smoke? The next afternoon he returned to the site. The bees, now with clean air, had returned home. He had an idea...What if instead of destroying the honeycomb, we drive the bees away with smoke? Maybe we can keep getting their honey for many moons ...

CORE TRAITS

Let us now return to the present, and with the investigative zeal of a true Type Five, let us delve into the fundamental traits of this temperament; those that will be shared by the vast majority of the men and women with this type of personality.

Eureka!: Fascination for understanding

The brain of a Type Five is predisposed to feel a fascination towards understanding the cause-and-effect relationships that surround them.

Naturally observant, they are able to concentrate over a long period of time and pay close attention to detail. They can perceive "the reality behind the reality," that is to say, to see beyond the "naked" eye.

As they observe, the perception of "systems" is imposed on them. These "systems" are natural (and sometimes social) phenomena, which generally obey a set of precise laws or variables, and therefore, tend to be inherently predictable and repetitive.

This passion has led many individuals of this type to make significant contributions to the world of knowledge, especially if they are also endowed with a normal or high level of intelligence.[186] And if the IQ is not very high, they will have the same fascination with understanding and analyzing, although their conclusions may not be particularly brilliant.

On top of that, the Sage tends to have an excellent memory for details, data, and information in general, which allows them to have great insights at the moments when their brain manages to establish associations regarding the problem that occupies them: the *Eureka* experience.

It is likely that once Types Five find an area of knowledge that most fascinates them, they will pour a lot of energy into it. They will want to know everything. They will want to understand deeply. They will keep their radar deployed to detect any information, conversation, or finding that relates to their topic of interest. They'll have fun reading books in their field, and they'll vigorously defend their views on the subject. In short, the Sage can have an intense emotional life linked to their area of expertise. They have the vocation to be an expert.

---

186 Let us remember that level of intelligence and personality are independent variables. Personality determines "cognitive style," the way to approach problems, not IQ.

"Insufficient facts always invite danger"[187]: Desire to predict and control

Their fascination with systems and with understanding phenomena around them has a downside. Anything that they cannot understand or predict becomes threatening to them. Type Five does not like chaos. They like to control the variables.

They want to count with more data, or if possible, with all of the data, before they take action. No guessing or risking based on few elements.

They do not like to improvise. They prefer to plan, to prepare, to study beforehand, to collect their thoughts, to observe how others do it. They want to maintain some control over what will happen. Keep that in mind, and when you want to invite them to do something, do not wait for the last moment. Anticipation will increase your chances of success.

"He who saves, wants for nothing": Thrifty and austere

This desire to control is often also expressed as an impulse to save. Types Five tend to store objects: bags, boxes, clothes that no longer fit, books, utensils in disuse. Just in case they could be useful in the future. How good it is to know that you will have everything whenever the need arises. It certainly gives you peace of mind ...

On the other hand, it seems that the Sage needs very few things to feel satisfied. Only basic personal comfort. Types Five do not like to waste resources, just as they don't like to waste their time and energy.

And their relationship with objects is often rather utilitarian. In the eyes of other people, Fives may prove to be of a Spartan austerity. *"Why*

---

187 From *Star Trek*, line by Spock, episode 24 of the first season of the series, entitled "Space Seed" (1968)

should I throw away this jacket? With a patch on the elbows, it will be as good as new." Even if the objects are old and worn out, if they still do their job, they should be preserved. Why waste?

"The only good is knowledge, and the only evil is ignorance"[188]: Focus on thinking

The "inner life" of Types Five is often occupied by their overactive mind. Knowing, experiencing, understanding, investigating. All of these things they are passionate about. Their life usually revolves around their intellectual curiosity and their ability to think.

Comparatively, they have little contact with their own emotional world. We have said "little contact" because their emotional life continues to exist, even if the Sage does not see it. It is only when emotions burst out forcefully, that they suddenly appear on their radar. That's when the Sage becomes baffled by the emotions he sees, for he cannot understand them.

The same goes for their "bodily" life. Often Fives experience little motivation for having physical experiences, for moving. It is easier to find them in front of their screen chasing a Quidditch ball than running after an actual ball on a soccer field.

Three's a crowd: Relationships are difficult

"Oh, I'm sorry. Did I insult you? Is your body mass somehow tied into your self-worth? Interesting..." (Sheldon Cooper)[189]

We said that everything that the Sage cannot understand or predict is a bit threatening to them. Perhaps most puzzling of all are interpersonal

---

188 In *Lives, Opinions and Judgments of the Most Illustrious Philosophers,* by Diogenes Laercio, important Greek historian believed to have been born in the 3rd century A.D.

189 From *The Big Bang Theory,* "The Luminous Fish Effect."

relationships and the emotional reactions of other people. Fives can feel baffled by the fact that they cannot really decode the subtle clues contained in facial gestures or messages "between the lines." They have difficulty "reading" the intentions of others quickly or accurately enough.

This difficulty generates confusion, distrust, a feeling of awkwardness and of not knowing what to do. Interpersonal relationships become an unpredictable and dangerous terrain.

It will almost always be difficult for them to "loosen up" and be spontaneous with people they don't fully trust. As a result, it will be harder for them to obtain satisfaction from their relationships. They become "exhausting," demanding a lot of energy from them.

And if communication and relationships with colleagues can be difficult, relationships with strangers even more so. Many social situations come to be regarded as a "necessary evil," and small talk becomes a tiresome and boring job.

Despite the above, Type Five can develop into a powerful speaker or an interesting presenter when it comes to their own area of expertise. And they will always enjoy a good intellectual discussion on those topics that interest them.

Far from the madding crowd[190]: Tendency to introversion

Fives protect their limits. They do not like to be "invaded," preferring to be the ones who seek the relationship, when they need it.

In private, they can rest and recharge their energy, clarify their feelings, and digest their experiences. The Sage enjoys the tranquility of those moments, when they can finally retreat to their "refuge." That's where they

---

190 Novel by Thomas Hardy, 1874.

feel most comfortable, with their understanding and their knowledge, safe from the disruption that emotions or other people can produce.

Recurring commitments are often an uphill battle. They may feel that they take away their freedom to do what is "important," that they "invade" their life, making them "lose control" of their own time.

It is likely that Five can only feel truly comfortable in the company of other people when those people are the select few closest to him.

Type Six: The Guardian

Or how a child who woke up in the night was able to save the clan

A FIRST GLANCE

The cavern is dark. Snores signal that inside, the whole band sleeps. Outside, croaks and chirps indicate that things are perfectly calm.

Suddenly, the faint sound waves of a branch that gave way to a weight reach the cavern. No one perceives it. No one? Wrong. Someone has opened his eyes and has got up with the speed of lightning. He sharpened all his senses and shouted on the spot: Attack! Just in time to wake up his companions, who shielded the entrance with their spears.

One of the most primitive strategies for survival, in any animal, is "fight or flight." Tens of thousands of years ago, some *Homo sapiens* carried a specific mutation affecting the area of their brain responsible for this response. They were better than their peers at detecting any sign of danger and reacting to it. Let us agree that it was a fundamental task, to be able to warn of the danger before it occurred, and that it gave enormous advantages over those who were surprised. We will call these hominids, of both genders, Type Six.

The Amygdala of these primal Sixes turned out to be more sensitive than average, easily activating in the face of any external sign of danger, however subtle, becoming the alarm system of the time. And when confronted with the alternative of fight or flight, it is likely that Type Six's first impulse was always flight. After all, a *caveman that fights and runs away, lives to fight another day.*

In the hunter-gatherer's time horizon there were multiple situations of danger. Average life expectancy hovered around 30 years, despite the fact that the physical limit of human life was not very different from what it is now.[191]

Almost half of the children did not reach 15 years of age, and of those who did, almost 40% did not reach 45. A contagious plague, a simple cold, an infected wound, or breaking a bone during a hunting raid could inevitably lead to the pyre, the grave, or the stomach of one or several happy wild cats. Being crushed by a mudslide or being murdered at the hands of

---

191 Gurven & Kaplan, 2007.

a sexual rival who attacked from behind was not a matter for the "news" of the bonfire hour. It was a matter of every day.

Many other risks did not necessarily involve death: a tribe of hostile "others" could invade your camp and steal the women or the hunt of the day. Or they could conspire to drive your tribe off the land where you camp and forage at this time of year. A male from your tribe could bully your companions, exclude them, or drive them out, leaving them alone, unprotected, away from their families, their clan, and everything they knew.

For all these reasons, a primitive Type Six who was able to see danger before it was too late was worth his weight in mammoth meat.

Now, let's empathize with Type Six. Not all were advantages; there was a price to pay. Let's imagine that in our brain there is a radar that is constantly announcing everything that could possibly go wrong and sending us images of the worst possible scenario that could be. The result would be a great deal of stress, wouldn't it?

BIOLOGICAL BASIS

Or how an Amygdala can defeat dragons

The amygdala is part of our limbic system, playing a key role in processing emotions, particularly fear, anxiety, and aggression. It plays an important part in memory fixation and decision making, and it is the main brain structure responsible for the "fight or flight" response.

Given the urgent nature of its function, our amygdala has evolved so that it receives critical sensory information about possible threats ASAP, that is, even before it reaches our cerebral cortex, thanks to a short cut feeding directly from the autonomic nervous system. This means that she knows about danger before "our conscious brain" becomes aware of it, and "decides" whether it is serious enough to trigger a stress response.[192] When the amygdala says it's a "go," it releases CRH,[193] sending urgency signals to the hypothalamus and other related areas in the brain, activating the sympathetic nervous system, and the release of glucocorticoids.[194]

It is then the turn of glucocorticoids to spring into action. They are stress hormones, sent as messengers to our whole body, signaling our organs that it's time to react to a threat and to enter into "survival mode."[195] Then it's time for the prefrontal cortex, the "manager in charge" within our brain, to enter the scene, directing thoughts and actions, and regulating the amygdala's emotional response.[196]

But that's not the end of the story. Glucocorticoids, in turn, also pour over the amygdala itself. When exposed to this shower of glucocorticoids, the amygdala's synapses become more excitable, causing its neurons to develop more robust interconnections with each other. This process, if prolonged over time, can make the entire amygdala increase in size, as has been observed to happen in people with post-traumatic stress.[197]

Thus far we've been discussing the response to threat of any *Homo sapiens*—and that of many other animals for that matter. Now we will focus on those people whose response to stress tends to be more intense and more frequent. What psychologists would describe as bearers of an anxious personality. Much has been studied about the causes of individual differences in the way and the strength with which we experience anxiety, and how this might be connected to individual differences in the way our amygdala works.

To begin with, an important body of evidence has established that people who are prone to anxiety tend to be so in a stable manner throughout

---

192 Sapolsky, 2004.
193 Also known as CRF, corticotropin releasing factor.
194 Sapolsky, 2004.
195 Cicchetti & Rogosch, 2012.
196 Bezdek & Telzer, 2017.
197 Sapolsky, 2004.

their lives[198]; and that this tendency is associated with a more sensitive or hyper-reactive amygdala.[199] Studies using fMRI[200] have shown that the amygdala of anxiety-prone people is activated more intensely and for a longer time, not only in the face of frightening stimuli but also when experiencing ambiguous ones. Patients with lesions or destruction of their amygdala have difficulty recognizing facial expressions of fear, show no signs of being afraid or anxious when exposed to frightening stimuli, and, in their personal life, seem to lack the instinct to avoid situations that are obviously dangerous.[201]

Evidence has been found indicating that the degree of sensitivity of our amygdala is, to a large extent, determined by hereditary factors. The main "suspect" is the CRHR1 variant of a gene that encodes for the CRH receptors.[202] As you might recall, CRH is a key substance in the activation of the stress response. In other words, this gene could be a candidate to explain an innate tendency to develop an "anxious personality."[203]

Now we invite you to apply, once again, our key idea Nº16, that is: normal and abnormal are different "degrees" on the same continuum. Let's take a look at some of the usual traits that characterize what could be the extreme version of this personality type, the anxiety personality disorder, because this will shed some light into the nuts and bolts of the normal, successful, well-adapted Type Six.

We will divide them into emotional, cognitive, and behavioral traits.

---

198   The first signs of this temperament have been detected at 5 or 6 months of age, in babies who avoid or limit their approach to unknown or high intensity stimuli (Posner, Rothbart, Sheese, & Voelker, 2012); (Thomaes, Bushman, Orobio De Castro, & Stegge, 2009); (Sleijpen, Heitland, Mooren, & Kleber, 2017). Other studies show that this disposition tends to remain stable during childhood (Pfeifer, Goldsmith, Davidson, & Rickman, 2002), adolescence (Schwartz, Snidman, & Kagan, 1999), and youth (Caspi & Silva, 1995).

199   Shackman et al., 2016.

200   Functional magnetic resonance imaging

201   Shackman et al., 2016.

202   Sleijpen et al., 2017.

203   Sleijpen et al., 2017; Weber et al., 2016.

1) Emotional traits:

- Tendency to anxiety and vulnerability to stress
- Emotional and autonomic overreaction in the face of threat and "danger"[204]
- Fear of social disapproval[205]
- Anxiety in the face of change, the uncertain, and the unknown, particularly during or after periods of acute stress[206]

2) Cognitive traits:

- Tendency to hypervigilance, even in the absence of any immediate danger
- High performance in tasks that require attention and alertness: fewer errors, less ups and downs in execution[207]
- Attentional bias towards anything that may constitute a threat, even when it is irrelevant to the task at hand[208]
- "Attentional capture" or difficulty in disconnecting their attention from stimuli that might be considered threatening, potentially leading to a slowdown in performance[209]
- Exaggerated risks assessment and tendency to overestimate the probability and severity of threats[210]
- Propensity to have intrusive thoughts of a distressing nature[211]

3) Behavioral traits:

- Great investment of effort to deal with stressors
- Tendency to suppress impulses or to inhibit appetite behavior[212]

---

204 Ewbank et al., 2009.
205 Sapolsky, 2004.
206 Shackman et al., 2016.
207 Nettle, 2006; Buss & Penke, 2012.
208 Shackman et al., 2016.
209 Shackman et al., 2016.
210 Stegmann, Reicherts, Andreatta, Pauli & Wieser, 2019.
211 Stout, Shackman, Pedersen, Miskovich & Larson, 2017.
212 Berridge & Kringelbach, 2015.

- Propensity to avoid danger and to react strongly in its presence[213]

As you may suspect, many of these traits are mutually reinforcing, since alertness to threats tends to support a state of anxiety, and vice versa.[214]

Life experiences, on the other hand, also have a fundamental role in the development of this tendency to anxiety. Evidence shows that people who carry the sensitive gene, will multiply their risk of suffering high levels of anxiety if they are exposed to any of the following environmental factors:

- Very high levels of glucocorticoids within the mother's uterus due to maternal stress[215]

- Traumatic experiences (of acute and excessive stress) during childhood, adolescence, or adulthood[216]

- Chronic stress situations at any stage in life[217]

It's not all bad news, though. The effect of the environment works both ways. The size of the amygdala and its excitability can decrease as a result of experiences that induce a state of calm and relaxation. Meditation, therapy, being involved in healthy relationships, and other similar experiences have the power to bring about physical changes in our brains.[218]

Many of the findings mentioned above are a work-in-progress. We are still on the early stages of a real and deeper understanding of the genetic underpinnings of anxious personality. There is much that we do not know.[219]

Yet, if we put everything together inside a single cauldron, and add some of the key ideas that we shared in our first chapter, we can come to the following conclusion: Type Six personality is associated with a higher

---

213 Elliot & Thrash, 2002.
214 LeDoux & Pine, 2016; Shackman et al., 2016.
215 Sapolsky, 2017.
216 Moffitt et al., 2007; Cicchetti & Rogosch, 2012.
217 Janke, Cominski, Kuzhikandathil, Servatius, & Pang, 2015.
218 Kopala-Sibley, Klein, Perlman, & Kotov, 2017; Roberts, Caspi, & Moffitt, 2003; Stout, Shackman, Pedersen, Miskovich, & Larson, 2017.
219 Janke et al., 2015.

sensitivity to anxiety; and this increased sensitivity has a clear biological basis and a likely hereditary origin.

Before moving on, here is another bit of interesting evidence about a neurological and behavioral pattern that might aid our comprehension of the internal wirings of Type Six. First, a little background information: in most situations and for most people, the amygdala and the prefrontal cortex work "in opposition." When one of them is screaming, the other one shuts up, and vice versa. However, there is an exception to that general rule. An ingenious experiment involving a computer game in which individuals played by themselves, secretly exposed them to the possibility to cheat. For all subjects knew, nobody would know if they had cheated or not. Three different behavioral patterns were observed. The first two made their choice without hesitation: Those who simply opted for "the right thing," right away; and those who gave in to temptation without a second thought. But there was a third group who hesitated. The interesting part comes now: the brain activity of all these subjects was being followed all along using an fMRI. The first two showed little activation of neither the prefrontal cortex nor the amygdala when deciding. In the case of the third group, both the prefrontal cortex and the amygdala showed intense and simultaneous activity, their fMRI flashing like a Christmas tree. This simple experiment might have stumbled on the neuroscience of doubt. According to Robert Sapolsky, this might be what happens when we need to make a decision in which, doing the "right" thing is the "scariest" thing to do.[220]

---

220 Sapolsky, 2010, Lecture 18.

EVOLUTIONARY ADVANTAGES

Or how a hunter-gatherer created a shift surveillance system

We can think that having a good hunter, a sage, or a warrior in our clan was the most important thing. But the fiercest warrior is of no use to us, if he did not know how to take his mallet in time and was attacked by surprise; neither is the most cunning hunter, if he did not measure the danger of hunting a beast that has fifty times his strength.

All the traits that we reviewed above can be explained by the evolutionary importance of: quickly perceiving those stimuli that might be crucial for survival, prioritizing relevant information and ignoring distractions, rapidly selecting the best course of action, applying it accurately, and being able to remember it later in case of need.

This mutation, random in its origin, turned out to be extremely relevant for the survival of Sixes and their descendants. Guardians survived, replicated, and multiplied, from ancient times until today.

From an evolutionary standpoint, Type Six personality may well be one of the oldest in terms of adaptation. In fact, in many species of mammals we can find equivalents to their pattern of behavior, both cautious and quick to react to danger.

If we look at it with perspective, we can say that, at the base of this personality, whether in human beings or animals, is the will to perpetuate life. It is life protecting itself from threat and destruction.

Type Six represents this absolute determination to survive.

It is perhaps this powerfully primal root that provides Type Six with its strength. This is an intense type. They feel intensely. They think and they react intensely, too. They carry a rollercoaster inside, although their visible actions might often appear prudent and moderate.

The will to preserve their own life is projected in many directions: the life of their children, their family, their groups and institutions to which they belong. The ideas with which they commune. They feel every threat as something visceral, as a menace to life itself. Their brain learned to codify dangers this way, even those dangers that "just" concern their belonging, prestige, or acceptance within the group.

They are alert, always ready to identify and detect dangers. And at the same time, they are willing to do whatever it takes to avoid or to confront them.

Hence arises the great adaptive value of the Six. They are willing to go above and beyond in order to protect what they value. They are able to put their commitment above every other interest, including their own comfort, and even their own well-being. They strive to establish solid bonds of collaboration and reciprocity with other people. And they strive to maintain and protect the group, since the collective, by itself, becomes a factor of protection and safety.

The day-to-day life of our hunter-gatherer ancestors was far from bucolic, as we have learned from studying primate societies. It would be hundreds of thousands of years before *Homo sapiens* were informed of the myth of the "good savage."[221]

Our first ancestors had to face droughts and glaciations, wild animals and famines, earthquakes and floods. The Six's will to protect their people and their determination to move forward, undoubtedly helped them to perpetuate their heritage and earn a place of respect in the eyes of their peers.

---

221 Proposed by French philosopher Jean-Jacques Rousseau (1712–1778).

THE FOOTPRINTS OF SAPIENS GUARDIAN

Scenes from a lost past

Scene 1:

He was not the fiercest warrior, nor was he the fastest. But he showed up in every battle. He was not an exceptional hunter, nor the most accurate with the arrow, but everyone wanted him to be part of their hunt. Anyone who had fought alongside him knew that he had their backs. Anyone who hunted by his side knew that they could count on him, always ready, with a timely collaboration. That is why she wanted to be with him. She knew that he would help take care of the children. She knew that she could trust him, and that there would be no lack of fruit or meat. She had seen him carrying the hides and the pots. Always willing to carry a little more, always attentive to be where a hand was missing. She wanted to share his bed in the cave. She wanted to enjoy his care and his eyes that conveyed truth. For many moons.

Scene 2:

From their hiding place, crouching behind the highest rocks in the gorge, they watched the bands of "others" advancing through the canyon. Two nights separated them from the cave. It was extremely risky to attempt the two-day journey to warn the rest of the clan. But necessary. Women, children, the elderly, and only a handful of men could not face this danger if they were attacked by surprise. The alarm had to be raised. But the distance was very long and the journey dangerous. They argued and decided to advance from the rear, trying not to be detected and thus, arrive on time to the aid of the cave. Although everyone knew in that instant that they would be late, and some would die in the attack. What if only one of them went ahead and gave notice? But who? If discovered, that would mean a sure death. They looked at each other. He stared at his mates, and as he volunteered, he was already taking the first steps of the long race ahead. He ran almost without stopping for two days and two nights, finally arriving on time to deliver the warning.

His feat would be told many times by the fire. And he was remembered as "the one who flew to save his clan."

Scene 3:

From the entrance of the cavern you could see the children helping with some domestic chores, the youngest ones playing or sleeping. Some mothers were nursing, and the elders were gathering wood for the night fire. The group that had gone out hunting and collecting fruits and seeds would arrive at any moment. That's when a huge bear appeared at the entrance of the cave. When those inside realized the situation, there was a sudden silence, and everyone held their breath. It would attack. The group of collectors was approaching the cavern, when they saw the scene and froze on the spot. In the blink of an eye, one of the returnees released a sudden squawk, throwing a sharp rock that hit the bear on the back of its head. The animal turned around and launched in angry pursuit of the woman. Before everyone could see what was happening, she had reached a huge tree and climbed it quickly, barely reached by the animal's claws. The bear growled in its frustration. This gave everyone just enough time to regroup, reinforce the cave entrance, and drive the animal away.

Scene 4:

Some animals began to group together and move forward. Birds that used to stay until late summer began to migrate. Usually aggressive beasts were passing by the cavern, without apparent interest to attack. The air took on a reddish hue. The old man felt the pungent, harsh, and acrid odor invading his nose. Then he remembered. When he was still a child, he saw the mountain spit fire. He immediately gave the alarm signal, giving enough time for the children and the sick to be prepared for the escape. He led everybody through a path he had already identified as the safest to evacuate the valley. As they began to cross the river, the mountain rained down orange ash and the earth moved under their feet.

CORE TRAITS

Let's now enter the world of Type Six in our day. More than other types, Sixes can be difficult to recognize if we only look at their visible behaviors, as we can see them sweet or confrontational, trusting or suspicious, sociable or reserved, cautious or impulsive. In the following section, we invite you to read between the lines to discover the "common thread," the motivation behind their behavior. This will we be the best way to truly get to know the inner world of the Guardian.

Warning, danger ahead: Hypersensitivity to risk

The Guardian is equipped with a true natural alarm system. As we just saw, this strong emotional and physiological reaction to any sign of risk has a clear evolutionary purpose[222]: to abandon everything that is being done and to activate oneself totally and completely in order to face or to escape from a danger. To save our skin.

In the old days, dangers could mean a tiger or the attack of a hostile sapiens. Over time, this alarm system has saved us from much more varied and subtle threats, such as being disowned by our tribe, losing one's job, being publicly shamed, or being late for a meeting.

The amygdala of the Six is wired to detect and activate itself against stressors of the most varied range, no matter how subtle. Very particularly, situations of "social risk." Holding a different opinion from the rest, realizing that we are dressed inappropriately for the ceremony, or having to present in front of a knowingly critical audience, are situations that accelerate our pulse, dilate our pupils, or dry up our mouth, if we happen to be a Six.[223]

This sensitivity to risk has its lights and its shadows. On one hand, their awakened mind is able to perceive real signs of danger, where others do not yet see anything. In a mental game of anticipatory imagination, their body's alarm system kicks in as if the future were already a reality. Their breathing quickens and a chill runs down their spine as they visualize the consequences of everything that could possibly go wrong. This allows them to plan for a line of action, and to react in advance, before events precipitate.

This talent for early detection, coupled with their lucid thinking, and the enormous driving force behind their desire to avoid danger, made the Guardian the greatest "mitigator," contingency planner, and disaster preventer in history. Not only is he capable of detecting and anticipating,

---

222 Ikemoto, Yang, & Tan, 2015; Ewbank et al., 2009; Elliot & Thrash, 2010.
223 Sapolsky, 2004.

but he also convinces and mobilizes his peers to take action, through the strength and the rationality of their arguments.

But as we have already mentioned, this excellent alarm system is expensive: it is paid for in comfortable installments of increased vulnerability to stress and anxiety. And when danger happens to be less visible than a tiger, it is even more difficult to escape.

Another cost of this trait, shaped by millennia of evolution to detect and react to subtle danger signals, is that it does not prepare them well to deal with those threats that might be "overwhelming." We see this in the animal kingdom. When danger is imminent and excessive, the deer is paralyzed. When the threat exceeds the dimensions for which Type Six is prepared, their habitual strategies tend to disarm, their thinking becomes "disorganized," and their behavior, usually prudent and moderate, could suddenly oscillate between two extremes: panicked "freezing" or impulsive "overreacting," sometimes to the point of aggression.

Something similar could happen to them when faced with stressful situations that continue over time. In the jungle, the "fight or flight" response lasted only as long as the danger was present. Then the Guardian could rest. Postmodern life, with diffuse and pervasive stressors, often involves high physiological and emotional wear and tear. They could end up suffering from ulcers, headaches, insomnia, or a wide range of stress-related disorders. Perhaps this is why Sixes may tend to resist change. They perceive the risks and suffer the uncertainty of what is to come much more strongly than others.

Open 24-hours…: Almost permanent state of "alert"

One of the best side benefits of the impulse to be alert to danger is, precisely, a great capacity to be alert. Sixes are equipped with an almost permanent state of hypervigilance that has proven to be of great adaptive power in many scenarios.[224]

For starters, they tend to be high performers in a range of cognitive tasks that require the ability to focus attention and direct thought in an orderly, logical, and sequential manner. Perhaps for this reason, Sixes are possibly the most rational of all the types, which is paradoxical if we consider that, at the same time, they are subject to very intense emotions.

Their focused attention and clarity of thought also allow them to forecast the future. Like expert chess players, their mind races ahead, anticipating possible consequences of decisions, actions, or inactions.

But there is also some bad news. Sixes do not dominate when this state of hyper-alertness is "switched on" or "switched off."[225] Even if they wanted to "disconnect" their attention to risks, even if they knew it was hurting their performance, even if they knew it was hurting them. It is useless. The state of alert is always there, always present, always prepared, like a *boy scout*.

A second problem is that the scale within their mind tends to tip towards the negative. Without them realizing it, when they weigh the risks against the opportunities, they tend to overestimate the first and underrate the latter. Forward-looking, yes, but with a bias towards seeing everything that can go wrong.

In the worst case, under extreme situations of intense or continuous stress, Sixes' attention span could be "captured" by their anxious emotions, triggering a vicious circle that accelerates and disorganizes their flow of thought, and exaggerates their risk assessment, flooding them with cata-strophic thoughts, and feeding their anxiety all over again.[226]

The great paradox of Sixes is that the evolutionary purpose of fear is to avoid harm; but it is fear itself that finally harms them.[227]

---

224 Buss & Penke, 2012.
225 Shackman et al., 2016.
226 Stegmann, Reicherts, Andreatta, Pauli and Wieser, 2019; Stout, Shackman, Pedersen, Miskovich & Larson, 2017; LeDoux & Pine, 2016; Shackman et al., 2016.
227 Sapolsky, 2004.

Between the lines: Wide and acute perception

One piece of good news is that Sixes can generally visualize many more sides of reality than their peers do. They usually are extremely perceptive. They are very good readers of other people's emotions. We believe that they develop this ability through their keen awareness of their own emotions and moods. And this is due, at least in part, to the fact that they experience many of their emotions as painful or annoying obstacles. Such as when they arise at inappropriate times, when they want to deliver a speech in public, ask their boss for a raise, confront the "bully" in their class, or disagree with the opinion of the majority.

And just as they are adept at picking up a slight gesture that betrays hostility in a coworker, or at reading between the lines what may be behind a seemingly inconsequential action, they will also be able to spot the subtle indicators of a failure in the production line.

When walking down the path that leads to the achievement of any project, their perception will collect all kinds of "evidence" and signs: both in the field of what needs to be done and in the area of relationships with others. Generally, the intuitions of the Six contemplate many elements at the same time.

"I will take the ring"[228]: Strong commitment and will-power

Sixes are intensely in contact with their own fear, it is true. But more than any other type, they are willing to make superhuman efforts to overcome their fear. Sometimes their motivation is to build a safe and secure environment for themselves and their family. Other times, it could be simply to prove to themselves what they are capable of.

---

228 Frodo Baggins, from *Lord of the Rings*, J.R.R. Tolkien

The protagonists of many epic tales are ordinary individuals, who, sometimes against their will, are pushed by extraordinary circumstances to become brave and heroic characters, committed to a cause far greater than themselves. In our imagination we can evoke the deeds of Frodo Baggins or Jon Snow.

Where does this strength come from? Fear is a primal, visceral emotion. How much are we willing to do to master it? To control it? To protect ourselves from it? Sixes' answer to these questions is: "A great deal. A very great deal."

And coming back down to earth, far from the extremes of heroism, we see that Sixes are usually disciplined and hardworking. They usually take good care of their duties and commit themselves to a cause. They often prepare and plan ahead. They study and they train. They compromise and collaborate.

We will also see them striving to build a secure future, to do things right, to detect problems and solve them. We will see them avoiding super-fluous and unnecessary dangers, but often facing far greater dangers, when it comes to their duty.

Can't live with you, can't live without you: Torn between trust and mistrust

We can see Sixes working hard to create bonds of loyalty and to establish collaborative relationships within their "tribe."

The Guardians instinctively perceive how important reciprocity is for survival. Many of their strongest emotions and motivations have to do with their wish to belong and their fear of being excluded. The group provides security, but the group is also the source of the main dangers. This is why Sixes often oscillate between their desire for togetherness and their fear of getting close, between their tendency to trust and their tendency to distrust.

Perhaps this is why many Sixes seem extroverted and introverted at the same time, going out to seek relationship, and then retiring to their winter quarters, to rest from exposure and vertigo. This is what psychologists would call "*ambiversion.*"

This ambivalence will be especially evident in the face of authority figures. Those who exercise power can be a source of security, of protection, of guidance. The Guardian is naturally predisposed to respect them and follow them. However, power can also be exercised in an excessive, abusive, unfair, or oppressive way. And to make things even more complicated, the same authority figure can be both at the same time.

As a consequence, the Guardian could fall into both extremes: into placing absolute loyalty and almost blind faith in a leader; or into total resentment and rebellion. This same ambivalence can turn painful when they are the ones in a position of power. In their imagination, the people they lead might be looking at them in the same light.

To be or not to be, that is the question: Tendency to doubt

Let's agree that avoiding "all dangers" is impossible. Everything that is done or not done, what is decided or not decided, the mistakes, the successes, everything can, eventually, bring about unwanted consequences.

When our attention is focused primarily on risks, it is obvious that you will have a hard time making decisions. It often happens that Sixes already have a decision made on an intuitive level. But almost invariably, their prefrontal cortex will stop them before they move forward, inviting them to carefully meditate, weigh, consider, second guess, and analyze all the factors involved. They will make a list of pros and cons. They will ask their friends and colleagues…how do you see it? What would you do in my place? It can become a long and exhausting process, because Sixes also realize the risk of not deciding, of delaying or procrastinating. Uff. It is difficult to decide if you are Six. Depending on the importance of the decision and on the circumstances, their doubt can bring along anxiety and thoughts racing at a thousand miles per hour.

Once they make up their minds, the Guardians often feel relief. Even if sometimes a voice still haunts them, saying, "What if you made a mistake? What was the road not taken like?"

Doubt is one of the mental traps of a Six, because it is not possible to anticipate all the risks, and it is not true that by giving so much thought to things one can make better decisions. It is the downside of having such an active mind, and such a strong concern for risks.

Type Seven: The Explorer

Or how a restless little boy crossed an ocean

A FIRST GLANCE

The young man began to remove the large leaves with which he had hidden his invention from curious and prying eyes. The rest of his little band looked at him in disbelief. They doubted that it was safe enough even to climb on, much less to sail. Yet his enthusiasm was such, and the wonders he described about the device were such, that it was difficult to reconcile what they saw with what they heard. When they put the artifact in the water, to everyone's surprise, it floated quite easily. As they climbed inside, it barely sank and displaced water. Stabilizers made of inflated animal skins added steadiness to the raft's movement. Of the eight initial enthusiasts, only six finally got on the boat. The oars made of bamboo proved to be extremely efficient and lightweight. The boat moved quickly into the sea, disappearing from sight with every wave that came down. In a short time, it became only a dot on the horizon. The two who had stayed on land waited until it was dark. One of them thought that he saw a fire on the land in front of them, but he could not be sure. What they were all sure of was that their six companions were never seen again.

When 70,000 years ago a group of "modern" Homo sapiens made the decision to leave their native Africa, a wave was unleashed that forever transformed life on earth, as it had been for millions of years. Their first cousins, the Neanderthals and the Denisovans, had lived successfully in Europe and Asia for more than 400,000 years.[229] Why did Homo sapiens prevail? What made us different from our cousins? Why are they relegated to a memory, a museum curiosity, while we dominate all the habitats on earth?

At least one of the elements that made the difference was our unflinching desire to travel.

Neanderthal men and women were intelligent and very much like us. They were humans. Their bodies were strong, they were well adapted to cold weather, and they could run for several days chasing after a deer or a bison. They took good care of their sick and their old, they had a varied diet, and they buried their dead with loving care. But they stayed all their lives more or less in the same place, only coming and going according to the seasons, to follow the migrations of the animals they knew. This tendency

---

229 Kolodny & Feldman, 2017.

to take root in their known lands caused them to interbreed mostly among themselves. There was little genetic variability, favoring the transmission of harmful mutations, and limiting their possibilities of "evolving" from the point of view of natural selection.

Homo sapiens, on the other hand, once they left Africa, never stopped again. In a few thousand years, they had spread across Asia and Europe, climbed mountains, crossed seas, ventured into jungles and swamps, waded through rivers and glaciers. They reached Oceania, and they populated America.

We believe that the gene that gave origin to Type Seven, partly explains this behavior of our species. Many Sevens must have been leading these early migrations. They must have gone ahead, leading the way, encouraging their fellows, enthusiastic and energetic, imagining a better future, beyond what was known "here."

They probably carried a mutation within their brains, a subtle change in the equilibrium of neurotransmitters, that exacerbated characteristics that all primates already have: restlessness and curiosity.[230]

BIOLOGICAL BASIS

Or how dopamine travels the entire earth and beyond

Our hypothesis is that the Type Seven would have emerged from a genetic mutation that has often been associated with a "difficulty in remaining

---

230 All mammals have a certain instinct to provoke movements (their own or those of others) in order to avoid inbreeding. In the case of primates, this instinct is even stronger: adolescent primates migrate voluntarily, not because anyone expels them. They are the ones that leave, attracted by a powerful and invisible force that drags them towards the novelty. They leave their families and begin journeys, sometimes for many days, alone and unprotected, until they find a new band to integrate (Sapolsky, 2017).

still" both physically and mentally; and a with a strong impulse towards stimulation and novelty.[231]

This mutation would be the 7R+ variant in the gene that encodes for dopamine D4 receptors (DRD4).[232] This variant would cause a lower level of dopaminergic activity (less amount of dopamine in the synapses) in the brain's reward system (ventral tegmental area, nucleus accumbens, and prefrontal cortex).[233]

How this gene operates and what is the mechanism by which it generates this hypo-functionality, are still open questions. Experts are still shuffling several theories: It could be a lower sensitivity of dopamine receptors at the postsynaptic level, a lower number of these receptors, or a greater presence of dopamine transporters, responsible for extracting it or eliminating it from the synaptic space.[234]

However, there is much agreement that this difference in dopamine functioning is associated with clearly identifiable patterns of behavior. We transcribe them here in detail, to reflect the wealth of information that exists about this genetic variant and its influence on how a person feels, thinks, and acts:

- Sensation-seeking, "craving for novelty," and "anticipation-excitement": the dopamine circuit is involved in activating anticipation and plea- sure-seeking in general.[235] Thanks to experiments carried out with monkeys, we know that the mere expectation of a reward already trig-

---

231 Several studies on behavioral neurogenetics suggest that genes that modulate the neurotransmission of dopamine mediate a variety of behavioral phenotypes associated with sensation-seeking (Garcia, Mackillop, Aller, Merriwether, & Sloan, 2010).

232 The dopamine D4 receptor is responsible for neuronal communication in the mesolimbic system, an area of the brain that regulates emotion and complex behavior. This receptor is activated by dopamine, but also by epinephrine and norepinephrine, as well as by numerous chemicals and synthetic drugs (Iversen & Iversen, 2007).

233 Iversen & Iversen, 2007; Krause, Dresel, Krause, La Fougere, & Ackenheil, 2003.

234 Krause et al., 2003

235 There is abundant evidence that people with this genetic variant have a strong "anticipatory" attitude towards pleasure and satisfaction, a continuous search for sensations and a "craving for novelty." This same relationship has been found in animals (Sapolsky, 2010).

gers a dopamine discharge, and that this anticipation seems to be far more addictive than pleasure itself. We also know that the dopamine attached to anticipation is even greater in the face of a "maybe" than when we are "sure" that we are getting the reward.[236] From an evolutionary perspective, we can imagine that this excitement in the face of uncertainty was extremely useful to boost genetic variability, making us abandon the world we know to venture into the unknown.

- Tendency to hyperactivity and attentional vulnerability to distraction: dopamine hypo-functionality is associated with difficulty in remaining physically in one place. At a cognitive level, it is associated to a greater difficulty in focusing attention. This translates into a greater tendency to be distracted by any stimulus coming from the environment or from within, such as thoughts, emotions, pain, or other sensations originated by our proprioceptive system. This is thought to be due to the fact that dopamine increases the brain's ability to exercise executive control of thought and inhibit sources of distraction. This hypo-functionality has also been associated with a greater tendency to develop attention deficit disorders with hyperactivity, which is why many of these disorders are treated with dopamine-based therapies.[237]

- High performance on tasks requiring cognitive agility: people who have a lower capacity for concentration may experience more difficulty in facing some academic tasks; but they have a clear advantage on tasks that require cognitive agility. This is because their brains spend less energy on "switching from one thing to another"; and they require less time to make the change.[238]

- Tendency to migrate: there is abundant evidence that this genetic variant predisposes to migration. Hence its nickname: the "Wanderlust

---

236 Sapolsky, 2017.

237 Hills, 2005; Iversen & Iversen, 2007.

238 Friedman & Miyake, 2017; propose that there is a trade-off between cognitive "agility" and "concentration" (or "target focus"); between cognitive stability and flexibility, regulated by dopamine.

Gene."[239] Evidence of this fact is the more frequent presence of this gene in geographical areas that have a high percentage of historical immigration, in populations descending from large human migrations, and in individuals with multiracial ancestors.[240]

- Higher vulnerability to substance abuse: alcohol, tobacco, drugs. People who carry this genetic variant have been shown to be more vulnerable to abuse of substances such as nicotine and amphetamines.[241] These substances are chemically related to dopamine and act upon the same neuronal circuits, so it is thought that this tendency might be an act of self-medication aimed at compensating for the lack of this neurotransmitter in their system.[242] Let's look at it with an analogy: Have you ever had an inexplicable desire to eat an orange? You may be lacking vitamin C...

- Greater tendency to engage in risky or impulsive behavior: people with this genotype are more likely to present impulsive behavior, to engage in gambling, or to take physical or financial risks.[243]

- Higher probability of having many sexual partners: this genetic variant has been associated with a greater tendency to change sexual partners more often throughout life, or, especially in men, to have several sexual partners at the same time. It has also been associated with the likelihood of having sexual contact earlier in life.[244] In fact, this genetic variant has been associated with lower levels of attachment to the reproductive partner in different species of mammals that are usually monogamous.[245]

---

239 Miller & Todd, 1993.

240 Chen, Burton, Greenberger, & Dmitrieva, 1999; Harpending & Cochran, 2002; Hills, 2006; Eisenberg et al., 2007; Garcia et al., 2010.

241 Palmiter, 2007; Sapolsky 2010b.

242 A high prevalence of smoking has been observed among people with Attention Deficit Hyperactivity Disorder, as a result of "self-medication with nicotine," to increase the release of dopamine in their synapses, and thus increase their capacity for attention and concentration (Mansvelder, Keath, & McGehee, 2002); (Potter & Newhouse, 2008).

243 Garcia et al., 2010; Sapolsky, 2017; Congdon, Lesch, & Canli, 2008.

244 Guo, Tong, Xie, & Lange, 2007; Eisenberg et al., 2007; Garcia et al., 2010.

245 Guo et al., 2007.

- High sensitivity to a detached parenting style: For some reason that is not yet clear, the people who carry this genetic variant seem to be especially vulnerable to what psychologists would call, the quality of "maternal attachment." There is evidence that the traits associated with this genetic variant become more acute when the individual has an early history with a cold, selfish, or withdrawn maternal figure. Just the opposite happens when the mother was sensitive, caring, and supportive, in which case, impulsivity and the need to seek sensations are still present, but greatly attenuated.[246]

EVOLUTIONARY ADVANTAGES

Or how a hunter-gatherer created activities just for fun

What do Marco Polo, Captain Cook, and Erik the Red have in common? They all felt the "itch," the restlessness, the curiosity to go out and see the world.

We do not know the history of the Marco Polo's from 30,000 to 50,000 years ago, but the traces of their footsteps have survived to this day. When modern *Homo sapiens* left Africa, it took them a few thousand years to cover the entire earth. A large majority must have migrated little by little, step by step, following the trail of food and climate, almost without realizing it.

Others, like Type Seven, must have volunteered to explore new territories, undertaking long journeys often driven only by their curiosity, their desire for novelty, or their dream of a better life.

Our history as *Homo sapiens* is strewn with travelers and migrants. And today we can guess that, to a large extent, these groups of travelers were made up of Type Seven.

---

246 Sapolsky, 2010a; Posner, Rothbart, Sheese, & Voelker, 2012.

Yet why was this mutation adaptive? And why has it been preserved to this day? Under many environmental conditions, our evolution must have favored the natural selection of "exploratory" and "flexible" behaviors. They often must have brought greater chances of survival for the carriers of this mutation and their entire families.

Whenever the search for food and resources had to be carried out in environments of scarcity or uncertainty, natural selection must have favored those with a capacity for "diffuse attention", inclined to perform quick searches over larger areas of land. These same situations must have hindered the survival of those who undertook slow and methodical searches over the smaller, usual territories, which most likely ended in failure.[247]

An example of this is every time our ancestors had to face the effects of a drought, sudden climate changes, or other natural disasters. Often these situations produced an evolutionary "bottleneck," that is, a sharp decline in population. In those cases, natural selection favored those more willing to migrate to unknown territories, to reproduce more frequently and with more sexual partners, and to solve difficulties in a more flexible and creative way.

On the other hand, their continuous displacement forced their brains to become deeply adaptable to the thousands of different habitats that they were finding. It also gave them access to watch and learn from "others," to exchange knowledge, and of course, to exchange DNA, over and over again, improving their "genetic makeup." And when the uncertainty and the bad times worsened, a decisive factor was to leave many offspring....At least some would be able to survive, wouldn't they?[248]

---

247 Hills, 2006.
248 In these particularly difficult environments, natural selection must have favored individuals who naturally tended to mate more and produce more offspring (Garcia et al., 2010); even if they had invested less effort in breeding (Eisenberg et al., 2007). A sign that the adaptive value of this trait varies strongly by habitat is that there are dramatic differences in the distribution of variants of this gene globally (Chen et al., 1999); (Harpending & Cochran, 2002).

We can also imagine an ancestral Romeo, driven by his natural curiosity and his search for new sensations, in furtive encounters with a Neanderthal or Denisovan Juliet, who nine months later would see the birth of a "genetic hybridization." Thanks to this, a modern child of European, Asian, or American descent will carry genes from some of those illustrious ancestors, benefitting from a more developed musculature or a better immune system. Although if this child decides to sunbathe on the beach looking for a beautiful tan, he will probably just turn as red as a lobster. And the culprit will probably be his Neanderthal great-grandfather.[249]

THE FOOTPRINTS OF SAPIENS EXPLORER

Scenes from a lost past

Scene 1:

It was the first time we had seen something like this. It was a pendant made of green stones and feathers. We had never seen anything so special and different. That whole group had similar ornaments. Spears with feathers and stones, warm furs with different colors. For their part, this group was very interested in our way of transporting water in animal skins. For a small animal skin, they gave us two spears and a pendant. We taught them how to make the water carriers, and they in turn showed us where to get the green stones. A whole moon later we packed up our things and said goodbye to the people who adorned themselves. When we returned to our clan, we told them stories, showed the new objects, and taught them what we had learned. A few young, enthusiastic, and motivated mates offered to come with us on our next trip. They too wanted to see the world beyond the highlands.

---

249 Borrowed from https://www.the-scientist.com

Scene 2:

The fruits looked really tasty. When opened, they were juicy and pulpy. There were quite a few in that place and they looked like they were sweet. The group looked at each other for an answer. Has anyone seen them before? Perhaps someone has heard an elder talking about them? But no one knew anything. They smelled good, but they had seen others bite into new fruit and end up with tremors in the body and foam in the mouth. Without saying anything, she stepped forward, took the open fruit, put it in her mouth, and tore off a large chunk. She savored it. It was sweet and different at the same time. Her face contracted because the taste was pungent and unknown. She had never tasted sour before. A big new piece confirmed that it was a delicious new flavor. The next day when she woke up, everyone was staring at her to check whether she was okay. The first thing she did was bite into another of those fruits. She had woken up hungry, and the abundance had to be exploited. Confident now that they were benign, everyone rushed to try the new fruit.[250]

Scene 3:

It had been a long journey to get there. But the river was truly threatening and there was no way to cross it. It was the kind of obstacle that could stop a journey and force a return. They asked the old traveler if they should come back after the rain season was over, or if there would still be some last resort. Perhaps he had experienced something similar or could come up with a new solution. Many times the old man had surprised them with his quips. The old man remembered that he had once seen how they had thrown logs into the water and the current had carried them down. But there were no large trees in this place. At that precise moment, a long line of beasts started crossing in herds to the other shore. That's when the old man came up with his idea: they should hold onto the back of one of those animals, and thus cross to the other side. No one would have thought of touching these animals out of fear of being gored. But the old man assured them that in the water, they would behave differently. Before they could even consider the idea, the old man was

---

250   Chen et al., 1999; Harpending & Cochran, 2002; Hills, 2006.

already in the water. And to everyone's surprise, he hung himself from one of the animals. Indeed, the beast did not seem upset. And if it was, swimming was already enough of a task. The old man let go as soon as his feet touched the bottom on the other side, and he waved his arms to the group. He had succeeded.

Scene 4:

Chewing those leaves gave her special powers to travel without moving from her place. She could see animals, colors, and fly to the top of the trees. Her discovery had been accidental, she was looking for similar leaves that she knew were good for the belly when one had eaten something one shouldn't have. When she chewed those other leaves, she had had the experience. She would laugh for a long time, not as she usually did, but with jumps and funny sounds. She was always a cheerful person, but this was something different. The others told her about the strange things she said and did while the influence of the herb lasted. She would imitate animals, run, jump and also remain totally still, like those who no longer breathe. After chewing herself, she would invite others to try them. She had always enjoyed trying new things. And for her, this experience was new every time.

CORE TRAITS

We are now going to distill the previous discussion, into a portrait of what these Explorers could look like in a world of airplanes and internet. In the following lines is a brief review of the personality traits towards which all Sevens would be genetically predisposed, to a greater or lesser degree.

The call to adventure: Sensation-seeking and crave for novelty

Sevens often experience an "anticipatory" state in relation to pleasure and satisfaction, a continuous search for sensations and a "craving for novelty"..." They want to feel intensely, and to experience new sensations. This trait, characteristic of this type, is expressed in many ways in the Explorer's personality.

Sevens feel great attraction for adventure and the unknown. They are perhaps the only type that have a taste for change ingrained in their biology. Change, if only for the sake of changing.

They often love traveling, trying strange flavors, smelling new scents, meeting different people. Perhaps for the same reason, they tend to dislike routine and get bored easily.

Their mind often tends to live in the future, in anticipation of something better to come. This leads them to have a huge imagination and an inclination to plan. However, we already saw that the rush of anticipation is usually greater than that of satisfaction. Perhaps this explains the experience of many Sevens. Once they succeed in achieving their plan, reality always seems more faded than they had imagined. This can cause Sevens to fall into spirals of dissatisfaction, which they seek to compensate for by trying increasingly different, and ever more intense sensations. In extreme cases, this can be a road to substance abuse or other sorts of immoderation.

"Viva la vida"[251]: Energetic, outgoing, and enthusiastic

Explorers enjoy being on the go. They find it difficult to remain physically still, silent, or without stimulation, even for short periods of time. They are vital and energetic, and they like speed. They move, they talk, they think fast. They love action, noise, variety, being with people. They enjoy being socially involved with others. They like to live in densely populated areas, where there is a lot of action, interaction, and intensity. More than other people, they tend to migrate.

---

251 Spanish for 'Long Live Life', song by British rock band Coldplay, written for their fourth album, *Viva la Vida or Death and All His Friends* (2008).

They often feel cheerful and full of energy. They love having fun and are entertaining to be with. They are beaming, sparkling, friendly, and outgoing, the "life of the party." They have a strong sense of humor, and they easily get excited about things. They are fascinated by interesting people, events, or ideas. Their enthusiasm, as well as their attention, often jumps from one thing to another, making it more difficult for them to delve into or follow through on their projects.

They may feel uncomfortable abiding emotions in the sadness range, and they may experience an urge to escape back into excitement, even if this means losing touch with their real emotions. This is why they can often come across as superficial.

We were sure we had written something to put here: Easily distracted and cognitively "agile"

Their difficulty in staying still is also manifested on a cognitive level. They find it difficult to focus their attention for a long time or to focus on just one thing at a time.

The good thing about this feature is that they can easily "switch from one thing to another" or from one topic to another, and they can deal with several tasks "at the same time" without getting tired and without lowering their performance. They are natural *multitaskers.*

This innate tendency to cognitive agility and distractibility has many consequences for the Explorer's "competency profile."

It is often easy for them to think "outside the box," that is, to interconnect ideas that might not be naturally connected; instead of maintaining a logical and sequential line of thought. If they also come endowed with a high intellectual capacity, they are likely to develop as creative and innovative persons, although they will probably tend to be more disorganized and fickle than their peers.

They are curious; everything interests them. They would like to know a bit about everything. But as they have trouble persevering, they often end up not digging too deep in any one area. The result is that they know very little about very many things. An ocean of knowledge, half-inch deep.

This combination of anticipatory mind, energy, and mental agility, make them imagine the future through a positive lens. In some cases they could become visionaries who dream of better worlds and excite their entourage to work for their achievement. They can be perceived as the engine and the inspiration of their teams.

Living to the limit: Prone to risk and impulsive behavior

This type is attracted to risk. Again, the explanation for this tendency could be found in the convolutions of their dopamine-thirsty brain. It is likely that some people of this type are literally "addicted to adrenaline."

Sevens love playing for high stakes, be it by engaging in an extreme sport, working as war reporters, or gambling their money on games of chance.[252] Explorers often need high doses of adrenaline to feel "alive" and stimulated. They look for intensity. In the extreme, they can put their life and their well-being in danger. And that of those around them.

Born free: Craving for freedom and hypersensitivity to restrictions

There is evidence that Sevens, from a very young age, are more sensitive to being restricted by an external constraint. This tendency seems to be maintained throughout their lives.

---

252   Justin Garcia, 2010; Congdon, 2008.

Explorers love freedom and flee from hierarchies, formalities, norms, and impositions of any kind. The very thought that they will not be able to move freely, do what they want and choose at will, deeply irritates them. They tend to establish horizontal relationships with everyone, may behave irreverently with authority figures, and often prefer informality in many areas of their life. In the case of adults, the way in which they speak or dress may give the impression of being lighthearted and younger than their chronological age.

They find it hard to establish commitments, as they appear to them as potential restrictions on their freedom. They may also find it difficult to fulfill these commitments, once established. Unconsciously, they may become angry at the person to whom or the situation to which they feel obligated, even if it was—and still is—their own choice.

It is often difficult for them to choose between several options, as they would prefer to always keep them all open.

Type Eight: The Warrior

Or how a little boy felt invincible

A FIRST GLANCE

Screams of terror shattered the quiet silence of the clan's sleep. A violent and deadly raid by the Barefoot people was advancing, killing not only warriors, but also women and children. Fear passed down

from gaze to gaze. They must flee swiftly, or they would die. The
Barefoot were fierce warriors and fought well in the dark. When he
saw the first people getting ready to run, the young warrior came
forward and stopped them. His eyes were swollen with blood as
he looked at them, his spear raised; and with a terrifying cry he
summoned them to battle. The clash with the Barefoot was fierce.
The young man smashed heads, arms, and legs with brutal force.
All those who saw him were flooded with the spirit of war. They felt
invincible. The enemy's blood watered the field, and the Barefoot
began to flee. Bathed in blood that was not his own, he cried out
again, "Death!" The warriors got the message. And they followed
him in a deadly race after those who fled. No one would be left alive.

Strength and aggressiveness are only separated by a matter of degree.
Courage and recklessness as well. The Warrior is a type that transits between
the different points of this continuum with extreme frequency. From raising the totem pole with an image of something resembling a bison and
encouraging his clan to advance into combat, to offering battle when their
numbers and strength are inferior by far. Today we can guess what was going
on inside the heads of these early Eights. They carried a genetic mutation
that made a slight difference in the amount of serotonin that circulated in
their brains. Without their even suspecting it, this unknown and invisible
substance was hiding behind this "volcanic force" they felt. What we now
call the "Warrior Gene" must have dictated to them that one never backs
down from a fight.

For years, university professors have challenged their students to partici-
pate in negotiation games and in different variants of the prisoner's dilemma.
In one part of the game, the dilemma is that apparently the only way to
make a profit is by betraying others. And we have been surprised to see how
some, feeling stabbed in the back, react with remarkable passion. Today, we
know of different studies that have replicated these negotiation games, in
combination with a genomic analysis of the participants. You might have

guessed it: those who carried the Warrior Gene were the most categorically willing to retaliate when they felt deceived or excluded.[253]

BIOLOGICAL BASIS

Or how serotonin wins a thousand battles and lives to tell the tale

Our exploration of the biological basis of Type Eight led us down two parallel paths. The impact of serotonin balance within our brain and the influence of testosterone on behavior.

Hypothesis 1. The impact of Serotonin

What is the real identity of this gene that hides behind the alias "Warrior Gene"? And how does it work? We will try to go by parts, as it is a complex mechanism, and one that is still under study. Let's check out what we know so far:

MAOA is the gene that codes for the production of a substance called monoamine oxidase A. This substance is an enzyme that catalyzes the breakdown of serotonin inside the brain. The MAOA-L variant of this gene has been associated with lower production of this enzyme, resulting in a decreased ability to degrade serotonin. The consequence of this all is that serotonin will tend to accumulate within the synaptic space.[254]

Watch out, because now comes the important point.

An excess of serotonin in the synapses of the prefrontal cortex has been associated with a lower capacity of the cortex to exert its role of containing the reactions of the amygdala. This, in turn, makes the amygdala more reactive, being more likely to trigger more frequent and intense aggressive

---

253 Sapolsky, 2017.
254 Sapolsky, 2017.

responses.[255] The result is a greater overall tendency to aggressiveness. This genetic variant must have emerged hundreds of thousands of years ago, and it was possibly behind the impulse that led the first Eights to become heroes or martyrs.

There are many things about this mechanism that we do not yet understand.[256] For example, why it acts differently in men and women. We do have some clues though. This gene is located on the X chromosome. When it is present in a man, perhaps it will have no "choice" but to express, since men only have one X chromosome. In the case of women, it is possible that this gene becomes "silent," while the "partner" gene on the other X chromosome is expressed.[257] Remember Mendel's peas?

Then, to complicate matters even further, there is evidence that in the case of women, it is another variant of the same gene that generates similar behavioral patterns.[258] In short, this is still a developing story.

Despite all this confusion, the jury has almost reached a verdict on the most important issue: this gene, and the serotonergic balance it causes in the brain, would be the main suspects of causing a higher inclination to aggressiveness as a stable personality trait,[259] both within normal and pathological ranges.[260]

Let us remember once again that one of our assumptions, based on findings from genetics and academic psychiatry, is that there is a continuum between normal traits and pathological traits that resemble them.

---

255 Duke, Bègue, Bell, & Eisenlohr-Moul, 2013; Garcia, Aluja, Fibla, Cuevas, & García, 2010; Eccles, MacArtney-Coxson, Chambers, & Lea, 2012.

256 Not all people who carry this gene are aggressive, and not all aggressive people carry this gene. The high level of serotonin in the synapses is only associated with aggression when its cause is hereditary (the MAOA-L or low activity), not when it is artificially induced (Smeijers, Bulten, Franke, Buitelaar, & Verkes, 2017) (Byrd et al., 2014).

257 Eme, 2013.

258 There is evidence that, in the case of women, it would be the MAOA-H variant (associated with lower levels of serotonin at synapses) that is associated with a greater tendency to aggression (Byrd et al., 2018).

259 Vicar, 2014.

260 Reti et al., 2011; Byrd et al., 2014.

The same traits that in normal degrees we may call strength, determination, or courage, in higher degrees we can call aggressiveness and even violence. They are expressions of the same continuum of traits, sharing a common genetic base.

The most extreme and pathological level of this continuum seems to coincide with what in psychiatry is diagnosed as antisocial personality disorder. Coincidentally, many researchers have associated the origin of this disorder with a serotonergic imbalance in the brain.

The symptoms that, according to the Mayo Clinic, are usually associated with this disorder, could be classified into five large groups:[261]

- Tendency towards insensitivity, lack of empathy, and lack of remorse for harming or mistreating other people.
- Difficulty in controlling impulses. Difficulty considering or learning from negative consequences of behavior. Lack of planning, recklessness, unnecessary risk-taking, failure to follow rules, history of irresponsibility, and failure to meet work or financial obligations, history of trouble with the law.
- Tendency to hostility, irritability, aggression, or violence.
- Propensity to deceive, use of charm or wit to manipulate others for personal gain or pleasure, poor or abusive relationships.
- Arrogance and feeling of superiority.

Let us now consider how the mechanisms associated with serotonin balance within the brain might explain these five groups of symptoms.

- Less sensitivity to physical and emotional pain. There is evidence that variations in the serotonin balance within the brain affect the level of sensitivity to physical pain in humans and other mammals, although this evidence is not yet entirely conclusive.[262] Let us remember that the

---

261 According to the Diagnostic and Statistical Manual of Mental Disorders (DSM-V), the above symptoms also include some that are associated with Narcissistic Personality Disorder, which has a high comorbidity with Antisocial Personality Disorder (Salavera Bordás, Puyuelo, Tricás, & Lucha, 2010).

262 Lindstedt et al., 2011; Hooten, Hartman, Black, Laures, & Walker, 2013.

perception of physical pain has two components: the merely sensory perception, and the emotional reaction that it triggers in our amygdala.[263] The latter is what determines how much the experience "affects" us, as well as the reaction of our autonomic nervous system. Let us also remember that, in our brain, the ability to feel our physical pain and the ability to feel our emotional "pain" are inextricably linked.[264] Many studies have shown that people with antisocial personality disorder are physiologically and subjectively less reactive to pain, and that their amygdalae are smaller and less responsive to frightening stimuli.[265]

- Less sensitivity to the pain of others. We know that, by extension, less sensitivity to our own pain also means less sensitivity to the pain of others, whether physical or emotional. Studies confirm that these patients have a weaker reaction to facial, vocal, or body signals of fear, sadness, or pain from others. The same effect has been observed in relation to other people's signs of joy, although to a lesser extent. Interestingly, their sensitivity to perceive other people's manifestations of anger and aversion, is completely preserved.[266] Studies using fMRI have been able to verify an inverse relationship between Orientation to Social Dominance at a psychological level, and the brain's reactivity to emotional pain.[267]

- Tendency to Impulsivity: Many studies have confirmed the role of serotonergic equilibrium on the ability to control impulses. The "Warrior Gene" and the action of serotonin have been associated with a lower metabolic activity in the prefrontal cortex, when it is in a "resting" state. Let us remember that the prefrontal cortex exercises a role of executive control over the amygdala's reactivity. A "lazier" cortex would make it harder to "count to ten" before exploding. On the other hand, it has been

---

263   Sapolsky, 2017.
264   Damasio, 2005.
265   Sapolsky, 2017.
266   R. James R. Blair, 2013.
267   Social Dominance Orientation (SDO), in Sapolsky, 2017.

observed that the prefrontal cortex of these individuals needs to activate more than normal when it is forced to face cognitive tasks that require its executive function: attention, concentration, directed thinking.[268]

- Propensity to aggression: It is thought that the MAOA-L gene variant would be associated with a greater tendency to react in a hostile way to aggressive or ambiguous external signals. At the base of this tendency would be a more excitable amygdala. These people seem to present an attribution bias that would lead them to perceive as hostile gestures or actions what others would perceive as neutral. Some argue that this mechanism would be at the root of these patients' vulnerability towards presenting aggressive behavior.[269] They interpret "aggression" more easily and react with aggression more frequently.[270] On the other hand, it seems that this mechanism would be mainly associated with aggressiveness of an impulsive nature, that which is not planned and is rather a product of the heat of the moment.[271]

- Superior capacity to "read" other people's intentions[272]: Our ability to empathize with other people's emotions, and our ability to read their motivations and thoughts, are two skills that run through independent circuits within our brain.[273] The exact mechanism is still unknown, but it has been observed that the lack of emotional empathy of these subjects does not affect at all their "cognitive" empathy, that is, their ability to intuit what other people are thinking. Many of these patients have a higher than normal capacity to "read minds" and to grasp the

---

268 Sapolsky, 2017.
269 Buckholtz & Meyer-Lindenberg, 2008.
270 Smeijers, Bulten, Franke, Buitelaar, & Verkes, 2017.
271 Garcia et al., 2010; Vicar, 2014; Montoya, Terburg, Bos, & van Honk, 2012; R.J.R. Blair, 2010).
272 Also known as "theory of mind" (Sapolsky, 2017).
273 Cognitive empathy involves primarily the dorsomedial prefrontal cortex, dorsal anterior cingulate cortex, and dorsal striatum; while emotional empathy involves primarily the ventromedial and orbitofrontal cortex, the anterior-ventral cingulate cortex, the amygdala, and the ventral striatum (Abu-Akel & Shamay-Tsoory, 2011).

intentions of others. This ability would allow them to stay "three steps ahead" to influence, deceive, or manipulate other people.[274]

- Feeling of powerfulness: Some authors have speculated about the relationship between serotonin imbalances, antisocial and narcissistic disorders, and what has been called *Hubris*, or "power syndrome."[275] This would be characterized by a tendency towards arrogant, self-referential behavior, messianic beliefs, and a strong attachment to power roles. It is possible to hypothesize that at the base of this phenomenon could be the sensation of physiological energization that rage confers, an emotion whose evolutionary meaning is to prepare the body for confrontation. And since nothing is so simple, we believe that this mechanism does not operate alone, but in conjunction with the effects of testosterone. More to come soon.

Up to now, we have reviewed the most pathological manifestations associated with this genetic variant. Several important questions remain in the air: What is it that makes the difference, the frontier line, between normality and disease? Are all carriers of this gene aggressive? To what extent? What about the influence of education, the good example of parents, the environment?

The answer to these questions came hand in hand with a study that marked a watershed in our understanding of the interaction between heredity and environment in the development of personality.[276]

---

274 R. James R. Blair, 2013; Sapolsky, 2017.
275 Owen et al., 2008; Claxton, Owen, & Sadler-Smith, 2015.
276 The "Dunedin Multidisciplinary Heath and Development Study" was a longitudinal study that followed the development of a group of 1037 children (52% male), from birth to age twenty-six, analyzing their genetics, different variables of their environment and education, and their behavior as adults. One of the most notable findings of this study was that those male individuals who carried the low-activity version of MAO-A, were three times more likely to manifest severe levels of aggressive behavior (differentiated by having convictions for violent crimes or a diagnosed antisocial personality disorder), but only in cases where they also had a history of abuse during their childhood (Moffitt T.E., Caspi A., Harrington H., 2002); (Caspi et al., 2002).

What these researchers found is that MAOA-L gene carriers who had been victims of violence, abuse, or mistreatment in childhood were three times more likely to exhibit severe levels of aggressive behavior in their youth and adulthood. The relationship was so direct that they even detected a correlation between the number of serious abuse events and the degree of aggression of the subjects.[277] On the other hand, the gene carriers who had no history of abuse turned out to be perfectly normal people.[278] From this vantage point we can guess that they were Eights—energetic, strong and determined, slightly more aggressive, but fully adapted and successful.

More recent investigations have tended to confirm that this genetic variant, while conferring a vulnerability to impulsive and aggressive behavior in general, may or may not be expressed depending on the presence of other biological and environmental factors during the individual's developmental period.[279] What other environmental factors can influence the expression of this gene is still being explored, such as the relationship dynamics with siblings or with peers, or more traumatic situations such as being subjected to *bullying*.

It is also thought that the expression of this gene could be affected by the presence of an excess of stress hormones in the intrauterine environment, during the prenatal brain development process.[280]

Hypothesis 2: The effect of testosterone

The Warrior Gene is not the only hypothesis that could explain a biological predisposition to develop as a Type Eight. There is evidence that exposure to higher than normal levels of testosterone inside the uterus has

---

277 Philibert et al., 2011.

278 Vicar, 2014; Reti et al., 2011; Sapolsky, 2017.

279 Booij et al., 2010; Sapolsky, 2017.

280 One hypothesis is that the variant of the MAOA-L gene has an impact on the brain development of males and is associated with a more labile socio-cognitive processing system, characterized by a greater tendency to interpret ambiguous stimuli as being hostile, and therefore, a greater tendency to react aggressively (Smeijers et al., 2017).

long-lasting impacts on behavior in adulthood. In the case of women, this higher exposure has been associated with increased levels of aggression and lower levels of sensitivity. In men, it has been shown to predict assertive or dominant personalities.[281]

When it comes to individuals who have completed their development, the relationship between testosterone and aggression is much more complex. In any case, this relationship gives us several clues about the biological mechanisms that could be at the root of Type Eight's behavior.

We already described the impact of testosterone on behavior when we reviewed Type Three, the Hunter. Let us briefly recall what we know today.

Contrary to what is usually believed, testosterone does not cause aggressive behavior. It is mostly the other way around; an aggressive reaction *triggers* an increase in testosterone secretion. Once this happens, testosterone acts by reinforcing, enhancing, and maintaining the aggressive response that was already present.[282]

Let us also remember that our body produces a testosterone discharge every time we feel like we are the winners in a competition, in what we call the "Winner Effect"; and that this rush occurs even when we anticipate a competitive situation, activating a whole set of behaviors aimed at winning it.[283]

This testosterone rush, designed to increase our level of aggressiveness in a defensive response, is equivalent to that which drives the lion to kill his rival to protect his territory, or the chimpanzees to defend their borders against the invasion of a rival gang.[284] In rodents, a testosterone discharge is a clear predictor of aggressive behavior in the face of intruders.[285]

---

281 Sometimes it has also been associated with greater mathematical ability, higher rates of Attention Deficit and Autism (disorders with male bias); and lower rates of depression and anxiety (disorders with female bias); (Sapolsky, 2017).

282 Sapolsky, 2017.

283 Schultheiss, Campbell, & McClelland, 1999.

284 Wingfield, Hegner, Dufty, & Ball, 1990; Wingfield, 2017.

285 Kloke et al., 2011.

Let's briefly remember the consequences that this testosterone discharge produces on behavior:[286]

- Exaggerated sense of self-confidence, well-being, and optimism
- Decreased levels of fear and anxiety
- Decreased level of empathy
- Increased reactivity, impulsiveness, and willingness to take risks
- Tendency to assume that one's own opinion is correct, and to ignore the opinions of others

An interaction has been reported between the presence of the Warrior Gene, and the strength of the association between testosterone discharge and aggressive behavior. Several studies report that the level of circulating testosterone in the blood predicts the degree of aggressive behavior, especially in individuals who either carry the Warrior Gene and/or have a "dominant personality" at the base.[287]

We believe that both the Hunter and the Warrior experience testosterone "highs" more often than their peers. The sensation they would get from these highs would be more or less the same. The interpretation that each would assign to these sensations would be related systemically to their overall set of personality traits. The Hunter will probably think "I am the best." The Warrior, "I am the strongest." And both will get ready to compete by implementing their own particular strategies.

Men and women endowed with the Warrior Gene must often have experienced the feeling of being winners, strong and invincible. Their determination, their tendency to face situations of danger or confrontation, and their foolproof self-confidence, must have often led their peers to give up power to them.

---

286 Sapolsky, 2017.
287 Sapolsky, 2017; Lobbestael, Baumeister, Fiebig, & Eckel, 2014; Archer, 2006; Carré, Putnam, & McCormick, 2009; Kloke et al., 2011; Montoya et al., 2012.

EVOLUTIONARY ADVANTAGES

Or how a hunter-gatherer united the clan to fight the invader

In game theory, the challenge known as the "Stag Hunt" poses a conflict between safety and social cooperation. This dilemma, initially described by Jean-Jacques Rousseau (1717–1778), describes the situation of two individuals who go out hunting. Each can choose between hunting a stag or a hare. Each player must select his move without knowing the choice of the other. If an individual chooses to hunt the stag, he can only succeed if he has the collaboration of the other. If the individual chooses the hare, he will be able to obtain it by his own means. In the equation he must weigh that the stag is a much more valuable reward than the hare, but success in that endeavor will depend on the choice his partner makes.[288]

This dilemma illustrates how we operate in a situation of social cooperation in which the decision to collaborate can lead us to gain or lose much more than the decision not to.

Throughout history, this type of situation has typically occurred when we *Homo sapiens* have had to coordinate in the face of a serious and urgent challenge, such as a war or a catastrophe. If everyone worked together to defeat the enemy, they could gain access to land, goods, and sexual partners. The opposite result could have meant losing everything, even one's life. However, there was always the option to flee and save at least one's own skin.

The theory says that human beings have evolved to instinctively seek strong leadership whenever we find ourselves in situations where there is much to lose or much to gain. We unconsciously sense that, under strong leadership, it is safer to assume that all members of the collective will have

---

288 Rooij, 2007.

a clear incentive to collaborate.[289] Either because we have been inspired by a powerful harangue sown with collective values, or out of the shared fear of possible reprisals.

And when the time comes, how do we recognize strong leadership? Again, the heritage of our species helps us identify the verbal and non-verbal signals of the testosterone discharge: strength, determination, and lack of fear in the face of imminent danger. Almost all of them are qualities that we can find in the Type Eight personality style.

Such behavior reminds us of a lion defending his territory. Or that of a buffalo, which charges without looking ahead. The Warrior is a visceral type, and its origin is likely to be lost in time, even before our species showed up.

We believe that since the time of the hunter-gatherers, the Warrior mutation gained evolutionary value each time the clan or tribe had to face these all-or-nothing challenges. The Warrior was always willing to step forward and face danger without fear. His almost absolute self-confidence, which could border on the delusional, was contagious to the collective, which for a moment was able to put aside its own fear. On a neurological level, it is very possible that the Warrior's harangue triggered a testosterone rush in all those who heard him, instilling for a few minutes a collective sense of strength and power. The phenomenon seems to be the same throughout history: William Wallace calling the Scots to battle in the 13th century, Jack Welch calling GE employees to stand up to competition a few decades ago, or a Warrior chief with his clan 60,000 years ago. Have you ever noticed what you feel when you watch the *Haka of the All Blacks?*

Still, let us agree that the Eight's optimism and confidence were no real guarantee of success. It is true that they improved the chances of uniting the group and increasing their fierceness and their confidence in the battle. But many of those incursions could have also ended badly. Even the bravest warriors can lose their lives in combat.

---

289 Grabo, Spisak, & Van Vugt, 2017.

Many of these ancient Eights must have formed part of the statistics of premature death from violent causes or by accident. We believe, however, that a shorter life did not prevent them from spreading their seed abundantly. As with other social animals, their instinct to behave as *alpha* males or females must have driven them to mate earlier and more often than their clan mates, thus ensuring the continuity of their mutation.[290]

And let us also agree that, if victorious, they would return at the head of the troops, covered in glory. Because, as if it were the destiny of this intense personality, their own lives incarnated this "all-or-nothing." Yesterday, as today, many must have been admired for their courage and determination. A few, however, must have ended their days wandering alone, expelled from their clans due to their violent acts.

One just needs to look at the biographies of many leaders throughout history. We can discover a Type Eight behind the lives and deeds of many of those impactful characters. Because the great contribution of this type seems to transcend the sphere of private life, to place itself behind some of the great accomplishments of our species. By dint of daring, many Eights must have led many human groups to make possible what seemed impossible.

---

290 According to many scholars, at that time, the relationship between men and women would have been much more egalitarian than in later millennia. Often, both men and women foraged equally. It is also likely that many hunter-gatherer bands were matrilineal, that is, women would have remained in their family of origin, sticking together with their blood relatives, and young males would have migrated to join a new band (Lee, 2018).

THE FOOTPRINTS OF SAPIENS WARRIOR

Scenes from a lost past

Scene 1:

We had never seen hair of such a light color. We knew the elders lost the color of their hair, but these were young and their hair was like the sun when it is high. They communicated with one another, but their speech was strange. We could tell from their gestures that they were hungry. He stepped forward and began to observe this strange group. Judging from their clothing, they must have come from the high lands. He looked into their eyes and saw no warrior spirit. He knew how to recognize when eyes have seen death. He tried to frighten them with a battle cry. He saw how their bodies shrank and how they moved closer together. Then he laughed heartily. These pale hairs would not withstand even the beginning of a battle, he said. He knew how to recognize fear in others. Also deception. So he stepped aside a little and invited them into our camp. We shared some meat and some fruit with them. We managed to understand, through their signs, that they had been attacked by a wolf pack and had been forced to flee. They would try to return to their cavern in a few moons. They wanted to stay until that moment. We looked at him to see if he would authorize it. And he bowed his head slightly, granting permission. The pale heads weren't a threat.

Scene 2:

The Clan had been walking for many days in search of water. Without it they would die. Finally they reached the riverbed. It was dry. For many, hope was gone. They began to advance along the old watercourse, but there weren't even small pools. Those who were still optimistic began to leave their bundles behind, to be able to walk with less weight. Most were already dragging their feet, feeling that these would be their last steps. Some of those who fell did not get up. News of the first deaths reached the leader that was heading the march. On hearing them, he quickened his pace and moved forward, distancing

198

himself further and further from the group. Some young men tried to keep up, but he stopped and ordered them to return. The group was devastated. Without him they could not continue. He had abandoned them at the worst moment, they thought. Nobody walked anymore, they just looked for the most comfortable place to wait. Some waited for the cold night; others, for death. It was almost night when they heard the steps of someone approaching quickly. It was him! He had returned! It took them two days to get the entire group to the lagoon. Most of them had to be carried like dead weight. He went on each of these trips, day and night. When they had all drunk and rested, and when they thought they had made the last trip, he gathered a troop to return and burn the corpses. No one would be left behind.

Scene 3:

It looked gigantic. It was the biggest acorn he had ever seen. He couldn't help but to open his mouth a little and make a sound of surprise, drawing the attention of all the other children. There were precious seconds that prevented him from reaching the prize first. Another boy, considerably older than him, had taken the trophy and was smiling happily. But he had seen that acorn first. That acorn was his. He felt the temperature of his face rise. And without thinking about the size of the prize bearer, he gave the big boy a strong push that made him stagger and fall to the ground. He approached the fallen one ready to finish the task and could see how he flinched and tensed up, waiting for the blow. Then he stretched out his hand and he received the acorn from the first of many opponents who, throughout his life, would not present resistance to him. It was the first time he felt it. He possessed a strength that was different from that of others. No matter the size or strength of his opponents, he could still make them feel his own power. And if they hit him, then he would hit back. And so it was on many occasions. And no one could ever receive or deliver as many blows as he.

Scene 4:

She put her mallet on the ground and set about relieving herself of body fluids. The moment she bent down, the huge hunter jumped onto her back. He was already prepared to penetrate her. She had been able to read this male's intentions for a long time. She had felt his gaze on her back several times. She had also seen him prowling around her bed. If she had wanted to breed with him, she would have already done so. She had understood the invitation. But she did not want to. She would only breed with a great warrior. So when the huge hunter tried to mate, she turned around fast, grabbed the bag that the males have between their legs, and squeezed with all her strength. The man screamed and jumped away and threatened her with a rock. He approached the woman, who had already picked up her mallet. Unlike him who still had his arm raised holding the stone, she did not move the mallet and only glared at him fiercely. Then the hunter understood that with this woman he would not copulate. He put down the stone and withdrew, making a sound like forced laughter. She bent down and finished relieving the liquids from her body.

CORE TRAITS

To describe Type Eight we must be respectful of their style. Let's cut to the chase. Without further ado, we propose that the biological mechanisms underlying this type would predispose toward the following core personality traits.

"It's just a scratch": Strong and unshakable

Pain does not move the Warrior. Nor are they moved by the wide range of emotions that usually come with pain. And we are not referring only to physical pain, but also to the "painful emotions" of the family of sadness or fear.

By virtue of the interactions they have with their environment, their innate inclinations give shape to an inner sense of "strength." Little by little, the young Warriors become familiarized with the intoxicating sensation of their own strength, capacity, energy, and self-confidence. The response they receive from others often only confirms this sensation.

They are intense, visceral, and physical. They feel the energy to face great challenges. They are willing to do whatever it takes in order to win. Without wavering. This is why an Eight can move mountains.

But not everything is un upside. Not feeling their own pain, they are not moved by the pain of others. When they move forward, they can do so without further contemplation or remorse. And if anyone whines, it is just a sign of their weakness. Because the Eight tends to divide people into strong and weak, respecting the first and despising the others, no matter if they are on their own side or on the enemy's.

This overestimation of strength could leave them trapped, forcing them to be strong at all costs, disregarding or despising any aspect of their own personality that could be considered a weakness. For the same reason, they may find it hard to open up and be vulnerable, even in their closest interpersonal relationships.

Ultimately, depending on their degree of maturity and their knowledge of themselves, the strength of the Eight will enable them either to build or to destroy, to win the war or to die after the first shot; to be admired or feared, loved or hated. In almost every case, the Warriors will inevitably leave their mark.

Veni, vidi, vici[291]: Self-confidence and determination

The Warrior radiates self-confidence. It is very easy to believe that they really know where they are heading. This ability is extremely useful for building trust and uniting hearts.

This assurance enables them to undertake great toils with optimism, to move forward smoothly where others stop, and to face life's challenges with courage.

Type Eight is a fast decision maker. They do not like to stop and think before they act, and often have little patience for lengthy explanations or detailed analyses. They prefer to move quick and make mistakes along the process, rather than delay the start of action. Even if this means having to rectify halfway through.

They usually perceive the "*big picture*," and quickly detect the important from the accessory, separating the grain from the chaff. They decide in a visceral way, following their own intuition, and sometimes, letting themselves be carried away by their impulses. Their hand does not waver when having to make unpopular decisions.

All the above can turn them into great leaders within contexts of danger and uncertainty, when one is forced to decide with only a few elements and at risk of facing serious consequences.

The "b" side of their unassailable sense of confidence is that it may lead them to overvalue their own judgment or to overestimate their own chances of success. Truth be told, they often find it difficult to anticipate the consequences of their own actions or decisions, and they would do well to listen to the analyses and apprehensions of those around them.

In extreme cases, they may succumb to the feeling of their own powerfulness, treating others with arrogance, assuming that their strength gives

---

291 Latin locution used by the general and Roman consul Julius Caesar in 47 BC, when addressing the Roman Senate, describing his recent victory over Pharnaces II of Pontus at the Battle of Zela.

them the right to abuse others just because they can, and believing themselves to be in possession of all the answers.

Strike first, strike hard, no mercy[292]: Willingness to confront

Type Eight's emotional spectrum is much more loaded towards anger and aversion than towards grief or fear. They can fall into outbursts of rage whenever they encounter a frustrating situation. Without them being fully aware of it, anger can make them feel energized and stimulated. And throughout their lives, they may learn that these outbursts of rage actually allow them to get away with just about anything. In addition to being innate, their aggression will tend to be reinforced based on their experience.

Their ebbed empathy makes it difficult for them to weigh the emotional costs that these outbursts can bring, both to themselves and to their relationship with others.

They are quick to come to confrontation. They are not afraid of conflict. All the contrary, it amuses them. In their experience, conflict almost always works out in their favor. Often, what for them was a small exchange of opinions, in the perception of others could be a pitched battle.

They tend to be skilled and tough negotiators, capable of waging psychological wars or subtly threatening until they find their opponent's weakness.

More particularly, Warriors tend to loathe feeling invaded or controlled, and often feel irritated when limits are placed on them or when they are restricted in any way.

They usually rebel against authority when they consider it to be weak, when it has been unfair, or simply because they consider that they should be in command. They essentially don't like being told what to do.

---

292 Motto of Cobra Kai, American action comedy-drama web television series based on film *The Karate Kid*.

They often find it difficult to regulate the strength of their own reactions, and they can easily become aggressive. Sometimes they let their anger express itself in a destructive way, even causing physical, emotional, or moral harm to other people.

In some extreme cases, they can fall into hostile or violent behavior, to the point of getting in trouble with the law. This is not only due to their innate impulsiveness, but also to the conscious or unconscious feeling that rules are made for the weak and do not really apply to them. They may actually believe that they are "above the law."

Staring danger in the face: Intensity, courage, and recklessness

Eights are spontaneous and like to live on the edge. To express themselves freely and to say exactly what they think, without any qualms. It is difficult for them to hold back their impulses and reactions, even if they later have to regret something they have said or done.

They relish adventure and intensity. Big challenges, big risks, big fights. Small things bore them, make them feel dull and lethargic. It is as if their mind can only truly "wake up" when faced with something "great."

They can go from adventurous to brave, or from risk-prone to audacious or reckless in the blink of an eye, especially if luck is smiling at them and they are feeling on a "winning streak." It is the effect of their own testosterone.

Occasionally, this impulsiveness can be expressed in a history of non-compliance with work or financial obligations, or in a general lack of willpower.

Playing Poker: The power of influence

The huge confidence of Type Eight gives them an aura of charisma that often exerts a seductive influence on others. On top of that, they are endowed with an innate ability to "read" the thoughts and intentions of those around them. They are skilled in perceiving, crystal clear, the power relationships, rivalries, and competition between factions and between individuals. They instinctively focus their attention on power, and on individuals who wield it.

They put forward their ideas with strength and conviction. They tend to push until they convince, persuade, or compel. Their "toolbox" has multiple strategies to deal with opposition and obstacles.

They usually have an impactful presence. They are adept at creating their own power base, and at establishing alliances and coalitions. All this gives them a natural ability to direct other people's will and to impact other people's emotions. At the end of the day, this translates into an enormous capacity to influence others. They exercise power with the naturalness of those who feel that "they are entitled".

But this same cocktail of skills, coupled with their usual disregard for others, can sometimes lead them to use their charm and wit to manipulate others to their own advantage.

Type Nine: The Peacemaker

Or how a smiling child avoided a war

A FIRST GLANCE

The assembly had become embroiled in a bitter dispute. Deciding whether to leave for an uncharted valley or whether it was better to stay in the highlands had divided the clan into two distinct factions.

The tone was escalating, and everyone could see that at any moment the situation would turn violent. The young man did not want to take sides for either faction, but he did stand up to take the floor. As he spoke, he brought back to their minds that they were all children of the spirit of the Bear and that, according to tradition, in the face of a disagreement like this it was necessary to hand over the decision to the elders. Just as it had been done when they had to decide whether to surrender the great cavern or to raise their spears against the Others. Just as it had been done when they decided to welcome and integrate the pale heads into the clan. They had always been the ones who had decided. The assembly fell silent and looked towards where the elders were. One of them stood up and thanked the young man for his serene tone. Then they announced that they would debate on the matter, and that the decision would be delivered when the night was over and there was light and heat outside. The young man sat down with those of his age, and they continued to clean up some grains that they had collected in the afternoon.

Our hunter-gatherer ancestors had many reasons to collaborate, and there is reason to believe that evolution put pressure to select those most capable of doing so.

As the size of groups expanded beyond the borders of family ties, their bonds became increasingly weaker and loyalties more unstable. As the force that brings the group together grows, so does the force that separates it. Action and reaction.

Still, the ability to establish collaborative networks within large groups of people seems to have been a hallmark of the evolutionary success of *Homo sapiens*. It seems to have been precisely this quality that allowed us to prevail, outsmarting our Neanderthal and Denisovan cousins, even though they had arrived thousands of years ahead of us.

The fact is that, in order to collaborate, both animals and humans were forced to develop the ability to modulate and restrain their own aggressive impulse. This functionality became so important for adaptation, that the mechanism could not be simply left to a "lesser activation" of the aggressive response. A specific area of the brain evolved, actively in charge of controlling and silencing the aggressive responses triggered by the amygdala. This area is called the Lateral Septum.[293]

Our hypothesis is that Type Nine's structural trait would be a hereditary predisposition to control or suppress one's aggressiveness, and a powerful and almost instinctive drive to maintain social harmony, even at the expense of one's own personal interests. This predisposition would be caused by a mutation that would have generated an overactive Septum.

It is interesting to note that, within the entire literature reviewed in connection with the biology of personality types, it is the behaviors associated with Type Nine that receive the least amount of attention. It seems a sort of existential joke for the personality with the highest degree of "humility" within the spectrum. A deeper explanation for this lack of attention might be, precisely, that this personality "does not generate problems."

BIOLOGICAL BASIS

Or how the Septum imagines caverns without borders

The literature review led us to generate two possible hypotheses regarding the biological basis of the Peacemaker's traits. The main one is related to the activity and the evolution of the Septum, this area of the brain responsible for the regulation of aggressive responses in animals. Later on we propose a second hypothesis, related to the neural mechanisms underlying the responses of "satisfaction" and "satiety."

As far as we know, these biological mechanisms and their relationship with behavior have been studied almost exclusively in animals. Given

---

293 Wong et al., 2016.

this, we will base our descriptions on an extrapolation of these behaviors to humans.

First Hypothesis: Control of own Aggression

Aggression is an animal behavior, adaptive to resolve competition for limited resources. It is a fundamental strategy to defend territory, to compete for sexual partners, food, or shelter, and to protect family and offspring. Fighting, however, is a physically strenuous activity, the results of which are not guaranteed and which can result in serious injury or death. It could eventually spawn only losers. This is why the central nervous system evolved a neural mechanism in charge of controlling and modulating its expression. The Lateral Septum is the part of the Limbic System "responsible" for inhibiting aggression.[294]

The Septum acts in opposition to the Amygdala. Every time the Amygdala is activated, the Septum tries to silence it, and vice versa. Like all limbic structures, the Septum "shouts" to the hypothalamus so that it pays attention to it and not to the other regions.[295]

There is multiple evidence for this function of the Septum in animals. In most mammals, and in many species of birds, Lateral Septum lesions have been found to be associated with a dramatic increase in the frequency of aggressive behaviors, and attacks on members of the same species. It is a phenomenon known as "septal fury." The same happens when the Septum is deactivated by chemical means. And exactly the opposite happens when the Lateral Septum is artificially stimulated. Both natural aggressiveness and that caused by injuries and drugs, are suppressed.[296]

What little we know about the role of the Lateral Septum in human behavior comes from the study of patients with tumors in this area. These

---

294 Sapolsky, 2010.
295 Wong et al., 2016.
296 Wong et al., 2016; Aleyasin, Flanigan, & Russo, 2018; Mirrione et al., 2014.

patients experience a high level of irritability and aggressiveness.[297] You can start making your own list of people who need electrical stimulation of the septum.

To our knowledge, there is still little evidence of innate individual differences in the functioning of the Lateral Septum.[298] We do know of a group of researchers, probably admirers of Hitchcock's movies, reporting that hyperaggressive individuals of a bird species present a lower level of activity in their Lateral Septum, probably of innate origin.[299]

Second hypothesis: Satiety response

Satisfaction is an emotional state that was originally associated with the feeling of satiety that humans and other mammals experience, after meeting our basic needs, such as food and shelter.

The theory says that the evolutionary function of satisfaction would be, at a behavioral level, to reduce a state of activation and lead us to find a safe, familiar, and comfortable place to recover and rest.

At the brain level, it would allow a memory consolidation process to remember those strategies that made it possible to satisfy the need.[300]

This satiety response would act by temporarily reducing the impact of environmental and emotional signals. This reaction would be mediated by serotonin, which would act in opposition to dopaminergic drugs, which prompt us to seek stimulation.[301]

It would be a "withdrawal" response, in order to rest once satiated. Physiologically very different from the "flight" response to danger. Now you know: if someone accuses you of running away from effort, you can

297 Zeman & King, 1958.
298 Talishinsky & Rosen, 2012.
299 Kasper et al., 2017.
300 Foster & Wilson, 2006; Bradshaw & Cook, 1996; Griskevicius, Shiota, & Nowlis, 2010; Berenbaum, 2002; Fredrickson, 1998.
301 Tops, Russo, Boksem, & Tucker, 2009.

explain that you are only "withdrawing in a state of satisfaction" to recover and rest. Don't forget to mention serotonin. This state is coupled with an emotional feeling of positive valence, a sense of subjective well-being.

On the other hand, many researchers have found that some individuals are genetically predisposed to experience "satisfaction" more easily and frequently than their peers.

Some scholars have even asserted that feelings of life satisfaction and subjective well-being would have a 70-80% heritability component.[302]

And in our era of genomic analysis, one study even managed to identify a genetic variant, rs322931, which could be associated with this greater tendency to "satisfaction" and general positive emotionality.[303] Although these studies are still preliminary and carried out with small and homogeneous populations, they promise that in the future we could find the heritable mechanisms at the base of this trait.

In summary, our second hypothesis to explain the biological basis of Type Nines is that they could come endowed with a genetic variant that makes them tend more easily towards satisfaction. Of course, we are talking here about satisfaction in much broader terms than mere satiety of basic needs. Again, we have learned that the areas of our brain work like this, extending their functions to other similar, but more sophisticated ones.

And finally, we think that the Peacemaker could also arise from a combination or an interaction between the two mechanisms. It could be a more active or sensitive Lateral Septum, in interaction, or combined with a greater tendency to enter this physiological and psychological state of satisfaction. In other words, you're sitting in a comfortable chair, John Lennon is singing "Imagine" in the background, you've already eaten and drunk, your bank account backs you up, and your partner is giving you a knowing look from

---

302   Nes & Røysamb, 2017.
303   Only the genome of 2522 African American individuals was mapped (Wingo et al., 2017)

across the room. If you get an email from a colleague telling you off right at that moment, you may feel too lazy to pick a fight...

EVOLUTIONARY ADVANTAGES

Or how a hunter-gatherer resolved a hunting dispute without taking up arms

The process of natural selection is eminently individualistic. There is no evolutionary equivalent in nature to sacrificing oneself for the sake of other individuals of my species, unless those individuals carry my own genetic material.

Moreover, according to the theory, the probability that we are willing to sacrifice ourselves for another human being is directly proportional to the percentage of genetic material that we share with them: 50% for a son or a brother; 25% for a nephew and 12.5% for a cousin...[304] In this context, the adaptive strategy of Type Nine can be counterintuitive. What did this calm, unaggressive, and noncompetitive individual really gain in this wild world that our ancestors had to face?

On a deeper look, they possess certain traits which may, at first sight, seem disadvantageous for the individual, but that in the long run end up benefitting them by enabling a better collaboration within the collective as a whole.

An example of the above is what happened to a farmer dedicated to poultry. One day he noticed that in one of his henhouses there was a "star" laying hen. It laid big, pink, spectacular eggs. And not only that: its production statistics were above all others in the pen. The farmer observed the reality of his other henhouses. He realized that in all of them there were some "star" laying hens. So he came up with a production strategy: he would gather all

---

304 Sapolsky, 2017; Dawkins, 1976.

these champions in one single pen, creating a "super-henhouse." The success would be unprecedented in the industry. He would become famous.

After a few days, what was unprecedented was his surprise: the production level of the "super-henhouse" was a fiasco. He had destroyed the production of the golden eggs. What had happened? He only realized after he observed for a while: these "super-hens" were actually "super-bullies" who were continuously pecking their less aggressive companions until they stressed them out of their egg-laying potential. The others ended up laying less as a result of stress. By bringing all the "bullies" together in one place, they stressed each other out, ultimately laying fewer eggs than the pen full of peaceful chickens.[305]

And if you don't like the examples of poultry, attention fishermen: even in fish societies natural selection has favored collaborative and affiliative personality traits, which would be transmitted through heredity, favoring the survival of the group as a whole.[306]

Evolutionarily, this sort of trait, aimed at the preservation of the collective, can become a strong competitive advantage when two groups are fighting for the same ecological niche.

Let us remember again that, 70,000 years ago, when our *Homo sapiens* ancestors made a second attempt to migrate from Africa reaching Europe and the Middle East, these lands were already inhabited by the Neanderthals for hundreds of thousands of years. They had brains as big as those of the newcomer, they knew the terrain, they made tools out of stone, and their body was better adapted to resist the cold.

One of the great factors that favored *Homo sapiens* in the competition for this ecological niche was our ability to organize ourselves into larger groups. And we believe that one of the key factors that made this cohesion possible was the existence of men and women, who, through the contagion

---

305 Sapolsky, 2017.
306 Kasper, Schreier, & Taborsky, 2019; Kasper et al., 2017.

of emotions, attitudes, and ideas of "peace," contributed to this cohesion. This is probably the great legacy, and one of the main contributions of Type Nine.

Let's acknowledge that Type Nine indirectly benefits from this contribution to the collective. Let's now see how, and under what circumstances, their adaptive strategies can also directly benefit them.

Let's take a look at societies of primates, our first cousins. These are generally very hierarchical. It is easy to imagine that the best thing is to have the power and make all the decisions. The mighty, after all, will have access to the biggest bananas, the sexiest females, or the best sunbathing spot. Or not?

Well, not always. Primatologists teach us that, under certain conditions, monkeys who do not compete for power experience less stress, are calmer, and ultimately have a better life.

This is what tends to happen in the context of species that organize themselves in more egalitarian societies, where males and females can choose more freely with whom they want to mate and where responsibility for breeding is shared. This is also the case in societies where there is high social mobility, where it is possible to move up or down the ranks more easily, and where there is considerable alternation in power, either because the systems are more egalitarian, or because of frequent fights between alpha males that take turns in displacing one another.[307]

And although these primates do not vote and do not choose parliaments, and although human beings may be somewhat more complicated, intuitively it does not sound so far from our reality. It is not in vain that we have so many genes shared with apes...

We can apply this wisdom to our own primate society and presume that the Peacemakers are likely to suffer less stress and live a longer and happier life than their more stressed or dominant peers, at least when the

---

307 Sapolsky, 2005.

environmental conditions allow. Likewise, when it comes to choosing a partner to share our home, it is not uncommon for us to opt for the one who we guess will be more helpful and kind.

It is not difficult to extrapolate to what must have happened 40,000 years ago, when a Peacemaker, female or male, with their friendly, non-threatening charm, became attractive and eligible as partners and as parents. In the old days, as well as today, it was nice to come home after the day's battles and find your partner who, instead of "giving you more war," was a haven of peace ...

THE FOOTPRINTS OF SAPIENS PEACEMAKER

Scenes from a lost past

Scene 1:

Upon entering the cave with his four rabbits and fourteen eggs, testimony to a magnificent morning of foraging, he found a huge and contentious warrior who was blocking the entrance. The same one who often got in trouble with others for taking their women. With his enormous strength, this guy was capable of splitting a man in two. The warrior's gaze lingered on the rabbits, and his massive head tilted to one side as his eyes made contact with those of the hunter. Without hesitation, the hunter bent down and divided his stock in two. He let him know that in the future, when the warrior had better hunting luck, he could return the favor and it would be very good for him when the time came. The warrior left his mallet on the ground and collected two rabbits and seven eggs. Those who were watching the situation breathed a sigh of relief.

Scene 2:

Everyone knew that the best way to fish in the sea was by dragging the braided vegetable fibers. That's why it was difficult to understand the endeavor of the old man, who spent entire afternoons sitting on the rocks fishing with a single strap tied to a small basket. Usually the old man managed to catch one fish, two at the most. Whether he fished or not, he entertained himself by imitating birds, speaking to the fish, or simply looking at the horizon. If someone went along with him, the old man would be happy and talk. If he was alone, he would smile all the same. On many occasions the fishermen invited him to adopt the new ways of fishing, much more productive than his old system. Invariably, he was surprised by what he was told and congratulated those who used these new techniques. He assured them that he would adopt them. However, the next day, others always saw him repeating his routine and throwing the basket into the sea with a cheerful smile.

Scene 3:

The little gray wolf turned his head and watched the young man from a prudent distance. He might have been a couple of months old. He was a curious little wolf. When the young man noticed the animal's presence, he hesitated whether to throw him a stone to scare him away. But then he thought, I'm the one in his territory, not he in mine. The two looked at each other for a long time. Then the young man took a piece of meat from the rabbit he was cutting up and threw it to the cub. The little wolf was frightened and quickly retreated a couple of meters, from where he looked at the young man again. He timidly advanced to where the chunk of meat had fallen, cleverly caught it between the fangs and backed away. This was the first of many encounters in which the young man fed him. It seemed that both enjoyed their encounters and, little by little, they eliminated the distance. His comrades never understood why he wasted food on this animal, but he smiled and repeated that he was his friend. Many times the young man moved to richer valleys and also to higher lands. And wherever he went, his friend always came out to receive his share of food. The young man became an adult and the wolf grew old with him. Eight times the rains came and went, until one afternoon the gray wolf did not show up for his appointment. So he searched for him by following his tracks. He found him hiding at the entrance of a small cavern. He was lying down and panting. Life was abandoning him. For the first time, the wolf felt the warm hand of his friend, who caressed him from the time the sun went down, until it rose again, with patience and affection, as his wolf spirit left his old body.

Scene 4:

The day had been extremely productive. She carried a basket with a rabbit and three small bowls with grains and fruits. It had been a fantastic day. The children, cheerful, were marching after her. All the little ones in the band liked to follow her in the morning work. She always smiled and told them stories, making them spend the time as if they were not really working at all. She seemed to enjoy their company. When one of the kids accidentally dropped the fruit or lost a prey, she gently and patiently explained how to do it correctly. When they quarreled, she would give them a shove or would roar like a tiger, they would laugh and it would all come to nothing. That night the bonfire was very lively. Several children had begun to fall asleep, when she entered the circle with a huge furry hide on her back, walking on her knees and imitating the growl of a bear. The children laughed and began to follow her on their knees, imitating everything she did. Until they were transformed into a small family of bears. Everyone celebrated the idea, and others were also encouraged to make their own imitations of animals and birds.

CORE TRAITS

We have said that Type Nine is perhaps the least documented by behavioral biology. However, although the features presented below represent an extrapolation, we believe that the evidence provided in the previous pages is more than sufficient to support the hypotheses that follow. We believe these to be the structural traits of Type Nine, arising from a greater tendency to control one's own aggression and to experience satisfaction.

Give peace a chance[308]: Controlling aggression and avoiding conflict

Peacemakers are strongly motivated to reduce conflict and create harmony. They experience confrontation as intensely threatening, something which must be avoided at all costs. In addition to this drive, they are endowed with a greater ability to control their own hostility.

From an early age, Nines learn to let go of the aggressions they receive from others, and to overlook any type of situation that potentially exposes them to conflict or confrontation, even if this implies some relinquishment on their part. This quality brings about both costs and benefits. Let's start with the benefits.

Their aversion to conflicts drives them to develop a complete "toolbox" to defuse them even before they have been declared. For example, sometimes they develop a great ease to lower the tension of a moment through funny, friendly, or diplomatic comments. And a special radar to perceive the atmosphere and any indicator of hostility or discomfort in people. They can empathize deeply and can easily visualize all sides of a problem.

Their desire for peace extends even beyond themselves, as they are able to use their innate abilities to mediate conflicts that arise between other people or groups. It is not in vain that we call them Peacemakers.

People of this type often perceive the world as an interconnected place, and are able to find common ground, even between the most divergent positions. They seek consensus, because they know that it is a fertile ground for peace.

But since nothing in life is free, this love of peace also brings about a problem. They often have a hard time saying no or showing their anger, no matter how justified. They will find it difficult to assert their rights or their

---

308 "Give Peace a Chance," song by John Lennon, 1972

views. And perhaps worst of all, this can make them more vulnerable to abuse or injustice.

Finally, the Nines' quest for harmony is not only about relationships. As this trait evolved, it also applied to the "inner climate" of the Nine. In other words, Peacemakers not only want to sow harmony in and with their environment, but they also want to cultivate harmony within their own inner self.

After you: Humble, noncompetitive, affable, and empathetic

Competition brings about the risk of confrontation and the threat of potential harm from an opponent. Peacemakers will be willing to give up competition, often sacrificing their own interests, in order to avoid this risk.

The positive side of their unwillingness to compete is that they are naturally humble and, in many cases, generous towards other people. Peacemakers often navigate under the radar and avoid the limelight, gladly giving it to others. They don't like the exposure of feeling the center of attention.

They are honest and unbiased when it comes to admitting their own mistakes. They are unpretentious, giving themselves little importance, and they can laugh at themselves easily, avoiding the clash with those who are speeding their way through life.

This affable and humble disposition allows them to be extraordinarily non-threatening in their relationships. They are always open to listen, they are naturally interested in others, it is easy for them to empathize, and to step into other people's "worlds." They have a special ability to make others feel accepted, included, or supported. It is easy to get along with them.

They often put the interests of the group above their personal interests, and therefore, they often have a holistic perception of situations.

One downside to this complexion is that Type Nines may eventually lose touch with their own needs and their own agenda. In some extreme cases, they can put all their own ambitions on hold in order to preserve what their nature forces them to feel as the greatest good: harmony with everything and everyone.

The glass half full: Calm, optimistic, and satisfied

It seems that Peacemakers tend to be satisfied with less. They often inhabit a calm and leisurely emotional state, and experience emotional ups and downs with less intensity than other people. Optimism is usually their most natural state, as they are naturally inclined to see the "glass half full" and the good side of people and things.

Sometimes they experience an impulse to withdraw from action, and others may perceive them as quiet, reserved, or placid. In many cases Nines are rather introverted, but always maintaining this air of bonhomie and openness, which makes it so easy to approach them.

The problem arises when these characteristics are taken to the extreme, when Nines go from being peaceful and gentle to being passive. This brings us to our next feature.

Don't push the river: Adaptable and conformist

An early 20th century statesman said: "There are only two kinds of problems, those that are solved by themselves and those that have no solution."[309] This statement, which may be surprising to some, contains part of the wisdom that characterizes the Type Nine.

---

309   Ramón Barros Luco (1835–1919) was president of Chile between 1910 and 1915.

Their humility, their avoidance of competition, and their tendency to be satisfied, can lead them to settle for what they have, adapting to their circumstances and what they have to live with. This predisposition turns them into deeply flexible and adaptable individuals.

Now, these qualities, taken to the extreme, can become one of the great Achilles' heels of the Peacemaker: a lower degree of activation or energy to change what does deserve to be changed. The line between "not pushing the river" and being carried away by the current, in many cases, is difficult for them to elucidate.

Returning to our statesman, history tells us that this man became president of his country because he stood up as a man of consensus. Once in office, he was able to guarantee dialogue between the different political factions existing in his country at that time, achieving the signing of a "Non-Aggression, Consultation and Arbitration" treaty with neighboring countries. A great accomplishment, typical of a Nine.

Don't say Yes when you want to say No[310]: Passive Resistance

The Peacemaker will often say "Yes," even when they want to say "No." The fateful outcome is that it will become very difficult for them to keep the commitments they never wanted to make, or to do the things they never wanted to do. And as a story of a foretold misfortune, by using this strategy, Peacemakers can provoke exactly what they most want to avoid: a conflict with others.

And don't be confused. Often, the Peacemaker is internally very sensitive to feeling mistreated or bossed around by others, even if we do not see it. Remember that they are sensitive to anything that might be interpreted as a sign of harshness. And whenever they have felt subdued, mistreated,

---

310   Title of a book by Herbert Fensterheim and Jean Baer (1975)

or their rights violated, the aggressiveness of the Nine will equally seek its course. It is then that they resort to passive aggression. They might simply forget, delay, or manage not to do what the other party wants them to do. Let it not be said that Peacemakers do not have their weapons.

SOME FINAL COMMENTS

We are convinced that this angle for looking at personality psychology can open the way to new perspectives. Not only to understand ourselves better, but to apply this knowledge to increase the effectiveness in our relationships, improve our impact on the world around us, increase our levels of happiness and well-being, or any other objective that we have set for ourselves.

We know that there is still a long way to go and that all the ideas contained in this book are susceptible to discussion, deepening, supplementing, and modification. Behavioral biology and genetics are producing findings that were unthinkable in previous decades, at an ever-increasing speed.

Having said that, we believe that there are some ideas that should serve as a starting point for future work or be subject of reflection in the forums where personality as a phenomenon is currently being discussed.

Unique and unrepeatable

We have talked about the biological determinants of our personality. However, one of the conclusions of our reflection is that each one of us is, in the end, unique and unrepeatable.

To begin with, the biological basis of our personality is composed of a chain of random coincidences. We have said that each of our personality traits has its origin in predispositions that can be more or less intense, and with different shades and colors, depending on our particular genetic load for those traits. Let us remember that the presence of a greater or lesser number of genes for a certain trait, and their combination with the presence of other genes, is what would ultimately result in our unique biological basis.

And this is only half the story.

The environment plays a fundamental role in the expression of our genes, since we were inside our mother's womb. An accumulation of thousands of micro and macro experiences, in continuous interaction with our genetic heritage, is what gradually makes us who we are. All the ingredients that compose the recipe for making you into yourself are unrepeatable, and the recipe includes events so early that even you don't keep them in your memory. All influencing each other, systemically, within a cauldron like a single great pottage. Therefore, it is not possible to assume that two people can be the same.

This does not ignore the fact that the careful observation of others, as well as the portraits that we see reflected in literature, cinema, or theater, show us patterns that are totally recognizable to us. And it does not impede us from making predictions about how the people we know will behave in the future, with a high degree of accuracy.

It seems that the most reasonable thing to do is to come to terms with both realities: the existence of personality patterns that can be clearly grouped together, and at the same time, the impossibility of capturing into a typology the enormous complexity of who we are.

There is nothing wrong with you

Our personality structure is an adaptive success. It is built on a set of more or less automatic responses, rooted in hereditary components of our brain, that allow us to adapt to certain recurrent challenges that we must face as a species. It is the result of thousands and thousands of years of evolution, of a natural mechanism that allows us to navigate our social environment successfully.

Our personality has aspects that are deeply rooted, connected to our most central traits, which exercise a powerful and mostly unconscious influence over our perception, our emotionality, and our behavior.

Each of us possesses a valuable set of traits that, when used correctly and in the right situations, will predict a high success rate.

If this were not the case, those traits, along with the genetic predisposition that sustains them, would have become extinct in some evolutionary nook and cranny thousands of years ago.

We do not mean to say that all manifestations of personality are equally adaptive. On the one hand, each trait is more or less adaptive depending on the type of challenge that lies ahead. One and the same trait is not good enough to face any challenge. Not all problems are solved by creating better norms or by applying more force. To learn how to dance the most appropriate way is not to read a book or evaluate the associated risks. When we use our "strengths" and we fail all the same, we are likely to feel frustration and believe that there is something wrong with us. And if we are not aware of our mistake, we will often try to fix this by doing even more of the same.

Sorry. There could be something wrong with you.

The *American Psychological Association* (APA) defines mental disorder as: "any condition characterized by cognitive and emotional disturbances, abnormal behaviors, impaired functioning, or any combination of these". [311]

And mental health like: "a state of mind characterized by emotional well-being, good behavioral adjustment, relative freedom from anxiety and

---

311   APA Dictionary of Psychology; https://dictionary.apa.org/

disabling symptoms, and a capacity to establish constructive relationships and cope with the ordinary demands and stresses of life".

Unfortunately, mental disorders do exist and almost always produce a mismatch in terms of adaptation to the environment. Mental health and adaptation, however, are not the same thing.

A person who is totally healthy from a psychological point of view, may have problems adjusting in an environment that is very alien to his or her natural inclinations.

Think of a Type Five trying to get along within a bubbly, sociable, and outgoing group of people. Or a Type Eight adapting to an environment that values social harmony above all else. Behavioral patterns that are adaptive in some environments or situations may be acutely ineffective in others.

At the other extreme, a psychologically ill person may go unnoticed, adapting relatively well to the needs and challenges of a particular environment. This is a real problem. Because they are apparently well integrated, their disorder may just seem to be "the way they are." A delusional optimism accompanied by a high dose of narcissism may well provide an individual with the certainty of having the absolute truth.

If we add a populist discourse and fool-proof self-confidence, that individual could well be elected to a major public office, affecting the destiny of millions of people. Any examples come to mind? Despite their apparent adaptation, we can detect that such a person would bear the hallmarks of mental illness.

Thus, as we can see, these pathologies do not always entail suffering or discomfort for the affected individual. Sometimes we can only recognize them by the suffering they inflict on others.

The real problem: ignorance and rigidity

It is likely that the one who raises his fist in the middle of the battle shouting "Victory or Death" and advances with sword blows cutting his enemies to pieces, may not be perceiving his fear, nor is he considering the quite definitive effects that death has. Or the one who says, "I will not make a pact with the opposition party, because it is a matter of principle, even if that implies that the country is destroyed," may not be considering that she might be wrong. The perceptual biases within our personality structure make us great experts in the use of some strategies, but leave us in total ignorance of others. There will always be a tendency in us to perceive one part of reality more clearly and to ignore, more or less radically, another part of it.

Without being exhaustive in this, since it will be the subject of new publications, we believe that the road to obtain the greatest benefit from this approach begins with self-awareness. We believe that real self-awareness is built on the basis of two intentional activities that require effort: self-observation from a state of calm, without judgment; and honest openness to the perception of others.

And the object of this effort should be, first of all, to understand our core type. How it behaves, how it acts on us, how it determines our perceptual biases, our deepest emotions, and our most ingrained behaviors. To perceive the "lens" through which we view the world, to observe the "observer," so as not to confuse our automatic perception with an "objective" reality. To observe ourselves in our day-to-day life, to recognize our patterns, to look at ourselves with perspective. To become aware of our subjectivity. To "watch" our structure in action. To know how and when it acts, to detect it, to know exactly which part of reality our perception emphasizes and which part it downplays.

And we have also mentioned the need to listen to others, since this is an irreplaceable source of two types of information that are key pieces in putting together this puzzle: The first, a window to the subjectivity of others can become a mirror to see our own subjectivity. And second, only others can tell us how we look "from the outside": how our actions impact those around us, and how this impact so often differs from our intentions.

In reviewing the types, we saw that there are some that are biologically more predisposed to optimism. They probably have a very favorable attitude toward their own personality structure and feel very comfortable with it. Other types come naturally inclined toward a critical view of themselves and reality, and may feel uncomfortable. They will feel that biology did not favor them and that they have to deal with a structure that offers little advantage. Both cases are equally subjective, equally biased, and in the long run, equally dangerous. If we do not know how to recognize which part of the "truth" we are missing, we will never be able to put the complete picture together.

Mistaking the "invitations" of our serotonin, oxytocin, or adrenaline with the truth will lead us to believe that what we see, think, or say is the "truth." This could have dire consequences for ourselves and others. This is the origin of fanatics, racists, dictators, gurus, possessors of truth, in their different guises. And it is also the source of a great deal of unnecessary suffering, of people who believe that their negative perception of themselves is "true."

Self-awareness is the base, the cornerstone from which to develop new answers that are more effective, fairer, more collaborative, safer, more informed, or more beautiful...choose your adjective according to your structure.

The next step to self-development is practice. There will be times when our most frequently used strategies will perfectly match the challenges that lie ahead. Eureka! For thousands of years that response was being prepared.

There will be other times when we can draw on behaviors and responses typical of our proximal types. All good, they are also comfortable for us.

They are resources and skills that we have at our fingertips. But there will be situations for which the best response, the most adaptive, is one that corresponds to our Absent Types. That's where the opportunity lies.

We propose that the second focus of our work should be to "practice" some behaviors that are distinctive of our Absent Types. We refer to a few, key behaviors, that we have identified as necessary to incorporate into our behavioral "toolbox."

Research in behavioral neurobiology has discovered that the effort to do things "differently" allows us to gradually generate new "neural pathways" in our brain.

The point is that it requires effort. It will feel new, alien, outside our comfort zone. We will resist and have thousands of internal voices telling us it is a bad idea. But only in this way can we expand our repertoire of responses, learn to react more flexibly, and better adapt to the environmental and relational challenges that are most difficult for us. And at the same time, we will trigger a virtuous circle, opening ourselves to a world of new and transforming experiences, which will lead us to emotions, thoughts, and sensations far beyond our usual "square meter."

The prize we will obtain at the end of this road will be the freedom to choose the person we want to be. It is not a total freedom, though. We still have to play with the biological and environmental cards we were given. But even under these restrictions we will be able to choose more freely how we want to live our lives, rather than simply reacting and enduring.

The model of the nine types is only a general map. But it is a powerful aid in taking the first step: it allows us to clarify where to look when we observe ourselves, and it energizes us to "want to change." It also allows us to "downplay" our own emotions and not take ourselves "so seriously."

In summary, once we know the map and are located on it, we believe that the way forward necessarily involves investing effort in self-awareness and practice.

In the long run, this will allow us to develop a more realistic and compassionate look at ourselves and others, gaining in tolerance, in flexibility, in "detachment" from our automatic reactions, and in perspective and depth to look at our life.

Epilogue

The difference was approximately seventy millivolts. A higher electrical charge within the cell allowed a discharge that traveled rapidly through dendrites and axons activating a series of synapses. Specific neurotransmitters circulated to and from the neocortex in perfect coordination between the emotional and the rational functions.

At that moment Trypto knew that this circular stone that collected rainwater would be extremely useful inside the cavern. Now it was left to decide how to move it. He pushed the rock and knew that it was totally impossible to move it even with the help of the strongest men in the band. At once, a quadrillion neural connections between both hemispheres, harmoniously coordinated with the folds of the neocortex, generated an idea in his mind: What if it was the cavern that moved to the stone of water and not the other way around?

He summoned his band together, and they began to build a protection of branches and trees around the stone. They created a shelter, that gave them protection almost as the real could give them.

Trypto reproduced his genetic makeup many times in his long 30 years of life. His descendants were able to process sensations and experiences generating action potentials in certain neurons, being transmitted at unimaginable speeds through synaptic pathways in specific areas of their brains, to generate ideas that would provide solutions to thousands of practical problems. Trypto and his descendants were great problem solvers.

Very close to the intersection of Pine and Nassau Streets, on the fifth floor of an old building, Tania Frolov had her small but comfortable flat. Her family had migrated to the United States from southern Russia in the early 20th century. They were involved in the railway business. Since she was a child, Tania showed great determination and tenacity in pursuing her goals. She excelled in everything she set out to do. For three years she had been operating in the stock market, which is why she had bought that small apartment a few blocks from the Stock Exchange.

That morning on the fifth floor of Pine Street, millions of neurons fired with the hyper-energization of Tania's goal-oriented behavior. She had to generate a strategy for the rapid sale of the shares of a large company. It was five o'clock in the morning. She put on her sneakers and began a four-mile run that ended at the 9/11 memorial, where she usually stopped to reflect and plan her day. The morning was cold, and when she finished her round, she needed a little more time than usual to stretch her muscles. As her head touched her knees, her ventral tegmental area, densely innervated by neurons from the lateral hypothalamus, through her dopaminergic system, made her clearly picture the path to the prize. Potential buyers should visualize the purchase of these shares as an opportunity in connection to a couple of high-profile political events going on at that time. She just had to build the story. She gave up her stretch and ran to her best dress, her Jimmy Choo's, and her high-protein breakfast.

It was 8:30 when she crossed the 11th gate on Wall Street. At 8:45, her computer screen gave her the figures for the markets that had already closed around the world. She mentally prepared herself for the day. She knew she would succeed. By her own experience and by the still traceable genes she had inherited from her ancient relative, Trypto, who, had he seen her, would have enjoyed her accomplishments as much as he had enjoyed his own, 60,000 years ago.

BIBLIOGRAPHY

Introduction

Capra, F. (2003). Las conexiones ocultas, Anagrama, España.

Naranjo, C. (1990). Ennea-type structures: Self-analysis for the seeker. Gateways/ IDHHB Incorporated; Nevada City, CA

Naranjo, C. (1994). Character and neurosis: An integrative view. Gateways/IDHHB; US, United States.

Panksepp, Jaak; Montag, C. (2017). Primary emotional systems and personality: An evolutionary perspective. *Frontiers in Psychology, 8*(AUG), 1414. https://doi. org/10.3389/fpsyg.2017.01414

Penke, L., Jokela, M., & Mu, G. E. (2016). The evolutionary genetics of personality revisited. *Current Opinion in Psychology, 7,* 104–109. https://doi.org/10.1016/j. copsyc.2015.08.021

Pinker, S. (2009). My Genome , My Self. *New York Times.*

Sutton, A. (2007). *Implicit and explicit personality in work settings : an application of Enneagram theory.* The University of Leeds.

Sutton, A. (2012). "But Is It Real?" a Review of Research on the Enneagram. *Enneagram Journal, 5*(1), 5–19. Retrieved from http://libweb.ben.edu/login?url=http://search. ebscohost.com/login.aspx?direct=true&db=a9h&AN=85641962&site=ehost-live

Three things you should know before finding yourself

Akey, J. M. (2009). Constructing genomic maps of positive selection in humans: Where do we go from here? Genome Research, 19(5), 711–722. https://doi. org/10.1101/gr.086652.108

Apicella, C. L., & Barrett, H. C. (2016). ScienceDirect Cross-cultural evolutionary psychology. Current Opinion in Psychology, 7, 92–97. https://doi.org/10.1016/j. copsyc.2015.08.015

Arslan, R. C., & Penke, L. (2014). Evolutionary Genetics. In Handbook of Evolutionary Psychology.

Avinun, R., & Knafo, A. (2014). Parenting as a Reaction Evoked by Children's Genotype: A Meta-Analysis of Children-as-Twins Studies. Personality and Social Psychology Review. https://doi.org/10.1177/1088868313498308

Barrett, H. C. (2006). Modularity and design reincarnation. The Innate Mind: Culture and Cognition, Ed. P. Carruthers, S. Laurence & S. Stich.

Brembs, B., & Hempel De Ibarra, N. (2006). Different parameters support generalization and discrimination learning in Drosophila at the flight simulator. Learning and Memory. https://doi.org/10.1101/lm.319406

Briley, D. A., & Tucker-Drob, E. M. (2014). Genetic and environmental continuity in personality development: A meta-analysis. Psychological Bulletin. https://doi.org/10.1037/a0037091

Buss, D. M., & Hawley, P. H. (2011). The Evolution of Personality and Individual Differences. The Evolution of Personality and Individual Differences. https://doi.org/10.1093/acprof:oso/9780195372090.001.0001

Buss, D. M., & Penke, L. (2012). Evolutionary Personality Psychology. In Handbook of Personality Processes and Individual Differences.

Chabris, C. F., Lee, J. J., Cesarini, D., Benjamin, D. J., & Laibson, D. I. (2015). The Fourth Law of Behavior Genetics. Current Directions in Psychological Science. https://doi.org/10.1177/0963721415580430

Cloninger, R. C., & Zwir, I. (2018). What is the natural measurement unit of temperament: Single traits or profiles? Philosophical Transactions of the Royal Society B: Biological Sciences, 373(1744). https://doi.org/10.1098/rstb.2017.0163

Davis, K. L., & Panksepp, J. (2011). The brain's emotional foundations of human personality and the Affective Neuroscience Personality Scales. Neuroscience and Biobehavioral Reviews, 35(9), 1946–1958. https://doi.org/10.1016/j. neubiorev.2011.04.004

Davis, L. K., Yu, D., Keenan, C. L., Gamazon, E. R., Konkashbaev, A. I., Derks, E. M., ... Scharf, J. M. (2013). Partitioning the Heritability of Tourette Syndrome and Obsessive-Compulsive Disorder Reveals Differences in Genetic Architecture. PLoS Genetics. https://doi.org/10.1371/journal.pgen.1003864

Friedman, N. P., & Miyake, A. (2017). Unity and diversity of executive functions: Individual differences as a window on cognitive structure. Cortex, 86, 186–204. https://doi.org/10.1016/j.cortex.2016.04.023

Garcia, J. R., Mackillop, J., Aller, E. L., Merriwether, A. M., & Sloan, D. (2010). Associations between Dopamine D4 Receptor Gene Variation with Both Infidelity and Sexual Promiscuity. https://doi.org/10.1371/journal.pone.0014162

Gaugler, T., Klei, L., Sanders, S. J., Bodea, C. A., Goldberg, A. P., Lee, A. B., ... Buxbaum, J. D. (2014). Most genetic risk for autism resides with common variation. Nature Genetics. https://doi.org/10.1038/ng.3039

Gratten, J., Wray, N. R., Keller, M. C., & Visscher, P. M. (2014). Large-scale genomics unveils the genetic architecture of psychiatric disorders. Nature Neuroscience. https://doi.org/10.1038/nn.3708

Hill, W. D., Arslan, R. C., Xia, C., Luciano, M., Amador, C., Navarro, P., ... Penke, L. (2018). Genomic analysis of family data reveals additional genetic effects on intelligence and personality. Molecular Psychiatry, 23(12), 2347–2362. https://doi.org/10.1038/s41380-017-0005-1

Insel, T., Cuthbert, B., Garvey, M., Heinssen, R., Pine, D. S., Quinn, K., ... Wang, P. (2010). Research Domain Criteria (RDoC): Toward a new classification framework for research on mental disorders. American Journal of Psychiatry. https://doi.org/10.1176/appi.ajp.2010.09091379

Iversen, S. D., & Iversen, L. L. (2007). Dopamine: 50 years in perspective. Trends in Neurosciences, 30(5), 188–193. https://doi.org/10.1016/j.tins.2007.03.002

Kasper, C., Schreier, T., & Taborsky, B. (2019). Heritabilities, social environment effects and genetic correlations of social behaviours in a cooperatively breeding vertebrate. Journal of Evolutionary Biology, 32(9), 955–973. https://doi.org/10.1111/jeb.13494

Keightley, P. D. (2012). Rates and fitness consequences of new mutations in humans. Genetics. https://doi.org/10.1534/genetics.111.134668

Keller, M. C., & Miller, G. (2006). Resolving the paradox of common, harmful, heritable mental disorders: Which evolutionary genetic models work best? Behavioral and Brain Sciences. https://doi.org/10.1017/S0140525X06009095

Klahr, A. M., & Burt, S. A. (2014). Elucidating the Etiology of Individual Differences in Parenting: A Meta-Analysis of Behavioral Genetic Research. Psychological Bulletin. https://doi.org/10.1037/a0034205

Klei, L., Sanders, S. J., Murtha, M. T., Hus, V., Lowe, J. K., Willsey, A. J., ... Devlin, B. (2012). Common genetic variants, acting additively, are a major source of risk for autism. Molecular Autism. https://doi.org/10.1186/2040-2392-3-9

Lee, S. H. (2018). Close Encounters with Humankind: A Paleoanthropologist Investigates Our Evolving Species. WW Norton & Company; United States of America

Lenton, A. P., Fasolo, B., & Todd, P. M. (2009). The relationship between number of potential mates and mating skew in humans. Animal Behaviour. https://doi.org/10.1016/j.anbehav.2008.08.025

Lukaszewski, A. W. (2013). Testing an Adaptationist Theory of Trait Covariation: Relative Bargaining Power as a Common Calibrator of an Interpersonal Syndrome. European Journal of Personality. https://doi.org/10.1002/per.1908

McAdams, T. A., Gregory, A. M., & Eley, T. C. (2013). Genes of experience: Explaining the heritability of putative environmental variables through their association with behavioural and emotional traits. Behavior Genetics. https://doi.org/10.1007/s10519-013-9591-0

McGue, M., Zhang, Y., Miller, M. B., Basu, S., Vrieze, S., Hicks, B., ... Iacono, W. G. (2013). A genome-wide association study of behavioral disinhibition. Behavior Genetics. https://doi.org/10.1007/s10519-013-9606-x

Montag, C., Widenhorn-müller, K., Panksepp, J., & Kiefer, M. (2017). ScienceDirect Individual differences in Affective Neuroscience Personality Scale (ANPS) primary emotional traits and depressive tendencies. Comprehensive Psychiatry, 73, 136–142. https://doi.org/10.1016/j.comppsych.2016.11.007

Nettle, D. (2006). The Evolution of Personality Variation in Humans and Other Animals, 61(6), 622–631. https://doi.org/10.1037/0003-066X.61.6.622

Panksepp, J. (2011). The basic emotional circuits of mammalian brains: Do animals have affective lives? Neuroscience and Biobehavioral Reviews, 35(9), 1791–1804. https://doi.org/10.1016/j.neubiorev.2011.08.003

Penke, L. (2010). Bridging the Gap Between Modern Evolutionary Psychology and the Study of Individual Differences. In The evolution of personality and individual differences (pp. 241–279).

Penke, L., Denissen, J. J. A., & Miller, G. F. (2007). The Evolutionary Genetics of Personality. European Journal of Personality, 21(January), 549–587. https://doi.org/10.1002/per

Penke, L., Jokela, M., & Mu, G. E. (2016). The evolutionary genetics of personality revisited. Current Opinion in Psychology, 7, 104–109. https://doi.org/10.1016/j.copsyc.2015.08.021

Persico, A. M., & Napolioni, V. (2013). Autism genetics. Behavioural Brain Research, 251, 95–112. https://doi.org/10.1016/j.bbr.2013.06.012

Plomin, R., Defries, J. C., Knopik, V. S., & Neiderhiser, J. M. (2016). Top 10 Replicated Findings From Behavioral Genetics. Perspectives on Psychological Science, 11(1), 3–23. https://doi.org/10.1177/1745691615617439

Plomin, R., Haworth, C. M. A., & Davis, O. S. P. (2009). Common disorders are quantitative traits. Nature Reviews Genetics. https://doi.org/10.1038/nrg2670

Plomin, R., & Simpson, M. A. (2013). The future of genomics for developmentalists. Development and Psychopathology. https://doi.org/10.1017/S0954579413000606

Polderman, T. J. C., Benyamin, B., De Leeuw, C. A., Sullivan, P. F., Van Bochoven, A., Visscher, P. M., & Posthuma, D. (2015). Meta-analysis of the heritability of human traits based on fifty years of twin studies. Nature Genetics. https://doi.org/10.1038/ng.3285

Rietveld, C. A., Cesarini, D., Benjamin, D. J., Koellinger, P. D., De Neve, J. E., Tiemeier, H., ... Bartels, M. (2013). Molecular genetics and subjective well-being. Proceedings of the National Academy of Sciences of the United States of America. https://doi.org/10.1073/pnas.1222171110

Roth, G., & Dicke, U. (2005). Evolution of the brain and intelligence. Trends in Cognitive Sciences. https://doi.org/10.1016/j.tics.2005.03.005

Sapolsky, R. M. (2017). Behave: The biology of humans at our best and worst. New York, NY; Penguin.

Sapolsky, R. M. (2010). Course entitled Human Behavioral Biology, Lecture 15, https://www.youtube.com/watch?v=LOY3QH_jOtE&t=12s; May 2010; Stanford University: http://www.stanford.edu/ Stanford Department of Biology: http://biology.stanford.edu/ Stanford University Channel on YouTube: http://www.youtube.com/stanford

Sinervo, B., & Lively, C. M. (1996). The rock-paper-scissors game and the evolution of alternative male strategies. Nature. https://doi.org/10.1038/380240a0

Turkheimer, E., Pettersson, E., & Horn, E. E. (2014). A Phenotypic Null Hypothesis for the Genetics of Personality. Annual Review of Psychology, 65(1), 515–540. https://doi.org/10.1146/annurev-psych-113011-143752

Verweij, K. J., Yang, J., Lahti, J., Veijola, J., Hintsanen, M., Pulkki-Råback, L., ... & Taanila, A. (2012). Maintenance of genetic variation in human personality: testing evolutionary models by estimating heritability due to common causal variants and investigating the effect of distant inbreeding. Evolution: International Journal of Organic Evolution, 66(10), 3238-3251.

Vinkhuyzen, A. A. E., Pedersen, N. L., Yang, J., Lee, S. H., Magnusson, P. K. E., Iacono, W. G., ... Wray, N. R. (2012). Common SNPs explain some of the variation in the personality dimensions of neuroticism and extraversion. Translational Psychiatry. https://doi.org/10.1038/tp.2012.27

Warrier, V., Toro, R., Won, H., Leblond, C. S., Cliquet, F., Delorme, R., ... Baron-Cohen, S. (2019). Social and non-social autism symptoms and trait domains are genetically dissociable. Communications Biology, 2(1). https://doi.org/10.1038/s42003-019-0558-4

Personality Types

Lee, S. H. (2018). Close Encounters with Humankind: A Paleoanthropologist Investigates Our Evolving Species. WW Norton & Company; United States of America

Meyer-Lindenberg, A., & Weinberger, D. R. (2006). Intermediate phenotypes and genetic mechanisms of psychiatric disorders. Nature Reviews Neuroscience, 7(10), 1–10. Retrieved from papers2://publication/uuid/7FC754D5-397D-4887-86C8-6DB218F64D38

Wynn, T., Coolidge, F., & Bright, M. (2009). Hohlenstein-Stadel and the evolution of human conceptual thought. Cambridge Archaeological Journal. https://doi.org/10.1017/S0959774309000043

Type One: The Regulator

Boehm, C. (2012). Costs and benefits in hunter-gatherer punishment. Behavioral and Brain Sciences. https://doi.org/10.1017/S0140525X11001403

Boehm, C. (2014). The moral consequences of social selection. Behaviour. https://doi.org/10.1163/1568539X-00003143

Foa, E. B., Huppert, J. D., Leiberg, S., Langner, R., Kichic, R., Hajcak, G., & Salkovskis, P. M. (2002). The obsessive-compulsive inventory: Development and validation of a short version. Psychological Assessment. https://doi.org/10.1037/1040-3590.14.4.485

Gogolla, N. (2017). The insular cortex. Current Biology, 27(12), R580–R586. https://doi.org/10.1016/j.cub.2017.05.010

Hu, X. Z., Lipsky, R. H., Zhu, G., Akhtar, L. A., Taubman, J., Greenberg, B. D., ... Goldman, D. (2006). Serotonin transporter promoter gain-of-function genotypes are linked to obsessive-compulsive disorder. American Journal of Human Genetics. https://doi.org/10.1086/503850

Krolak-Salmon, P., Hénaff, M. A., Isnard, J., Tallon-Baudry, C., Guénot, M., Vighetto, A., ... Mauguière, F. (2003). An attention modulated response to disgust in human ventral anterior insula. Annals of Neurology, 53(4), 446–453. https://doi.org/10.1002/ana.10502

Matsumoto, R., Ichise, M., Ito, H., Ando, T., Takahashi, H., Ikoma, Y., ... Suhara, T. (2010). Reduced serotonin transporter binding in the insular cortex in patients with obsessive-compulsive disorder: A [11C]DASB PET study. NeuroImage, 49(1), 121–126. https://doi.org/10.1016/j.neuroimage.2009.07.069

Moller, H. J., Borwin, B., Bauer, M., Hampel, H., Herpertz, S., Soyka, M., ... Maier, W. (2015). DSM-5 reviewed from different angles : goal attainment, rationality , use of evidence , consequences — part 2 : bipolar disorders , schizophrenia spectrum disorders , anxiety disorders , obsessive – compulsive disorders , trauma- and stressor-related dis. European Archives of Psychiatry and Clinical Neuroscience, 87–106. https://doi.org/10.1007/s00406-014-0521-9

Nicholson, E., & Barnes-Holmes, D. (2012). Developing an implicit measure of disgust propensity and disgust sensitivity: Examining the role of implicit disgust propensity and sensitivity in obsessive-compulsive tendencies. Journal

of Behavior Therapy and Experimental Psychiatry, 43(3), 922–930. https://doi.
org/10.1016/j.jbtep.2012.02.001

Perlis, R. H., Holt, D. J., Smoller, J., Blood, A., Lee, S., Kim, B. W., … Breiter, H. C.
(2008). Association of a Polymorphism Near CREB1 With Differential Aversion
Processing in the Insula of Healthy Participants. Archives of General Psychiatry,
65(8), 882–892.

Rosario-Campos, M. C., Miguel, E. C., Quatrano, S., Chacon, P., Ferrao, Y., Findley,
D., … Leckman, J. F. (2006). The Dimensional Yale-Brown Obsessive-Compulsive
Scale (DY-BOCS): An instrument for assessing obsessive-compulsive symptom
dimensions. Molecular Psychiatry. https://doi.org/10.1038/sj.mp.4001798

Rozin, P., & Haidt, J. (2013). The domains of disgust and their origins: Contrasting
biological and cultural evolutionary accounts. Trends in Cognitive Sciences,
17(8), 367–368. https://doi.org/10.1016/j.tics.2013.06.001

Sadri, S. K., McEvoy, P. M., Egan, S. J., Kane, R. T., Rees, C. S., & Anderson, R.
A. (2017). The Relationship between Obsessive Compulsive Personality and
Obsessive Compulsive Disorder Treatment Outcomes : Predictive Utility and
Clinically Significant Change. Behavioural and Cognitive Psychotherapy, (April),
524–529. https://doi.org/10.1017/S1352465817000194

Sapolsky, R. M. (2004). Why zebras don't get ulcers: The acclaimed guide to stress,
stress-related diseases and coping. Holt paperbacks; St Martin's Press; New
York, United States

Sapolsky, R. M. (2010). Course entitled Human Behavioral Biology, Lecture 15,
https://www.youtube.com/watch?v=LOY3QH_jOtE&t=12s ; May 2010; Stanford
University: http://www.stanford.edu/ Stanford Department of Biology: http://
biology.stanford.edu/ Stanford University Channel on YouTube: http://www.
youtube.com/stanford

Sapolsky, R. M. (2011). Course entitled Human Behavioral Biology, Lecture
on The Biological Underpinnings of Religiosity; https://www.youtube.com/
watch?v=4WwAQqWUkpI; Stanford University: http://www.stanford.edu/
Stanford Department of Biology: http://biology.stanford.edu/ Stanford University
Channel on YouTube: http://www.youtube.com/stanford

Sapolsky, R. M. (2017). Behave: The biology of humans at our best and worst. New
York, NY; Penguin.

Shapira, N. A., Liu, Y., He, A. G., Bradley, M. M., Lessig, M. C., James, G. A., … Goodman, W. K. (2003). Brain activation by disgust-inducing pictures in obsessive-compulsive disorder. Biological Psychiatry, 54(7), 751–756. https://doi.org/10.1016/S0006-3223(03)00003-9

Stengler-Wenzke, K., Müller, U., Angermeyer, M. C., Sabri, O., & Hesse, S. (2004). Reduced serotonin transporter-availability in obsessive-compulsive disorder (OCD). European Archives of Psychiatry and Clinical Neuroscience. https://doi.org/10.1007/s00406-004-0489-y

Watson, D., & Wu, K. D. (2005). Development and validation of the Schedule of Compulsions, Obsessions, and Pathological Impulses (SCOPI). Assessment. https://doi.org/10.1177/1073191104271483

Wicker, B., Keysers, C., Plailly, J., Royet, J. P., Gallese, V., & Rizzolatti, G. (2003). Both of us disgusted in My insula: The common neural basis of seeing and feeling disgust. Neuron, 40(3), 655–664. https://doi.org/10.1016/S0896-6273(03)00679-2

Wu, K. D., Clark, L. A., & Watson, D. (2006). Relations between Obsessive-Compulsive Disorder and personality: Beyond Axis I-Axis II comorbidity. Journal of Anxiety Disorders. https://doi.org/10.1016/j.janxdis.2005.11.001

Wu, K. D., & Cortesi, G. T. (2008). Relations between perfectionism and obsessive – compulsive symptoms : Examination of specificity among the dimensions. Journal of Anxiety Disorders, 23, 393–400. https://doi.org/10.1016/j.janxdis.2008.11.006

Ying, X., Luo, J., Chiu, C. yue, Wu, Y., Xu, Y., & Fan, J. (2018). Functional dissociation of the posterior and anterior insula in moral disgust. Frontiers in Psychology, 9(JUN), 1–10. https://doi.org/10.3389/fpsyg.2018.00860

Type Two: The Social Weaver

Apicella, C. L., & Barrett, H. C. (2016). ScienceDirect Cross-cultural evolutionary psychology. Current Opinion in Psychology, 7, 92–97. https://doi.org/10.1016/j.copsyc.2015.08.015

Aragona, B. J. (2009). Dopamine regulation of social choice in a monogamous rodent species. Frontiers in Behavioral Neuroscience, 3(August), 1–11. https://doi.org/10.3389/neuro.08.015.2009

Aspé-Sánchez, M., Moreno, M., Rivera, M. I., Rossi, A., & Ewer, J. (2016). Oxytocin and vasopressin receptor gene polymorphisms: Role in social and psychiatric traits. *Frontiers in Neuroscience, 9*(JAN). https://doi.org/10.3389/fnins.2015.00510

Campbell, A. (2010). Oxytocin and human social behavior. *Personality and Social Psychology Review, 14*(3), 281–295. https://doi.org/10.1177/1088868310363594

Centro de Secuenciación del Genoma Humano (Baylor College of Medicine); retrieved from: https://www.hgsc.bcm.edu/

Curtis, J. T., Yu, Y. J., Insel, T. R., Detwiler, J. M., Aragona, B. J., Liu, Y., & Wang, Z. (2005). Nucleus accumbens dopamine differentially mediates the formation and maintenance of monogamous pair bonds. *Nature Neuroscience, 9*(1), 133–139. https://doi.org/10.1038/nn1613

De Dreu, C. K. W., Greer, L. L., Van Kleef, G. A., Shalvi, S., & Handgraaf, M. J. J. (2011). Oxytocin promotes human ethnocentrism. *Proceedings of the National Academy of Sciences of the United States of America.* https://doi.org/10.1073/pnas.1015316108

Domes, G., Heinrichs, M., Michel, A., Berger, C., & Herpertz, S. C. (2007). Oxytocin Improves "Mind-Reading" in Humans. *Biological Psychiatry.* https://doi.org/10.1016/j.biopsych.2006.07.015

Dyble, M., Thompson, J., Smith, D., Salali, G. D., Chaudhary, N., Page, A. E., … Migliano, A. B. (2016). Networks of Food Sharing Reveal the Functional Significance of Multilevel Sociality in Two Hunter-Gatherer Groups. *Current Biology, 26*(15), 2017–2021. https://doi.org/10.1016/j.cub.2016.05.064

Hamilton, M. J., Buchanan, B., & Walker, R. S. (2018). SCALING the SIZE, STRUCTURE, and DYNAMICS of RESIDENTIALLY MOBILE HUNTER-GATHERER CAMPS. *American Antiquity, 83*(4), 701–720. https://doi.org/10.1017/aaq.2018.39

Hercules, D. M., Curtis, J. T., Yu, Y. J., Insel, T. R., Detwiler, J. M., Aragona, B. J., … Aragona, B. J. (2016). Variation in the β-endorphin, oxytocin, and dopamine receptor genes is associated with different dimensions of human sociality. *Proceedings of the National Academy of Sciences, 3*(3), E4898. https://doi.org/10.1073/pnas.1708178114

Israel, S., Lerer, E., Shalev, I., Uzefovsky, F., Riebold, M., Laiba, E., … Ebstein, R. P. (2009). The oxytocin receptor (OXTR) contributes to prosocial fund allocations in the Dictator Game and the social value orientations task. *PLoS ONE*. https://doi.org/10.1371/journal.pone.0005535

Jacob, S., Brune, C. W., Carter, C. S., Leventhal, B. L., Lord, C., & Cook, E. H. (2007). Association of the oxytocin receptor gene (OXTR) in Caucasian children and adolescents with autism. *Neuroscience Letters*. https://doi.org/10.1016/j.neulet.2007.02.001

Knobloch, H. S., Charlet, A., Hoffmann, L. C., Eliava, M., Khrulev, S., Cetin, A. H., … Grinevich, V. (2012). Evoked axonal oxytocin release in the central amygdala attenuates fear response. *Neuron, 73*(3), 553–566. https://doi.org/10.1016/j.neuron.2011.11.030

Kosfeld, M., Heinrichs, M., Zak, P. J., Fischbacher, U., & Fehr, E. (2005). Oxytocin increases trust in humans. *Nature*. https://doi.org/10.1038/nature03701

Lee, S. H. (2018). Close Encounters with Humankind: A Paleoanthropologist Investigates Our Evolving Species. WW Norton & Company; United States of America

Liu, X., Kawamura, Y., Shimada, T., Otowa, T., Koishi, S., Sugiyama, T., … Sasaki, T. (2010). Association of the oxytocin receptor (OXTR) gene polymorphisms with autism spectrum disorder (ASD) in the Japanese population. *Journal of Human Genetics*. https://doi.org/10.1038/jhg.2009.140

McDonald, N. M., Baker, J. K., & Messinger, D. S. (2016). Oxytocin and parent-child interaction in the development of empathy among children at risk for autism. *Developmental Psychology*. https://doi.org/10.1037/dev0000104

Rodrigues, S. M., Saslow, L. R., Garcia, N., John, O. P., & Keltner, D. (2009). Oxytocin receptor genetic variation relates to empathy and stress reactivity in humans. *Proceedings of the National Academy of Sciences of the United States of America*. https://doi.org/10.1073/pnas.0909579106

Sapolsky, R. M. (2010). Course entitled Human Behavioral Biology, Lecture 15, https://www.youtube.com/watch?v=LOY3QH_jOtE&t=12s ; May 2010; Stanford University: http://www.stanford.edu/ Stanford Department of Biology: http://biology.stanford.edu/ Stanford University Channel on YouTube: http://www.youtube.com/stanford

Sapolsky, R. M. (2017). Behave: The biology of humans at our best and worst. New York, NY; Penguin.

Savaskan, E., Ehrhardt, R., Schulz, A., Walter, M., & Schächinger, H. (2008). Post-learning intranasal oxytocin modulates human memory for facial identity. *Psychoneuroendocrinology*. https://doi.org/10.1016/j.psyneuen.2007.12.004

Shamay-Tsoory, S. G., Fischer, M., Dvash, J., Harari, H., Perach-Bloom, N., & Levkovitz, Y. (2009). Intranasal Administration of Oxytocin Increases Envy and Schadenfreude (Gloating). *Biological Psychiatry*. https://doi.org/10.1016/j.biopsych.2009.06.009

Skuse, D. H., Lori, A., Cubells, J. F., Lee, I., Conneely, K. N., Puura, K., ... Young, L. J. (2014). Common polymorphism in the oxytocin receptor gene (OXTR) is associated with human social recognition skills. *Proceedings of the National Academy of Sciences of the United States of America*. https://doi.org/10.1073/pnas.1302985111

Smeltzer, M. D., Curtis, J. T., Aragona, B. J., & Wang, Z. (2006). Dopamine, oxytocin, and vasopressin receptor binding in the medial prefrontal cortex of monogamous and promiscuous voles. *Neuroscience Letters*, *394*(2), 146–151. https://doi.org/10.1016/j.neulet.2005.10.019

Walum, H., Westberg, L., Henningsson, S., Neiderhiser, J. M., Reiss, D., Igl, W., ... Lichtenstein, P. (2008). Genetic variation in the vasopressin receptor 1a gene (AVPR1A) associates with pair-bonding behavior in humans. *Proceedings of the National Academy of Sciences*, *105*(37), 14153–14156. https://doi.org/10.1073/pnas.0803081105

Wu, S., Jia, M., Ruan, Y., Liu, J., Guo, Y., Shuang, M., ... Zhang, D. (2005). Positive association of the oxytocin receptor gene (OXTR) with autism in the Chinese Han population. *Biological Psychiatry*. https://doi.org/10.1016/j.biopsych.2005.03.013

Zak, P. J. (2017). The neuroscience of trust. Harvard Business Review, 95(1), 84-90.

Zak, P. J., Stanton, A. A., & Ahmadi, S. (2007). Oxytocin increases generosity in humans. *PLoS ONE*. https://doi.org/10.1371/journal.pone.0001128

Type Three: The Hunter

Aston-Jones, G., Smith, R. J., Sartor, G. C., Moorman, D. E., Massi, L., Tahsili-Fahadan, P., & Richardson, K. A. (2010). Lateral hypothalamic orexin/hypocretin neurons: A role in reward-seeking and addiction. *Brain Research*. https://doi.org/10.1016/j.brainres.2009.09.106

Briers, B., Pandelaere, M., Dewitte, S., & Warlop, L. (2006). Hungry for money. *Psychological Science*, *17*(11), 939–943. https://doi.org/10.1111/j.1467-9280.2006.01808.x

Friedman, N. P., & Miyake, A. (2017). Unity and diversity of executive functions: Individual differences as a window on cognitive structure. *Cortex*, *86*, 186–204. https://doi.org/10.1016/j.cortex.2016.04.023

Harari, Yuval N. (2014). Sapiens: A brief history of humankind. Random House, London.

Hills, T. T. (2005). Animal Foraging and the Evolution of Goal-Directed Cognition Thomas. *Cognitive Science*, *37*(2), 3–41. https://doi.org/10.1016/j.neuron.2017.12.022

Ikemoto, S., Yang, C., & Tan, A. (2015). Basal ganglia circuit loops, dopamine and motivation: A review and enquiry. *Behavioural Brain Research*, *290*, 17–31. https://doi.org/10.1016/j.bbr.2015.04.018

Li, J., Hu, Z., & De Lecea, L. (2014). The hypocretins/orexins: Integrators of multiple physiological functions. *British Journal of Pharmacology*. https://doi.org/10.1111/bph.12415

Pantazis, C. B., James, M. H., Bentzley, B. S., & Aston-Jones, G. (2019). The number of lateral hypothalamus orexin/hypocretin neurons contributes to individual differences in cocaine demand. *Addiction Biology*. https://doi.org/10.1111/adb.12795

Sapolsky, R. M. (2012). The Trouble with Testosterone (And Other Essays on the Biology of the Human Predicament). *The American Biology Teacher*. https://doi.org/10.2307/4450505

Sapolsky, R. M. (2017). Behave: The biology of humans at our best and worst. New York, NY; Penguin.

Thompson, M. D., Xhaard, H., Sakurai, T., Rainero, I., & Kukkonen, J. P. (2014). OX1 and OX2 orexin/hypocretin receptor pharmacogenetics. *Frontiers in Neuroscience*. https://doi.org/10.3389/fnins.2014.00057

Tyree, S. M., & de Lecea, L. (2017). Lateral Hypothalamic Control of the Ventral Tegmental Area: Reward Evaluation and the Driving of Motivated Behavior. *Frontiers in Systems Neuroscience*, *11*(July), 1–9. https://doi.org/10.3389/fnsys.2017.00050

Wingfield, J. C., Hegner, R. E., Dufty, A. M., & Ball, G. F. (1990). The "challenge hypothesis": theoretical implications for patterns of testosterone secretion, mating systems, and breeding strategies." *American Naturalist.* https://doi.org/10.1086/285134

Wingfield, John C. (2017). The challenge hypothesis: Where it began and relevance to humans. *Hormones and Behavior.* https://doi.org/10.1016/j.yhbeh.2016.11.008

Type Four: The Wizard

Bernhardt, B. C., & Singer, T. (2012). The Neural Basis of Empathy. Annual Review of Neuroscience. https://doi.org/10.1146/annurev-neuro-062111-150536

Bonenberger, M., Plener, P. L., Groschwitz, R. C., Grön, G., & Abler, B. (2015). Polymorphism in the µ-opioid receptor gene (OPRM1) modulates neural processing of physical pain, social rejection and error processing. Experimental Brain Research, 233(9), 2517–2526. https://doi.org/10.1007/s00221-015-4322-9

Coghill, R. C., McHaffie, J. G., & Yen, Y. F. (2003). Neural correlates of interindividual differences in the subjective experience of pain. Proceedings of the National Academy of Sciences of the United States of America, 100(14), 8538–8542. https://doi.org/10.1073/pnas.1430684100

Fuchs, P. N., Peng, Y. B., Boyette-Davis, J. A., & Uhelski, M. L. (2014). The anterior cingulate cortex and pain processing. Frontiers in Integrative Neuroscience, 8(MAY), 1–10. https://doi.org/10.3389/fnint.2014.00035

Goleman, D., & Boyatzis, R. (2017). Emotional intelligence has 12 elements. Which do you need to work on. Harvard Business Review, 84(2), 1-5.

Iannetti, G. D., Salomons, T. V., Moayedi, M., Mouraux, A., & Davis, K. D. (2013). Beyond metaphor: Contrasting mechanisms of social and physical pain. Trends in Cognitive Sciences. https://doi.org/10.1016/j.tics.2013.06.002

Marsh, A. A., Finger, E. C., Fowler, K. A., Adalio, C. J., Jurkowitz, I. T. N., Schechter, J. C., … Blair, R. J. R. (2013). Empathic responsiveness in amygdala and anterior cingulate cortex in youths with psychopathic traits. Journal of Child Psychology and Psychiatry and Allied Disciplines, 54(8), 900–910. https://doi.org/10.1111/jcpp.12063

Navratilova, E., Xie, J. Y., Meske, D., Qu, C., Morimura, K., Okun, A., … Porreca, F. (2015). Endogenous opioid activity in the anterior cingulate cortex is required for relief of pain. Journal of Neuroscience, 35(18), 7264–7271. https://doi.org/10.1523/JNEUROSCI.3862-14.2015

Rainville, P. (2002). Brain mechanisms of pain affect and pain modulation. Current Opinion in Neurobiology. https://doi.org/10.1016/S0959-4388(02)00313-6

Sapolsky, R. M. (2017). Behave: The biology of humans at our best and worst. New York, NY; Penguin.

Shackman, A. J., Salomons, T. V., Slagter, H. A., Fox, A. S., Winter, J. J., & Davidson, R. J. (2011). The integration of negative affect, pain and cognitive control in the cinculate. Nature, 12, 154–167.

Shackman, A. J., Stockbridge, M. D., Tillman, R. M., Kaplan, C. M., Tromp, D. P. M., Fox, A. S., & Gamer, M. (2016). The Neurobiology of Dispositional Negativity and Attentional Biases to Threat: Implications for Understanding Anxiety Disorders in Adults and Youth. Journal of Experimental Psychopathology, 7(3), 311–342. https://doi.org/10.5127/jep.054015

Tolkien, J. R. R. (2012). The Fellowship of the Ring: Being the first part of The Lord of the Rings (Vol. 1). Houghton Mifflin Harcourt

Villemure, C., & Bushnell, M. C. (2009). Mood influences supraspinal pain processing separately from attention. Journal of Neuroscience. https://doi.org/10.1523/JNEUROSCI.3822-08.2009

Wager, T. D., Atlas, L. Y., Lindquist, M. A., Roy, M., Woo, C. W., & Kross, E. (2013). An fMRI-based neurologic signature of physical pain. New England Journal of Medicine. https://doi.org/10.1056/NEJMoa1204471

Wynn, T., Coolidge, F., & Bright, M. (2009). Hohlenstein-Stadel and the evolution of human conceptual thought. Cambridge Archaeological Journal. https://doi.org/10.1017/S0959774309000043

Type Five: The Sage

Abrahams, B. S., & Geschwind, D. H. (2008). Advances in autism genetics: On the threshold of a new neurobiology. *Nature Reviews Genetics*. https://doi.org/10.1038/nrg2346

Aron, E. N., & Aron, A. (1997). Sensory-Processing Sensitivity and Its Relation to Introversion and Emotionality. *Journal of Personality and Social Psychology*, 73(2), 345–368. https://doi.org/10.1037/0022-3514.73.2.345

Baron-Cohen, S., Richler, J., Bisarya, D., Gurunathan, N., & Wheelwright, S. (2003). The systemizing quotient: An investigation of adults with Asperger syndrome or high-functioning autism, and normal sex differences. *Philosophical Transactions of the Royal Society B: Biological Sciences.* https://doi.org/10.1098/rstb.2002.1206

Baron-Cohen, S., & Wheelwright, S. (2004). The empathy quotient: An investigation of adults with asperger syndrome or high functioning autism, and normal sex differences. *Journal of Autism and Developmental Disorders.* https://doi.org/10.1023/B:JADD.0000022607.19833.00

Blatt, G. J., Fitzgerald, C. M., Guptill, J. T., Booker, A. B., Kemper, T. L., & Bauman, M. L. (2001). Density and Distribution of Hippocampal Neurotransmitter Receptors in Autism: An Autoradiographic Study. *Journal of Autism and Developmental Disorders.* https://doi.org/10.1023/A:1013238809666

Brix, M. K., Ersland, L., Hugdahl, K., Grüner, R., Posserud, M. B., Hammar, Å., ... Beyer, M. K. (2015). "Brain MR spectroscopy in autism spectrum disorder—The GABA excitatory/inhibitory imbalance theory revisited." *Frontiers in Human Neuroscience,* 9(JUNE), 1–12. https://doi.org/10.3389/fnhum.2015.00365

Cederlund, M., Hagberg, B., Billstedt, E., Gillberg, I. C., & Gillberg, C. (2008). Asperger syndrome and autism: A comparative longitudinal follow-up study more than 5 years after original diagnosis. *Journal of Autism and Developmental Disorders.* https://doi.org/10.1007/s10803-007-0364-6

Collins, A. L., Ma, D., Whitehead, P. L., Martin, E. R., Wright, H. H., Abramson, R. K., ... Pericak-Vance, M. A. (2006). Investigation of autism and GABA receptor subunit genes in multiple ethnic groups. *Neurogenetics,* 7(3), 167–174. https://doi.org/10.1007/s10048-006-0045-1

Constantino, J. N., & Todd, R. D. (2005). Intergenerational transmission of subthreshold autistic traits in the general population. *Biological Psychiatry.* https://doi.org/10.1016/j.biopsych.2004.12.014

Courchesne, E., & Pierce, K. (2005). Why the frontal cortex in autism might be talking only to itself: Local over-connectivity but long-distance disconnection. *Current Opinion in Neurobiology.* https://doi.org/10.1016/j.conb.2005.03.001

Diógenes Laercio (412-323 AC); Vidas, opiniones y sentencias de los filósofos más ilustres, retrieved from (https://es.wikipedia.org/wiki/Di%C3%B3genes_Laercio)

Greenberg, D. M., Warrier, V., Allison, C., & Baron-Cohen, S. (2018). Testing the empathizing–systemizing theory of sex differences and the extreme male brain theory of autism in half a million people. *Proceedings of the National Academy of Sciences of the United States of America.* https://doi.org/10.1073/pnas.1811032115

Harari, Yuval N. (2014). Sapiens: A brief history of humankind. Random House, London.

Hoekstra, R. A., Bartels, M., Verweij, C. J. H., & Boomsma, D. I. (2007). Heritability of autistic traits in the general population. *Archives of Pediatrics and Adolescent Medicine.* https://doi.org/10.1001/archpedi.161.4.372

Hussman, J. P. (2001). Suppressed gabaergic inhibition as a common factor in suspected etiologies of autism [1]. *Journal of Autism and Developmental Disorders.* https://doi.org/10.1023/A:1010715619091

Jing-Quiong, K., & Barnes, G. (2012). A Common Susceptibility Factor of Autism and Epilepsy: Funcional Deficiency of GABAa Receptors. *Journal of Autism and Developmental Disorders.*

Mahdavi, M., Kheirollahi, M., Riahi, R., Khorvash, F., Khorrami, M., & Mirsafaie, M. (2018). Meta-Analysis of the Association between GABA Receptor Polymorphisms and Autism Spectrum Disorder (ASD). *Journal of Molecular Neuroscience, 65*(1), 1–9. https://doi.org/10.1007/s12031-018-1073-7

Maximo, J. O., Cadena, E. J., & Kana, R. K. (2014). The implications of brain connectivity in the neuropsychology of autism. *Neuropsychology Review, 24*(1), 16–31. https://doi.org/10.1007/s11065-014-9250-0

McPheeters, M. L., Warren, Z., Sathe, N., Bruzek, J. L., Krishnaswami, S., Jerome, R. N., & Veenstra-VanderWeele, J. (2011). A systematic review of medical treatments for children with autism spectrum disorders. *Pediatrics.* https://doi.org/10.1542/peds.2011-0427

Noonan, S. K., Haist, F., & Müller, R. A. (2009). Aberrant functional connectivity in autism: Evidence from low-frequency BOLD signal fluctuations. *Brain Research.* https://doi.org/10.1016/j.brainres.2008.12.076

Perreault, C., & Mathew, S. (2012). Dating the origin of language using phonemic diversity. *PLoS ONE, 7*(4). https://doi.org/10.1371/journal.pone.0035289

Persico, A. M., & Napolioni, V. (2013). Autism genetics. *Behavioural Brain Research, 251*, 95–112. https://doi.org/10.1016/j.bbr.2013.06.012

Rubenstein, J. L. R. (2010). Three hypotheses for developmental defects that may underlie some forms of autism spectrum disorder. *Current Opinion in Neurology.* https://doi.org/10.1097/WCO.0b013e328336eb13

Sapolsky, R. M. (2010a). Course entitled Human Behavioral Biology, Lecture 8: Recognizing Relatives; https://www.youtube.com/watch?v=P388gUP-Sq_I&list=PL848F2368C90DDC3D&index=9&t=0s; April 2010; Stanford University: http://www.stanford.edu/ Stanford Department of Biology: http://biology.stanford.edu/ Stanford University Channel on YouTube: http://www.youtube.com/stanford

Sapolsky, R. M. (2010b). Course entitled Human Behavioral Biology, Lecture 22: Emergence and Complexity, https://www.youtube.com/watch?v=o_ZuWbX-CyE&list=PL848F2368C90DDC3D&index=22; Stanford University: http://www.stanford.edu/ Stanford Department of Biology: http://biology.stanford.edu/ Stanford University Channel on YouTube: http://www.youtube.com/stanford

Sapolsky, R. M. (2017). Behave: The biology of humans at our best and worst. New York, NY; Penguin.

Smolewska, K. A., McCabe, S. B., & Woody, E. Z. (2006). A psychometric evaluation of the Highly Sensitive Person Scale: The components of sensory-processing sensitivity and their relation to the BIS/BAS and "Big Five." *Personality and Individual Differences, 40*(6), 1269–1279. https://doi.org/10.1016/j.paid.2005.09.022

Sucksmith, E., Roth, I., & Hoekstra, R. A. (2011). Autistic traits below the clinical threshold: Re-examining the broader autism phenotype in the 21st century. *Neuropsychology Review.* https://doi.org/10.1007/s11065-011-9183-9

Warren, Z., McPheeters, M. L., Sathe, N., Foss-Feig, J. H., Glasser, A., & Veenstra-VanderWeele, J. (2011). A systematic review of early intensive intervention for autism spectrum disorders. *Pediatrics.* https://doi.org/10.1542/peds.2011-0426

Warrier, V., Toro, R., Won, H., Leblond, C. S., Cliquet, F., Delorme, R., ... Baron-Cohen, S. (2019). Social and non-social autism symptoms and trait domains are genetically dissociable. *Communications Biology, 2*(1). https://doi.org/10.1038/s42003-019-0558-4

Type Six: The Guardian

Bezdek, K. G., & Telzer, E. H. (2017). Have No Fear, the Brain is Here! How Your Brain Responds to Stress. *Frontiers for Young Minds.* https://doi.org/10.3389/frym.2017.00071

Buss, D. M., & Penke, L. (2012). Evolutionary Personality Psychology. In *Handbook of Personality Processes and Individual Differences.*

Caspi, A., & Silva, P. A. (1995). Temperamental Qualities at Age Three Predict Personality Traits in Young Adulthood : Longitudinal Evidence from a Birth Cohort Author (s): Avshalom Caspi and Phil A . Silva Published by : Wiley on behalf of the Society for Research in Child Development. *Wiley on Behalf of the Society for Research in Child Development, 66*(2), 486–498.

Cicchetti, D., & Rogosch, F. A. (2012). Gene × environment interaction and resilience: Effects of child maltreatment and serotonin, corticotropin releasing hormone, dopamine, and oxytocin genes. *Development and Psychopathology, 24*(2), 411–427. https://doi.org/10.1017/S0954579412000077

Desimone, R., & Duncan, J. (1995). Neural Mechanisms of Selective Visual Attention. *Annual Review of Neuroscience.* https://doi.org/10.1146/annurev.ne.18.030195.001205

Elliot, A. J., & Thrash, T. M. (2010). Approach and Avoidance Temperament as Basic Dimensions of Personality. *Journal of Personality.* https://doi.org/10.1111/j.1467-6494.2010.00636.x

Ewbank, M. P., Lawrence, A. D., Passamonti, L., Keane, J., Peers, P. V., & Calder, A. J. (2009). Anxiety predicts a differential neural response to attended and unattended facial signals of anger and fear. *NeuroImage.* https://doi.org/10.1016/j.neuroimage.2008.09.056

Gurven, M., & Kaplan, H. (2007). Longevity Among Gatherers Examination: A Cross-Cultural Examination. *Population and Development Review, 33*(2), 321–365.

Ikemoto, S., Yang, C., & Tan, A. (2015). Basal ganglia circuit loops, dopamine and motivation: A review and enquiry. *Behavioural Brain Research, 290*, 17–31. https://doi.org/10.1016/j.bbr.2015.04.018

Janke, K. L., Cominski, T. P., Kuzhikandathil, E. V., Servatius, R. J., & Pang, K. C. H. (2015). Investigating the role of hippocampal BDNF in anxiety vulnerability using classical eyeblink conditioning. *Frontiers in Psychiatry.* https://doi.org/10.3389/fpsyt.2015.00106

Kopala-Sibley, D. C., Klein, D. N., Perlman, G., & Kotov, R. (2017). Self-criticism and dependency in female adolescents: Prediction of first onsets and disentangling the relationships between personality, stressful life events, and internalizing psychopathology. *Journal of Abnormal Psychology.* https://doi.org/10.1037/abn0000297

LeDoux, J. E., & Pine, D. S. (2016). Using neuroscience to help understand fear and anxiety: A two-system framework. *American Journal of Psychiatry.* https://doi.org/10.1176/appi.ajp.2016.16030353

Moffitt, T. E., Caspi, A., Harrington, H., Milne, B. J., Melchior, M., Goldberg, D., & Poulton, R. (2007). Generalized anxiety disorder and depression: Childhood risk factors in a birth cohort followed to age 32. *Psychological Medicine, 37*(3), 441–452. https://doi.org/10.1017/S0033291706009640

Nettle, D. (2006). The Evolution of Personality Variation in Humans and Other Animals, *61*(6), 622–631. https://doi.org/10.1037/0003-066X.61.6.622

Pfeifer, M., Goldsmith, H. H., Davidson, R. J., & Rickman, M. (2002). Continuity and change in inhibited and uninhibited children. *Child Development.* https://doi.org/10.1111/1467-8624.00484

Posner, M. I., Rothbart, M. K., Sheese, B. E., & Voelker, P. (2012). Control networks and neuromodulators of early development. *Developmental Psychology.* https://doi.org/10.1037/a0025530

Roberts, B. W., Caspi, A., & Moffitt, T. E. (2003). Work Experiences and Personality Development in Young Adulthood. *Journal of Personality and Social Psychology.* https://doi.org/10.1037/0022-3514.84.3.582

Sapolsky, R. M. (2004). Why zebras don't get ulcers: *A guide to stress, stress related diseases, and coping.* Holt paperbacks; St Martin's Press; New York, United States https://doi.org/10.1002/cir.3880060119

Sapolsky, R. M. (2010). Course entitled Human Behavioral Biology, Lecture 18: Aggression II, retrieved from: https://www.youtube.com/watch?v=wLE71i4JJiM&list=PL848F2368C90DDC3D&index=18; May 2010; Stanford University: http://www.stanford.edu/ Stanford Department of Biology: http://biology.stanford.edu/ Stanford University Channel on YouTube: http://www.youtube.com/stanford

Sapolsky, R. M. (2017). Behave: The biology of humans at our best and worst. New York, NY; Penguin.

Schwartz, C. E., Snidman, N., & Kagan, J. (1999). Adolescent social anxiety as an outcome of inhibited temperament in childhood. *Journal of*

the American Academy of Child and Adolescent Psychiatry. https://doi.
org/10.1097/00004583-199908000-00017

Shackman, A. J., Stockbridge, M. D., Tillman, R. M., Kaplan, C. M., Tromp, D. P. M.,
Fox, A. S., & Gamer, M. (2016). The Neurobiology of Dispositional Negativity and
Attentional Biases to Threat: Implications for Understanding Anxiety Disorders
in Adults and Youth. *Journal of Experimental Psychopathology, 7*(3), 311–342.
https://doi.org/10.5127/jep.054015

Sleijpen, M., Heitland, I., Mooren, T., & Kleber, R. J. (2017). Resilience in refu-
gee and Dutch adolescents: Genetic variability in the corticotropin releasing
hormone receptor 1. *Personality and Individual Differences, 111,* 211–214. https://
doi.org/10.1016/j.paid.2017.02.002

Stegmann, Y., Reicherts, P., Andreatta, M., Pauli, P., & Wieser, M. J. (2019). The
effect of trait anxiety on attentional mechanisms in combined context and cue
conditioning and extinction learning. *Scientific Reports.* https://doi.org/10.1038/
s41598-019-45239-3

Stout, D. M., Shackman, A. J., Pedersen, W. S., Miskovich, T. A., & Larson, C.
L. (2017). Neural circuitry governing anxious individuals' mis-allocation of
working memory to threat. *Scientific Reports, 7*(1), 1–11. https://doi.org/10.1038/
s41598-017-08443-7

Thomaes, S., Bushman, B. J., Orobio De Castro, B., & Stegge, H. (2009). What makes
narcissists bloom? A framework for research on the etiology and development
of narcissism. *Development and Psychopathology, 21*(4), 1233–1247. https://doi.
org/10.1017/S0954579409990137

Tolkien, J. R. R. (2012). The Fellowship of the Ring: Being the first part of The Lord
of the Rings (Vol. 1). Houghton Mifflin Harcourt

Weber, H., Richter, J., Straube, B., Lueken, U., Domschke, K., Schartner, C., … Reif,
A. (2016). Allelic variation in CRHR1 predisposes to panic disorder: Evidence for
biased fear processing. *Molecular Psychiatry.* https://doi.org/10.1038/mp.2015.125

Type Seven: The Explorer

Akst, Jef (2019). Neanderthal DNA in Modern Human Genomes Is
Not Silent. Retrieved from: https://www.the-scientist.com/features/
neanderthal-dna-in-modern-human-genomes-is-not-silent-66299

Chen, C., Burton, M., Greenberger, E., & Dmitrieva, J. (1999). Population migration and the variation of dopamine D4 receptor (DRD4) allele frequencies around the globe. *Evolution and Human Behavior.* https://doi.org/10.1016/S1090-5138(99)00015-X

Congdon, E., Lesch, K. P., & Canli, T. (2008). Analysis of DRD4 and DAT polymorphisms and behavioral inhibition in healthy adults: Implications for impulsivity. *American Journal of Medical Genetics, Part B: Neuropsychiatric Genetics.* https://doi.org/10.1002/ajmg.b.30557

Eisenberg, D. T. A., Campbell, B., MacKillop, J., Modi, M., Dang, D., Lum, J. K., & Wilson, D. S. (2007). Polymorphisms in the Dopamine D4 and D2 Receptor Genes and Reproductive and Sexual Behaviors. *Evolutionary Psychology.* https://doi.org/10.1177/147470490700500402

Friedman, N. P., & Miyake, A. (2017). Unity and diversity of executive functions: Individual differences as a window on cognitive structure. *Cortex, 86,* 186–204. https://doi.org/10.1016/j.cortex.2016.04.023

Garcia, J. R., Mackillop, J., Aller, E. L., Merriwether, A. M., & Sloan, D. (2010). Associations between Dopamine D4 Receptor Gene Variation with Both Infidelity and Sexual Promiscuity. https://doi.org/10.1371/journal.pone.0014162

Guo, G., Tong, Y., Xie, C. W., & Lange, L. A. (2007). Dopamine transporter, gender, and number of sexual partners among young adults. *European Journal of Human Genetics.* https://doi.org/10.1038/sj.ejhg.5201763

Harpending, H., & Cochran, G. (2002). In our genes. *Proceedings of the National Academy of Sciences of the United States of America.* https://doi.org/10.1073/pnas.012612799

Hills, T. T. (2006). Animal foraging and the evolution of goal-directed cognition. *Cognitive Science, 30*(1), 3–41. https://doi.org/10.1207/s15516709cog0000_50

Iversen, S. D., & Iversen, L. L. (2007). Dopamine: 50 years in perspective. *Trends in Neurosciences, 30*(5), 188–193. https://doi.org/10.1016/j.tins.2007.03.002

Kolodny, O., & Feldman, M. W. (2017). A parsimonious neutral model suggests Neanderthal replacement was determined by migration and random species drift. *Nature Communications.* https://doi.org/10.1038/s41467-017-01043-z

Krause, K. H., Dresel, S. H., Krause, J., La Fougere, C., & Ackenheil, M. (2003). The dopamine transporter and neuroimaging in attention deficit hyperactivity

disorder. In *Neuroscience and Biobehavioral Reviews*. https://doi.org/10.1016/j.
neubiorev.2003.08.012

Mansvelder, H. D., Keath, J. R., & McGehee, D. S. (2002). Synaptic mechanisms
underlie nicotine-induced excitability of brain reward areas. *Neuron*. https://
doi.org/10.1016/S0896-6273(02)00625-6

Miller, G. F., & Todd, P. M. (1993, August). Evolutionary wanderlust: Sexual
selection with directional mate preferences. In From Animals to Animats 2:
Proceedings of the Second International Conference on Simulation of Adaptive
Behavior (Vol. 2, p. 21). MIT Press, Bradford Books.

Palmiter, R. D. (2007). Is dopamine a physiologically relevant mediator of feeding
behavior? *Trends in Neurosciences*, *30*(8), 375–381. https://doi.org/10.1016/j.
tins.2007.06.004

Posner, M. I., Rothbart, M. K., Sheese, B. E., & Voelker, P. (2012). Control networks
and neuromodulators of early development. *Developmental Psychology*. https://
doi.org/10.1037/a0025530

Potter, A. S., & Newhouse, P. A. (2008). Acute nicotine improves cognitive deficits
in young adults with attention-deficit/hyperactivity disorder. *Pharmacology
Biochemistry and Behavior*. https://doi.org/10.1016/j.pbb.2007.09.014

Sapolsky, R. M. (2010a). Course entitled Human Behavioral Biology, Lecture 7:
Behavioral Genetics II, retrieved from: https://www.youtube.com/watch?v=RG-
5fN6KrDJE&list=PL848F2368C90DDC3D&index=7; April 2010; Stanford
University: http://www.stanford.edu/ Stanford Department of Biology: http://
biology.stanford.edu/ Stanford University Channel on YouTube: http://www.
youtube.com/stanford

Sapolsky, R. M. (2010b). Course entitled Human Behavioral Biology, Lecture
14: Limbic System, retrieved from: https://www.youtube.com/watch?v=CA-
OnSbDSaOw&list=PL848F2368C90DDC3D&index=14; April 2010; Stanford
University: http://www.stanford.edu/ Stanford Department of Biology: http://
biology.stanford.edu/ Stanford University Channel on YouTube: http://www.
youtube.com/stanford

Sapolsky, R. M. (2017). Behave: The biology of humans at our best and worst. New
York, NY; Penguin.Shapira, N. A., Liu, Y., He, A. G., Bradley, M. M., Lessig, M.
C., James, G. A., … Goodman, W. K. (2003). Brain activation by disgust-inducing

pictures in obsessive-compulsive disorder. Biological Psychiatry, 54(7), 751–756. https://doi.org/10.1016/S0006-3223(03)00003-9

Type Eight: The Warrior

Abu-Akel, A., & Shamay-Tsoory, S. (2011). Neuroanatomical and neurochemical bases of theory of mind. *Neuropsychologia*, *49*(11), 2971–2984. https://doi.org/10.1016/j.neuropsychologia.2011.07.012

Archer, J. (2006). Testosterone and human aggression: An evaluation of the challenge hypothesis. *Neuroscience and Biobehavioral Reviews.* https://doi.org/10.1016/j.neubiorev.2004.12.007

Blair, R. J.R. (2010). Psychopathy, frustration, and reactive aggression: The role of ventromedial prefrontal cortex. *British Journal of Psychology.* https://doi.org/10.1348/000712609X418480

Blair, R. James R. (2013). The Neurobiology of Psychopathic traits in youths. *Nature.*

Booij, L., Tremblay, R. E., Leyton, M., Séguin, J. R., Vitaro, F., Gravel, P., ... Benkelfat, C. (2010). Brain serotonin synthesis in adult males characterized by physical aggression during childhood: A 21-year longitudinal study. *PLoS ONE.* https://doi.org/10.1371/journal.pone.0011255

Buckholtz, J. W., & Meyer-Lindenberg, A. (2008). MAOA and the neurogenetic architecture of human aggression. *Trends in Neurosciences.* https://doi.org/10.1016/j.tins.2007.12.006

Byrd, A. L., Manuck, S. B., Hawes, S. W., Vebares, T. J., Nimgaonkar, V., Chowdari, K. V., ... Stepp, S. D. (2018). The interaction between monoamine oxidase A (MAOA) and childhood maltreatment as a predictor of personality pathology in females: Emotional reactivity as a potential mediating mechanism. *Development and Psychopathology, 31,* 1–17. https://doi.org/10.1017/S0954579417001900

Carré, J. M., Putnam, S. K., & McCormick, C. M. (2009). Testosterone responses to competition predict future aggressive behaviour at a cost to reward in men. *Psychoneuroendocrinology.* https://doi.org/10.1016/j.psyneuen.2008.10.018

Caspi, A., Mcclay, J., Moffitt, T. E., Mill, J., Martin, J., Craig, W., ... Poulton, R. (2002). Role of Genotype in the Cycle of Violence in Maltreated Children. *Science, 297*(5582), 851–854.

Claxton, G., Owen, D., & Sadler-Smith, E. (2015). Hubris in leadership: A peril of unbridled intuition? *Leadership, 11*(1), 57–78. https://doi.org/10.1177/1742715013511482

Damasio, A. (2005). En busca de Spinoza. Neurobiología de la emoción y los sentimientos. Ed: Crítica; Barcelona

Duke, A. A., Bègue, L., Bell, R., & Eisenlohr-Moul, T. (2013). Revisiting the serotonin-aggression relation in humans: A meta-analysis. *Psychological Bulletin, 139*(5), 1148–1172. https://doi.org/10.1037/a0031544

Eccles, D. A., MacArtney-Coxson, D., Chambers, G. K., & Lea, R. A. (2012). A unique demographic history exists for the MAO-A gene in Polynesians. *Journal of Human Genetics*. https://doi.org/10.1038/jhg.2012.19

Eme, R. (2013). MAOA and male antisocial behavior: A review. *Aggression and Violent Behavior, 18*(3), 395–398. https://doi.org/10.1016/j.avb.2013.02.001

Garcia, L. F., Aluja, A., Fibla, J., Cuevas, L., & García, O. (2010). Incremental effect for antisocial personality disorder genetic risk combining 5-HTTLPR and 5-HTTVNTR polymorphisms. *Psychiatry Research, 177*(1–2), 161–166. https://doi.org/10.1016/j.psychres.2008.12.018

Grabo, A., Spisak, B. R., & van Vugt, M. (2017). Charisma as signal: An evolutionary perspective on charismatic leadership. *Leadership Quarterly, 28*(4), 473–485. https://doi.org/10.1016/j.leaqua.2017.05.001

Hooten, W. M., Hartman, W. R., Black, J. L., Laures, H. J., & Walker, D. L. (2013). Associations between serotonin transporter gene polymorphisms and heat pain perception in adults with chronic pain. *BMC Medical Genetics*. https://doi.org/10.1186/1471-2350-14-78

Kloke, V., Jansen, F., Heiming, R. S., Palme, R., Lesch, K. P., & Sachser, N. (2011). The winner and loser effect, serotonin transporter genotype, and the display of offensive aggression. *Physiology and Behavior, 103*(5), 565–574. https://doi.org/10.1016/j.physbeh.2011.04.021

Lee, S. H. (2018). Close Encounters with Humankind: A Paleoanthropologist Investigates Our Evolving Species. WW Norton & Company; United States of America

Lindstedt, F., Berrebi, J., Greayer, E., Lonsdorf, T. B., Schalling, M., Ingvar, M., & Kosek, E. (2011). Conditioned pain modulation is associated with common Polymorphisms in the serotonin transporter gene. *PLoS ONE*. https://doi.org/10.1371/journal.pone.0018252

Lobbestael, J., Baumeister, R. F., Fiebig, T., & Eckel, L. A. (2014). The role of grandiose and vulnerable narcissism in self-reported and laboratory aggression and testosterone reactivity. *Personality and Individual Differences, 69*, 22–27. https://doi.org/10.1016/j.paid.2014.05.007

Mayo Clinic, Antisocial personality disorder, Symptoms; retrieved from https://www.mayoclinic.org/diseases-conditions/antisocial-personality-disorder/symptoms-causes/syc-20353928

Moffitt T.E., Caspi A., Harrington H., M. B. J. (2002). Males on the life-course-persistent and adolescence-limited antisocial pathways. *EmbaseDevelopment and Psychopathology, 14*, 179–207.

Montoya, E. R., Terburg, D., Bos, P. A., & van Honk, J. (2012). Testosterone, cortisol, and serotonin as key regulators of social aggression: A review and theoretical perspective. *Motivation and Emotion, 36*(1), 65–73. https://doi.org/10.1007/s11031-011-9264-3

Owen, D., Gee, S., George, D. L., Thatcher, M., George, W., & Blair, T. (2008). Hubris syndrome. *Clinical Medicine, 8*(4).

Philibert, R. A., Wernett, P., Plume, J., Packer, H., Brody, G. H., & Beach, S. R. H. (2011). Gene environment interactions with a novel variable Monoamine Oxidase A transcriptional enhancer are associated with antisocial personality disorder. *Biological Psychology, 87*(3), 366–371. https://doi.org/10.1016/j.biopsycho.2011.04.007

Reti, I. M., Xu, J. Z., Yanofski, J., McKibben, J., Uhart, M., Cheng, Y. J., … Nestadt, G. (2011). Monoamine oxidase A regulates antisocial personality in whites with no history of physical abuse. *Comprehensive Psychiatry, 52*(2), 188–194. https://doi.org/10.1016/j.comppsych.2010.05.005

Rooij, R. van. (2007). The Stag Hunt and the Evolution of Social Structure. *Studia Logica*. https://doi.org/10.1007/s11225-007-9024-2

Salavera Bordás, C., Puyuelo, M., Tricás, J. M., & Lucha, O. (2010). Comorbilidad de trastornos de personalidad: estudio en personas sin hogar. *Universitas Psychologica, 9*(2), 457–468. https://doi.org/10.11144/javeriana.upsy9-2.ctpe

Sapolsky, R. M. (2017). Behave: The biology of humans at our best and worst. New York, NY; Penguin.

Schultheiss, O. C., Campbell, K. L., & McClelland, D. C. (1999). Implicit power motivation moderates me testosterone responses to imagined and real dominance success. *Hormones and Behavior.* https://doi.org/10.1006/hbeh.1999.1542

Smeijers, D., Bulten, E., Franke, B., Buitelaar, J., & Verkes, R. J. (2017). Associations of multiple trauma types and MAOA with severe aggressive behavior and MAOA effects on training outcome. *European Neuropsychopharmacology*, 1–9. https://doi.org/10.1016/j.euroneuro.2017.06.016

Vicario, C. M. (2014). Aggression traits in youth psychopathy: the key role of serotonin. *Frontiers in Psychiatry*, 5(March), 289–320. https://doi.org/10.1007/7854

Wingfield, J. C. (2017). The challenge hypothesis: Where it began and relevance to humans. *Hormones and Behavior.* https://doi.org/10.1016/j.yhbeh.2016.11.008

Type Nine: The Peacemaker

Aleyasin, H., Flanigan, M. E., & Russo, S. J. (2018). Neurocircuitry of aggression and aggression seeking behavior: nose poking into brain circuitry controlling aggression. *Current Opinion in Neurobiology*, 49(Figure 1), 184–191. https://doi.org/10.1016/j.conb.2018.02.013

Berenbaum, H. (2002). Varieties of joy-related pleasurable activities and feelings. *Cognition and Emotion.* https://doi.org/10.1080/0269993014000383

Biblioteca Nacional de Chile, Memoria Chilena: Ramón Barros Luco; retrieved from http://www.memoriachilena.gob.cl/602/w3-article-3666.html

Blum, K., Oscar-berman, M., Bowirrat, A., Giordano, J., Madigan, M., Braverman, E. R., ... Borsten, J. (2013). Neuropsychiatric Genetics of Happiness, Friendships, and Politics: Hypothesizing Homophily ("Birds of a Feather Flock Together") as a Function of Reward Gene Polymorphisms. *NHI Public Access*, 3(112). https://doi.org/10.4172/2157-7412.1000112.Neuropsychiatric

Bradshaw, J. W. S., & Cook, S. E. (1996). Patterns of pet cat behaviour at feeding occasions. *Applied Animal Behaviour Science.* https://doi.org/10.1016/0168-1591(95)01011-4

Dawkins, R. (1976). The selfish gene; New York: Oxford University Press.

Foster, D. J., & Wilson, M. A. (2006). Reverse replay of behavioural sequences in hippocampal place cells during the awake state. *Nature.* https://doi.org/10.1038/nature04587

Fredrickson, B. L. (1998). What good are positive emotions? *Review of General Psychology.* https://doi.org/10.1037/1089-2680.2.3.300

Griskevicius, V., Shiota, M. N., & Nowlis, S. M. (2010). The Many Shades of Rose-Colored Glasses: An Evolutionary Approach to the Influence of Different Positive Emotions. *Journal of Consumer Research, 37*(2), 238–250. https://doi.org/10.1086/651442

Kasper, C., Schreier, T., & Taborsky, B. (2019). Heritabilities, social environment effects and genetic correlations of social behaviours in a cooperatively breeding vertebrate. *Journal of Evolutionary Biology, 32*(9), 955–973. https://doi.org/10.1111/jeb.13494

Kasper, C., Vierbuchen, M., Ernst, U., Fischer, S., Radersma, R., Raulo, A., ... Taborsky, B. (2017). Genetics and developmental biology of cooperation. *Molecular Ecology, 26*(17), 4364–4377. https://doi.org/10.1111/mec.14208

Mirrione, M. M., Schulz, D., Lapidus, K. A. B., Zhang, S., Goodman, W., & Henn, F. A. (2014). Increased metabolic activity in the septum and habenula during stress is linked to subsequent expression of learned helplessness behavior. *Frontiers in Human Neuroscience.* https://doi.org/10.3389/fnhum.2014.00029

Nes, R. B., & Røysamb, E. (2017). Happiness in Behaviour Genetics: An Update on Heritability and Changeability. *Journal of Happiness Studies, 18*(5), 1533–1552. https://doi.org/10.1007/s10902-016-9781-6

Okbay, A. (2016). Genetics of Well being. *Nature Genetics, 48*(6).

Sapolsky, R. M. (2004). Social Status and Health in Humans and Other Animals. *Annual Review of Anthropology, 33*(1), 393–418. https://doi.org/10.1146/annurev.anthro.33.070203.144000

Sapolsky, R. M. (2005). The Influence of Social Hierarchy on Primate Health. *Science, 308*(5722), 648–652.

Sapolsky, R. M. (2010). Course entitled Human Behavioral Biology, Lecture 14: Limbic System, retrieved from: https://www.youtube.com/watch?v=CAOnSbD-SaOw&list=PL848F2368C90DDC3D&index=14; April 2010; Stanford University: http://www.stanford.edu/ Stanford Department of Biology: http://biology.stanford.edu/ Stanford University Channel on YouTube: http://www.youtube.com/stanford

Sapolsky, R. M. (2017). Behave: The biology of humans at our best and worst. New York, NY; Penguin.

Sprangers, M. A. G., Thong, M. S. Y., & Bartels, M. (2014). Biological pathways, candidate genes, and molecular markers associated with quality-of-life domains: an update. *Quality of Life* Research, 23(7), 1710–1714. https://doi.org/10.1007/s

Tops, M., Russo, S., Boksem, M. A. S., & Tucker, D. M. (2009). Serotonin: Modulator of a drive to withdraw. *Brain and Cognition*, 71(3), 427–436. https://doi.org/10.1016/j.bandc.2009.03.009

Wingo, A. P., Almli, L. M., Stevens, J. S., Jovanovic, T., Wingo, T. S., Tharp, G., … Ressler, K. J. (2017). Genome-wide association study of positive emotion identifies a genetic variant and a role for microRNAs. *Molecular Psychiatry*, 22(5), 774–783. https://doi.org/10.1038/mp.2016.143

Wong, L. C., Wang, L., D'Amour, J. A., Yumita, T., Chen, G., Yamaguchi, T., … Lin, D. (2016). Effective Modulation of Male Aggression through Lateral Septum to Medial Hypothalamus Projection. *Current Biology*, 26(5), 593–604. https://doi.org/10.1016/j.cub.2015.12.065

Meet *Nine Sapiens*, a totally new version of the Enneagram model, that incorporates recent findings in genetics, neurobiology, and evolutionary psychology into a unique vision of personality structure. Learn about the neurobiological mechanisms that might explain the core traits of each type. Step into an exciting recreation of our prehistoric past and discover how your personality strategies emerged tens of thousands of years ago. Nine Sapiens, an adventure of self-exploration, and a powerful tool for people development.

Claudia Nario and **Hugo Krüger** are psychologists, with postgraduate studies in Organizational Behavior and Mental Health. For over 25 years, they have been working with their clients to improve their quality of life and their ability to lead, through a deeper understanding of their own personality. They live in Barcelona from where they travel around the world, delivering lectures, consulting and training.